# FIRE & ROSES

# FIRE &
# ROSES

*The Burning of the Charlestown Convent, 1834*

NANCY LUSIGNAN SCHULTZ

NORTHEASTERN UNIVERSITY PRESS    BOSTON

Northeastern University Press

Copyright 2000 by Nancy Lusignan Schultz

Originally published in 2000 by The Free Press, a division of Simon & Schuster, Inc.
First paperback edition published by Northeastern University Press in 2002
by agreement with Simon & Schuster, Inc.

An earlier version of some of the material on Rebecca Reed and Maria Monk
appears in my introduction to *Veil of Fear: Nineteenth-Century Convent Tales*
(Purdue University Press, 1999) and in my article on captivity narratives in
*Studies in Puritan Spirituality: Literary Calvinism and Nineteenth
Century Women Authors,* Vol. 6, 1997, 71–99.

*Library of Congress Cataloging-in-Publication Data*
Schultz, Nancy Lusignan, 1956–
Fire & roses : the burning of the Charlestown Convent, 1834 /
Nancy Lusignan Schultz.—1st pbk. ed.
p. cm.
Includes bibliographical references and index.
ISBN 1-55553-514-3 (pbk. : acid-free paper)
1. Ursuline Convent (Charlestown, Boston, Mass.)—History—19th century. 2. Riots—
Massachusetts—Boston—History—19th century. 3. Fires—Massachusetts—Boston—
History—19th century. 4. Charlestown (Boston, Mass.)—History—19th century.
5. Boston (Mass.)—History—19th century. 6. Anti-Catholicism—Massachusetts—
Boston—History—19th century. I. Title: Fire and roses. II. Title.
F74.C4 S35 2002
974.4'61—dc21          2002016538

Designed by Ellen R. Sasahara

Printed and bound by Quebecor World, Martinsburg, West Virginia.
The paper is QW Liberty, an acid-free stock.

MANUFACTURED IN THE UNITED STATES OF AMERICA
06   05   04   03   02       5   4   3   2   1

FOR JACKSON, JACKSON III, AND JONAS

AND

IN MEMORY OF HENRY ABRAM

# CONTENTS

# PRINCIPAL CHARACTERS

**James T. Austin**: Attorney general and the prosecuting attorney in the trial of the convent rioters.

**Mary Barber**: Sister Mary Benedict, the beautiful daughter of Virgil and Jerusha Barber, who became the third superior of the Boston-area Ursulines.

**Mrs. Barrymore**: The dancing instructor at the convent.

**Reverend Lyman Beecher**: Congregationalist minister and father of Harriet Beecher Stowe who gave three anti-Catholic sermons on the day before the riot.

**Elizabeth Bennett**: Sister Ambrose, choir nun.

**James Bowman**: Painter of portraits of Benedict Fenwick and Mary Anne Moffatt.

**John R. Buzzell**: Brick maker and leader of the convent rioters who was acquitted of the crime to cheers and acclamation.

**Sarah Chase**: Sister Mary Ursula, lay sister.

**Bishop Jean Louis Cheverus**: First bishop of Boston, recalled to France in 1823.

**Maria Cotting**: Silver-medal-winning student to whose home Sister Mary John fled on the night of her escape.

**Reverend William Croswell**: Episcopalian rector of Christ Church ("Old North") in Boston, who encouraged Rebecca Reed to write *Six Months in a Convent*.

**Edward Cutter**: Member of the Massachusetts legislature and owner of a local brickyard who investigated the case of Elizabeth Harrison.

**Rebecca DeCosta**: Sister Mary Claire, lay sister.

**Commodore Jesse Elliott**: Catholic Commander of the Charlestown Navy Yard and friend of Mary Anne Moffatt.

**George F. Farley, and Samuel H. Mann**: Counsel for most of the accused convent rioters.

**Reverend Benedict Joseph Fenwick**: Jesuit priest and second Roman Catholic bishop of Boston, for whom Mount Benedict was named.

**Mary Anne and Jane Fraser**: Probable nieces of Mary Anne Moffatt.

**Elizabeth Harrison**: Sister Mary John, the mother assistant and music teacher of the convent, who suffered a fit of insanity and ran away two weeks before the convent was attacked.

**Ann Janet Kennedy**: Sister Mary Francis, dissatisfied young novice from New York who befriended Rebecca Reed.

**Peter A. Kielchen**: The Russian consul stationed in Boston, and friend of Mary Anne Moffatt.

**Father Maguire**: Confessor to the nuns in Quebec, sent to Boston to escort Mother St. George to Quebec.

**Marvin Marcy**: The boy who burned Bishop Fenwick's books on the night of the fire and the only convicted rioter.

**Father François Antoine Matignon**: Executor of John Thayer's will and a benefactor of the Ursulines.

**Mary Louise McLaughlin**: Mother St. Henry, superior of the Quebec Ursulines.

**Jane (Genevieve) Moffatt**: Mother of Mary Anne Moffatt, still living in 1836.

**Mary Anne Ursula Moffatt**: Sister Mary Edmond St. George, superior of the Charlestown Ursulines.

**William Moffatt**: Father of Mary Anne Moffatt, a loyalist who fled to Canada and died before 1810.

**Catherine Molineaux**: Sister Mary Angela, cousin of the Ryan sisters and one of the four foundresses of the Boston Ursulines.

**Grace O'Boyle**: Sister Bernard, lay sister.

**The O'Keefe sisters from Ireland**: Margaret, Sister Mary Magdalene, who, according to Rebecca Reed, had her life shortened by the "austerities" imposed on the religious; Frances, Sister Mary Austin, mistress of the junior class; and Ellen, Sister Mary Joseph.

**Sister St. Henry Quirck**: Niece of the foundresses who succumbed to tuberculosis shortly after the destruction of the convent.

**Rebecca Reed**: The novice who "escaped" from Mount Benedict in 1832 and wrote a best-selling exposé called *Six Months in a Convent*.

**Peter Rossiter**: Irish caretaker at Mount Benedict who was beaten by John R. Buzzell two months before the convent was attacked.

**John Runey**: The selectman who was present when the convent was burned and whose daughter later suffered a fit of insanity.

**Catherine Ryan**: Sister Mary Magdalene, one of the four foundresses of the Boston Ursulines.

**Margaret Ryan**: Sister Mary Austin or Augustine. One of the four original foundresses and beloved friend of Mary Anne Moffatt.

**Mary Ryan**: Sister Mary Joseph, foundress and the first superior of the Boston-area Ursulines.

**Lemuel Shaw**: Chief Justice of the Massachusetts Supreme Judicial Court who presided over the trial of the convent rioters.

**Reverend Joseph Signay**: Bishop of Quebec who recalled Mother St. George to Quebec.

**Reverend William Taylor**: Priest in charge of the diocese of Boston, 1823–25, and friend of Mary Anne Moffatt.

**Lucy Thaxter**: Former student who wrote a letter in defense of the community at Mount Benedict.

**Father John Thayer**: Protestant convert and benefactor of the Boston Ursulines.

**Dr. Abraham Thompson**: Physician at the Mount Benedict convent whose daughters had attended the school.

**Louisa Goddard Whitney**: Former student at the Mount Benedict Academy and author of *The Burning of the Convent* (1877).

**Catherine Wiseman**: Sister Mary Frances, one of the original trustees in Boston.

# FIRE &
# ROSES

# PROLOGUE

THE ANGRY THUNDERSTORMS that shook the Massachusetts coastline early on Wednesday, August 13, 1834 may have seemed to some like God's retribution for the events of the previous forty-eight hours. In the fishing town of Newburyport, about forty miles north of Boston, in a bar called the Bite Tavern, lay the blood-soaked corpse of Henry Creesy. His hand still held the jackknife that he had used to slit his own throat. Earlier that evening, drenched with rain and sweat, he had stumbled into the dark tavern and ordered the first of several whiskeys. As the night stretched on, his behavior had become more and more erratic. Dark mutterings over the glass had escalated into horrified glances over his shoulder. Then, when a neighbor from the town rested his hand in friendly greeting on Creesy's arm, the distraught man jumped up from his stool at the bar, spun wildly around, and flashed his knife. As the barman and others moved to subdue him, he broke from their grasp and stood frozen in the middle of the room. In the candlelit tavern, he must have imagined dozens of glittering demons' eyes staring at him, as he stood helpless in the center of a magic circle of fire. The knife flashed once more in the candlelight, and Creesy toppled onto the wooden floor. His severed windpipe gurgled, then was quiet, and as the stunned patrons watched, a red stain spread, outlining his head in his own gore, like an infernal halo.

Minutes later, Creesy's wife, responding to a frantic summons from her neighbor, ran her hand over his still chest and brushed against something in his breast pocket. Reaching inside, she pulled out three round wafers embossed with crosses. Shuddering, she returned them quickly to his pocket. Turning to the tavern-keeper, she begged him to send immediately for the minister.[1] When the clergyman arrived, Creesy's body had been removed to a room upstairs in the tavern. His wife met the minister's condolences with a glazed look, and she directed him to examine the vest pockets.

"My God," he gasped, as he pulled out the communion wafers. "Where did your husband get these?"

But then the answer dawned on him.

"From the Charlestown convent! He was one of the men who attacked the school that night. And he stole these consecrated hosts! God is already taking vengeance on those who profaned that sacred place."

## CHAPTER ONE

# THE SEED IS PLANTED

*All the brick-kilns had been set burning, and as night concealed the ugly brickyards and clay-fields in which they were erected, nothing was visible but the magic circle of fire that seemed to be drawn around the Convent.*

—LOUISA WHITNEY, *The Burning of the Convent,* 1877

IN THE TWILIGHT of a sweltering August evening in 1834, groups of men are gathering on the Winter Hill Road in the Charlestown neighborhood of Boston, near the main gate of a Roman Catholic convent. It is Monday, and they have come here after rounds of drinks at the local tavern, following another backbreaking day's work. They are brickmakers, sailors, firemen, apprentices, and hooligans, Charlestown's poorest and least educated, and tonight they have a job to do. Cloistered inside are about a dozen Ursuline nuns who, in the last eight years, have built an elegant brick boarding school for wealthy girls high on a hill encircled by the brickyards of Charlestown, where most of those in the crowd at the gate eke out a meager living. Tall, sturdy fences fully enclose Mount Benedict, the nuns' lush twenty-four-acre farm, with its fragrant orchards of apple and pear, its heavily laden vineyards, its bounteous herb and vegetable gardens, its pebbled maze of walks through roses, a veritable self-contained Eden.

The men at the gate are angry. They're angry about a lot of things. Many have come down to the city from New Hampshire, leaving wives and children behind to manage as best they can the failing farms where the men once made decent livings growing alfalfa and clover for animal feed. As generations passed, the farms had been subdivided, and New

Hampshire's sons had inherited fewer and fewer acres. Even with their thrifty Presbyterian Scots backgrounds, the men were finally unable to sustain a living from the exhausted soil of their parcels. Now they lived in dirty, crowded all-male dormitories owned by the brickyard boss, and worked with their backs for a dollar or two a day, supplying bricks for the rapidly growing city of Boston.[1] Daily, as they wiped the sweat from their eyes, they glanced up from the brickyards to see verdant Mount Benedict, where the daughters of some of Boston's most prominent Protestant families were receiving an expensive European-style education from a community of Ursuline nuns. On this night, August 11, 1834, there were about ten Catholic and forty Protestant girls inside, many from elite Unitarian families in Boston, who paid a yearly tuition to the nuns equivalent to a brickmaker's wages for six months' labor.

Though many of the men had indirectly won their livelihood from the extensive construction work at the boarding school, lately the convent's relationship with the neighboring brickyards had deteriorated. Rumors had been circulating around Charlestown that something was amiss. A novice named Rebecca Reed had escaped over the convent wall two years before and told disturbing tales of the abuse she and other nuns suffered within. A convert to Catholicism, Miss Reed had been admitted to the school as a charity pupil, and had aspirations to become a nun. But she became dissatisfied with her life in the community, and fancied that a plot was afoot to imprison her in a Canadian convent. She had found a ready audience for her stories in anti-Catholic Yankee Boston, foreshadowing the wild success in 1835 of her published exposé of convent life. And just two weeks before, another nun named Sister St. John had run away from the convent to the home of one of the brickyard bosses, begging him to take her safely away. That nun had been brought back, against her will, or so the locals believed, by the Roman Catholic bishop, Benedict Joseph Fenwick, after whom Mount Benedict had been named. Now the *Mercantile Journal* was publishing rumors that St. John, whose given name was Elizabeth Harrison, was dead or held captive within the convent walls. When the selectmen of Charlestown had been sent in to investigate on the day before the riot, they had been treated with contempt by the convent's feisty mother superior, Sister St. George, née Mary Anne Moffatt.

Though Harrison, the escaped nun, assured the selectmen that she now wished to remain in the community, Moffatt's haughty demeanor disgusted them. One ringleader of the rioters, a strapping six-foot-six brick maker named John R. Buzzell, later said that Moffatt was "the sauciest woman I ever heard talk."[2] Yesterday, the Superior had berated the selectmen for interfering with the running of her business. Today, as darkness deepened and the crowd grew, she threatened destruction of their homes and businesses. Standing at the front window, Moffatt ordered the crowd to disperse. If they didn't, she said, "The bishop has at his command an army of twenty thousand Catholic Irishmen who will burn your houses."

Bottles of rum and whiskey were passed around by the men at the gate, some of whom had painted their faces like Indians for the occasion. Around half past nine, a shout went up from the crowd, "Down with the Pope! Down with the convent!" alarming the nuns and students. The mother superior quickly assembled her sisters and ordered them to take the nightgown-clad girls, who ranged in age from six to fourteen, to the rear of the building. She then came to an upper window to face the crowd below, and demanded to know what they wanted.

"We want to see the nun who ran away!"

When Moffatt disdainfully shook her head in denial, two gunshots were fired in the air as a warning. At eleven o'clock the crowd began to tear down the convent fence, and lit a bonfire of fencing and tar barrels on the neighboring property of brickyard owner Alvah Kelley. Its light was visible for miles around. Local church bells began to peal out the signal for fire, and engine companies from Charlestown and Boston raced to the scene. But many of the firemen had friends in the crowd, and escaped nun Rebecca Reed's brother-in-law, Prescott Pond, was a member of Boston Engine No. 13. Instead of fighting the fire, the men from No. 13 provided cover for the rioters as they raced up the hill toward the convent. Stones and bricks shattered the rows of windows in the three-story building and its adjoining wings. A farmhand grabbed a stake to batter in the front door, and the rioters burst into the building. Moffatt ordered the nuns to take the flock of children down the back stairway to the convent garden. She then quickly returned to her office, and put something in her pocket, a miniature of her mother, she would later claim. Two other nuns ran to the chapel and wrenched the mahogany tabernacle from the center of the altar. Inside was an antique silver ciborium, a sacred chalice holding the consecrated bread that in Roman Catholic belief is the body of Christ. The nuns hid the tabernacle in a rosebush blooming in the garden.

By midnight, the rioters had penetrated to the heart of the cloister. Some of them broke up furniture and heaped it in the center of the large assembly room. Others gleefully hurled musical instruments out the windows, violins, harps, and even pianos. Amid cheers and jeers, the Bible, the ornaments of the altar, and the cross were tossed on the pyre and with their torches, the rioters ignited a fire. The firemen outside stood idly by, or returned to their engine houses as a crowd of about four thousand looked on. Hearing the shouts of the rioters inside the convent, the nuns and students, who had been cowering near the mausoleum in the garden where the convent buried its dead, fled through an opening they had made in the fence. In their nightgowns, the women and girls ran through the field in the light of the second-quarter moon, and took shelter half a mile away at the home of Mr. Adams, a neighbor. By one-thirty in the morning they could see that the entire building was engulfed in flames.

The rioters, who for sport had donned the slate gray uniforms and white dresses of the students, began to whoop it up at the bishop's lodge. This was a small cottage tucked away in a quiet corner of the property, where Benedict Fenwick, the second bishop of Boston, would occasionally spend the night after an afternoon happily puttering in the convent's gardens. Fenwick did not have much leisure time in these early days of establishing the diocese of Boston, and gardening in the lovely enclosures on Mount Benedict was one of his few recreations. But on this night, a fresh-faced boy named Marvin Marcy conducted a mock auction with Fenwick's small but well-stocked library, calling out "Sold!" as he consigned books to the flames.

Not satisfied with this vandalism, the rioters moved on to the mausoleum in the garden. This was a tiny chapel of brick where prayers for the dead were offered, and the bodies of deceased nuns lay in the crypt below. The rioters battered their way in, lifted the trap door, and raced down the stone steps of the nether chamber, looking for the bodies of murdered Protestant girls. Only the corpses of six or seven nuns lay in coffins. With pickaxes, they pried off the tops, and pulled the bodies out onto the floor. Turning over a corpse with the toe of his boot, one of the rioters took a cudgel to the skull, and some teeth went skittering across the stone floor. Laughing and joking, still swigging whiskey, the men pocketed the teeth for souvenirs. Next, they moved on to destroy the remaining buildings on the premises: the barn, the stables, the ice-house, and a restored farmhouse. By daybreak, the magnificent convent was a heap of smoldering ruins.

Only one part of the property stood relatively untouched—the convent's lush terraced gardens. After a day recovering from their business of the previous evening, the men returned as soon as darkness fell to finish the job. Crossing the drawbridge to Charlestown once more, they again streamed up the center road to Mount Benedict. Tonight their object was the end of Eden. They pulled the vines laden with ripening grapes from trellises. They swung axes at apple and pear trees heavy-hung with fruit. They trampled neat green rows of lettuce and broccoli, and hurled tomatoes and bean plants skyward. Finally, they trampled the rose bushes, even as the thorns tore at their clothes and skin.

The night before, two men had found the mahogany tabernacle hidden in an especially beautiful rosebush, covered with voluptuous red blooms of an overpowering fragrance. Tonight, one of these men again stood before the bush with a scythe, recalling how he and his companion, a wagon-hand from Newburyport named Henry Creesy, had rejoiced when they spotted the tabernacle hidden there. Creesy, known in his native town as having "a melancholy temper, but inoffensive and industrious," made a slim living from the patronage of the wagoners, whom he followed around the city and offered assistance where needed.[3] The teamsters or truckmen—a hardy crew who manned the long, two-wheeled carts then in use—could be frequently found at disturbances around town. On this night, Creesy assisted the truckmen in perpetrating one of the most notorious acts of anti-Catholic violence in American history. When the wagon-hand pulled the silver ciborium from the tabernacle hidden in the rosebush, he shoved a few of the wafers it held into his breast pocket, and laughed as he announced, "Now I have God's body in my pocket!" At the same moment, he looked up to see flames coming from the convent window. Shrieking with glee, the wagon-hand hurled the silver vessel into a thick hedge.

Creesy must have been pretty drunk, thought his companion, to toss away a valuable silver goblet and just keep the wafers. Last night, the man with the scythe had hunted a long time for it, but darkness and the thickness of the hedge obscured it from his view.

"Drunken fool," he murmured, shaking his head with disgust, as he stood before the imposing bush.

Then he raised his scythe and hacked and hacked at the rose bush until the branches all lay broken, and red petals were strewn like bloodstains on the white stones of the pathway.

\* \* \*

Old and hackneyed as they may seem;—threadbare as they may be supposed to have become, by the continual wear and tear . . . in the public papers, in private conversation, in the reports of the Committees, and in the arguments of the Bar,—I yet venture to say that there are not only unexhausted, but almost unnoticed incidents in the history of this transaction, which, in the hand of one skilled and practised [sic] in touching the strings and sounding the stops of the human breast, might be made to harrow up the sternest soul, and freeze the youngest blood among us. . . .[4]

ROBERT CHARLES WINTHROP made these observations about narrating the burning of the Ursuline convent on March 12, 1835, just as the trials of the convent rioters were winding down, and a few short days before the appearance of escaped nun Rebecca Reed's best-selling exposé of the Charlestown community, *Six Months in a Convent*. Winthrop modestly went on to demur, "I have no such skill," and left the challenge to others. Though his speech before the legislature in favor of compensating the Ursulines for their losses was compelling, it was ultimately not successful. During the nearly seventeen decades that have followed, many lawyers, commentators, and scholars have taken up Winthrop's challenge to harrow the soul and freeze the blood through the telling of this tale.[5]

And the themes *are* harrowing. They include the *real* secrets of the Ursuline convent in Charlestown: mysticism, alcoholism, a secret burial, a possible illegitimate birth, and the mysterious fate of the mother superior, Mary Anne Moffatt, whose strange and troubling disappearance remains an unsolved mystery. Persons connected with the riot suffered a variety of devastating effects. Some went mad, including escaped nuns Rebecca Reed and Elizabeth Harrison, convent rioters Henry Creesy and Marvin Marcy, the daughter of the buffoonish Charlestown selectman John Runey, and possibly Mary Anne Moffatt herself. Others developed permanent disfigurements or disabilities. This was the case with William Croswell, Rebecca Reed's minister, whose once handsome appearance was marred by a worsening facial tic that developed after his stressful involvement in the controversy. At least two deaths indirectly resulted from the catastrophe at the convent. A young Irish nun named Sister St. Henry was the first victim, dying within six weeks of shock and tuberculosis. The father of the only convicted rioter, seventeen-year-old Marvin Marcy, apparently died of shame or grief during the course of the trials. Within four years of the event, Rebecca Reed herself had succumbed to tuberculosis, which the twenty-six-year-old claimed to have contracted at the convent. The terrifying legends that arose after this event are intertwined with larger historical themes of class warfare, erupting tensions over religion and gender, and the struggle to define a democratic society in the years following the American Revolution. In many ways, the story of this riot in antebellum Charlestown, Massachusetts remains the story of today's America.

Henry Creesy's suicide and the snapshot of the riot contain many of the larger threads of the story. But history begins with people, not events, and the story of the destruction of the Charlestown convent is the story of intersecting lives: Mary Anne Moffatt, the convent's powerful mother superior; the ambitious second bishop of Boston, Benedict Fenwick; the impressionable and romantic novice Rebecca Reed and her high-strung minister William Croswell; the beautiful and eccentric nun, Mary Barber; and the unflappable leader of the convent rioters, John R. Buzzell, the strapping brick maker from New Hampshire. The lives of these main characters, as well as of a host of supporting players, help weave the tapestry of this formative event in American history, which itself has ancient origins. Members of the Charlestown Ursuline community and their attackers were actors in a centuries-old tradition with both European and colonial American roots.

The story of the Charlestown Ursulines dates back to the settling of North America. The first nuns on the continent were Ursulines, arriving from France in 1639, and settling in Canada to teach Indian girls and the daughters of French settlers in their Quebec monastery. For a century before their arrival in the New World, the Ursulines had been pioneers in women's education. As in many religious orders, Ursuline nuns take vows of poverty, chastity, and obedience, but for five hundred years, this venerable order has made a fourth commitment: to devote their lives to educating women. In 1727, with the arrival of ten sisters in New Orleans, the Ursulines founded what was to be the first permanent establishment of religious women in the United States. Half a century before the Revolution, the New Orleans Ursulines became in fact the first professional elementary school teachers in the United States.[6] Though other orders later founded houses, the Ursulines remained one of the most elite, enjoying the friendship and patronage of American founding fathers Samuel Adams, George Washington, and Thomas Jefferson.[7]

In fact, the first-rate schools run by these women had historically attracted the daughters of the upper classes, both Protestant and Catholic, and the order developed its prestigious reputation. Ursulines heroically adjusted their mission and nursed American soldiers during the Revolutionary War and the War of 1812.[8] Roman Catholic Church leaders in the United States also appreciated the excellent work of the Ursulines in women's education. The first Catholic bishop in the United States, John Carroll, was advised by Rome in 1788 to bring in more Ursuline sisters to help with setting up the first diocese.[9] Mary Anne Moffatt, Mary Barber, and the other Charlestown Ursulines, then, were continuing this long and distinguished tradition of service in establishing the Ursuline Academy in Charlestown, Massachusetts during the early nineteenth century.

Other Roman Catholic nuns followed. Between 1790 and 1829, twelve different orders of nuns established convents in the United States, though only about half of these communities flourished and grew.[10] An Ursuline house in New York that had been founded in 1812 by sisters from Ireland was one of the early casualties. Summoned by the state's vicar-general, Anthony Kohlmann, the sisters had some success in attracting pupils, but not American postulants, girls who would prepare to join the order.[11] To remain a viable institution, the New York Ursulines needed to attract Americans who could afford a dowry of $2,000. As a historian of this period notes, "Since no interested New Yorker of the day could afford the dowry, none entered, and the sisters returned to Ireland in 1815."[12]

The Boston Ursuline mission had been the dream of a priest, Father John Thayer, a former Congregationalist minister who had once served as chaplain to Massachusetts Governor John Hancock, the American statesman and first signer of the Declaration of Independence.[13] Born in Boston May 15, 1758, John Thayer was the fourth son in a family of eight boys, the children of Cornelius and Sarah (Plaisted) Thayer.[14] On a trip to Rome in 1783 after his graduation from Yale, the twenty-five-year-old Thayer converted to Catholicism, after witnessing miraculous cures at the shrine of the venerable Benedict Joseph Labré.[15] Thayer wrote a vivid account of his conversion experience that was widely read, reprinted in several editions, and translated into eight languages.[16] Almost immediately, the young man decided to enter the priesthood. Thayer was fervent in his new faith, but lacked tact and prudence. He often alienated both Protestants and Catholics with whom he came in contact, including John Adams, Quebec's Bishop Hubert, and Baltimore's John Carroll.[17] While on his way back to America from Europe, he had traveled to Boulogne-Sur-Mer in France and met with members of the Ursuline order there. Impressed with their way of life, he vowed to establish an Ursuline convent in his birthplace, Boston.[18] An Indian school run by the Catholics that had been in existence earlier had closed, leaving no Catholic schools in the city,[19] and the small population of children of this faith were educated in public or Protestant institutions.[20]

In 1790 Thayer returned to Boston, where Catholics numbered fewer than a hundred out of a population of 18,000, and began his ministry.[21] There the young priest proposed the radical idea of founding a convent in Boston. His Catholic opponents ridiculed Thayer for this plan, because until 1803, there were only two convents in the entire United States, the French Ursulines in New Orleans and the Carmelites of Maryland.[22] Thayer's vision of educating women was somewhat eccentric since there were no schools for young Catholic men in the area. Thayer probably saw the education of girls as a means of strengthening Catholic families, and thought that the poorest Catholics needed the greatest assistance. But in selecting the Ursuline order for this mission, Thayer may have inadvertently planted the seed for controversy. The

Ursulines had always had a dual mission in women's education, a commitment to helping the poor as well as to educate the daughters of the elite. With the move from Boston to Charlestown, the New England convent's mission easily shifted from Thayer's original intention, heightening Yankee anxieties about the convent's education of upper-class Protestant girls.

In Boston, Father Thayer quickly became enmeshed in disputes with local Protestant ministers, which convinced him that the hostile climate he perceived in turn-of-the-nineteenth-century New England would hinder his dream of bringing a monastic community into the city. He decided he would have to find outside financial backing in order to found an Ursuline convent in this Yankee stronghold. Thayer requested a transfer to Virginia, and Bishop Carroll of Baltimore agreed and sent a replacement for the Boston mission. Thayer subsequently embarked for Europe in 1803, and to Ireland in 1811, settling in Limerick to work among the poor and raise money for the Boston academy, which he was still intent on founding. In Limerick, the priest stayed with a cloth merchant's family by the name of Ryan, giving French lessons to the youngest daughter, Margaret.[23] Two of James Ryan's others daughters, Mary and Catherine, had been educated by Ursulines at Thurles, in Tipperary County, and Thayer believed the Ryans had the faith and education to open and operate a school in Boston. Surely by now, he believed, the city would have become more tolerant in its attitude toward Catholics.

During his stay with the Ryans, the charismatic Father Thayer spoke often of his vision of founding an Ursuline convent in Boston, and of his disappointment at the refusal of the Blackrock Ursulines of Cork to found another mission after their abortive attempt in New York in 1812.[24] Moved by the priest's description of the spiritual needs of New Englanders, Mary and Catherine Ryan, each independent of the other, offered to join the projected community.[25] That the two sisters volunteered is not surprising, since the Ryan family was notable for its vocations. James Ryan's four daughters all became Ursuline nuns. His daughter Anne, the only one to marry, bore three daughters and a son before she became a widow and followed her sisters into an Ursuline convent. All four of her children became members of a religious community, the son joining the Jesuits and the three daughters the Ursulines.[26]

Once he had a commitment from Mary and Catherine Ryan to found the Boston mission, Father Thayer arranged for the women to train for the sisterhood in the Ursuline Convent at Trois Rivières in Canada. Their sister Margaret and widowed cousin Catherine O'Connell Molineaux also signed on for the project, and planned to join them at Trois Rivières the following year. There the four women would train to become Ursuline nuns and study the administration of a convent, but would not enter as members of the Canadian community. Instead, they would be preparing to found their own in Boston. Thayer expected to accompany the Ryans to Canada but in 1815, the fifty-three-year-old priest fell suddenly and gravely ill. Realizing he would die without seeing his dream fulfilled, he wrote to Boston, entrusting his Ursuline project to a priest and former Sorbonne professor named Father François Antoine Matignon who was stationed in the city. Thayer bequeathed his considerable savings, a sum of over ten thousand dollars, to the Ursulines.[27] The whole estate was valued at $10,764—a large one for the day, consisting of a house on Prince Street valued at $1,000 and diverse stocks. Father Matignon, the assistant of Boston's first bishop, Reverend Jean Louis Anne Magdeleine Lefebre de Cheverus, was named his legatee.[28] Matignon, like Cheverus, was an aristocratic refugee from the French Revolution. Both men were admired and respected by many of Boston's Protestant leaders, and therefore were able to considerably improve the climate for opening a school in the city.[29]

The Ryans made the crossing on May 4, 1817, on the ship *Victory*, which sailed from Limerick to Boston.[30] Matignon then escorted them to the Ursuline convent at Trois Rivières to begin their training. In Boston, Matignon and Bishop Cheverus, who had arrived in Boston in 1796, together worked to foster the fledgling Catholic church and the planned Ursuline mission. Matignon invested Thayer's money wisely, and the original legacy nearly doubled.[31] When Matignon himself died on September 19, 1818, he also directed a third of his inheritance, $2,500, toward the future Ursuline foundation to be established in that city.[32]

A month after they were saddened by the death of Father Matignon, but with a renewed sense of mission, Mary and Catherine Ryan took preliminary vows in the Ursuline order at Trois Rivières in October 1818 under the religious names of Mary Joseph and Mary Magdalene.

Later that year, the Ryans were joined in their vocation by their sister Margaret and their cousin, Catherine Molineaux, who took the names Augustine and Angela. A year later, Mary and Catherine Ryan took lifetime vows.

By June 16, 1820, Bishop Cheverus was proceeding with plans to bring the Ursulines to Boston, and to bequeath them his rectory as their home. For the location of his new rectory, Cheverus purchased a lot adjacent to the Cathedral of the Holy Cross for $4,500, and welcomed the four sisters from Trois Rivières. Cheverus had long cherished the idea of a school for Catholic girls in Boston as the foundation for building strong Catholic families. Though he privately expressed a preference for Mother Elizabeth Ann Seton's Sisters of Charity, Thayer's will had been absolute in dictating that the Boston academy be opened by Ursulines. Father Thayer's protegée, Mary Ryan, now Sister Joseph, was named superior, and the sisters opened a day school for the education of poor girls as their benefactor had planned. The first professed American postulants who trained in Boston were Elizabeth Harrison, Sister Mary John, and Catherine Wiseman, Sister Mary Frances.[33] Two additional American converts would later join the order, Mary Rebecca Theresa DeCosta, Sister Mary Claire, and Sarah Chase, Sister Mary Ursula.[34] By 1822, the community numbered seven religious and two novices.[35] All of these accessions attracted public attention, and some discomforting rumbling was heard in the press about a growing Catholic presence in Boston. The popular Bishop Cheverus intervened with an editorial, appealing to the ideals of liberty and freedom that the nation stood for, and rhetorically asking what threat could be posed by a small number of people assembled for the just cause of teaching children.

The small band of Ursulines opened their school adjoining the Cathedral of the Holy Cross on Franklin Street in Boston, and welcomed about one hundred pupils as day scholars, half of whom attended in the morning and half in the afternoon.[36] With the inheritance they had received from Fathers Thayer and Matignon, the Boston Ursulines had sufficient support to operate their academy, so the girls, mostly poor and the daughters of Irish immigrants, paid no tuition. According to the second superior of the Ursuline convent, Thayer's will had dictated that "the property was to belong solely to the Ursuline Community."[37] Some of the money continued to be invested in public funds and stock, and was generating income from interest.[38] The revenue from these investments enabled the first Ursulines to offer free education and the school thrived immediately.

But their prosperity was to be short-lived. Soon the members of the Ryan family would begin suffering from symptoms of deadly tuberculosis. Then, in 1823, the king of France recalled the ailing Bishop Cheverus to France, despite a petition for him to remain in Boston signed by two hundred prominent citizens.[39] When the bishop returned to France in 1823, he too left a portion of his property to the Ursulines.[40] It is likely that among his gifts to the Ursulines was the antique ciborium that Henry Creesy so carelessly tossed aside on the night of the riot. Cheverus's replacement, Bishop Benedict Fenwick, did not arrive in Boston until 1825.[41]

During the final months of Cheverus's tenure, the Ursuline sisters were plagued with tuberculosis. Both Catherine Molineaux, Sister Mary Angela, and Catherine Ryan, Sister Mary Magdalene, died the same year. Ryan, who had been inspired by Father Thayer to cross the Atlantic and found the Boston convent, passed away on April 9, 1823 at age twenty-eight.[42] Three months after Bishop Cheverus left, the first Ursuline superior, Mary Ryan, Mother St. Joseph, also dying of tuberculosis, asked the Reverend William Taylor, whom Cheverus had appointed two years earlier to administer the diocese, to write to another community of Ursulines in Quebec City for help. By mid-1824, three of the four foundresses, all in their twenties and thirties, had died, leaving the community with very little leadership. The fourth, Margaret Ryan, Sister Mary Augustine, would die in 1827. Reverend Taylor turned to the elite Quebec Ursulines for help in maintaining the community, and the Canadian Monseignor Plessis was able to lend one sister from the Quebec monastery, thirty-year-old Mary Anne Ursula Moffatt, Mother Mary Edmond St. George.

Madame St. George, who gazed down from her window on the night of the fire with such angry disdain, had arrived in Boston in Spring 1824. Mary Ryan, the first Boston superior, then lay near death in the final stage of tuberculosis. When the plea for help came from the illness-decimated New England Ursulines, Mary Anne Moffatt had already been a member of the Quebec cloister for ten years, and had risen to the position of mistress of the *demi-pensionnaires,* wealthy day pupils, at the academy. Monseignor Plessis, the monastery's spiritual advisor, approached Moffatt as a possible superior for Boston, but she initially declined, citing her unworthiness. When his disappointment was reported back to her, "that he had believed her capable of greater generosity," she agreed to begin the long trip from Quebec to Boston.[43] Moffatt thus consented to undertake a radically different mission in Boston from that of Quebec's. She would be relocating from a community that dated back nearly two centuries to one that had been founded only four years before. And the school's clientele as envisioned by Father Thayer was quite different from the daughters of Canada's notaries, military officers, and physicians. One week after her community had voted to come to Boston's aid by lending her to the struggling Ursulines, Moffatt packed her nun's habit into a trunk, donned traveling clothes, and boarded a steamboat. She left her quiet home in the monastery and her native country of Canada to assume a central role in the tragedy that exploded in Charlestown, Massachusetts a decade later, but which began and ended with the gate of the Quebec cloister shutting behind her.

At her profession, Moffatt had taken the religious name of St. George, martyr and legendary slayer of dragons. Her choice of the knight as a personal patron was an appropriate choice for a woman of her strong character. Given her status as a convert, it is interesting that Moffatt chose St. George, a saint frequently associated with the English Protestant Church. The legend of Moffatt's patron saint, a Christianized variant of the Perseus and Andromeda myth,[44] however, echoes many of the threads of the historical narrative of the Charlestown convent riot.[45] Like Moffatt, St. George left his home and traveled to a new province, where he rose to prominence. The knight came to a town that bordered on a swamp where a terrible dragon lived. The people had mustered together to kill the beast, but its breath was so foul that they had to flee. To keep the monster away from their homes, then, each day the townspeople fed the dragon two sheep. When sheep became scarce, they drew lots for a human sacrifice. It was the king's daughter who made the unlucky choice. When no one volunteered to take the princess's place, the young girl bravely arrayed herself in her bridal finery and went out to meet her doom.

Riding his horse through the forest, St. George spied the virgin about to be sacrificed. The brave knight attacked the monster and transfixed it with his lance. He then borrowed the maiden's girdle, fastened it around the dragon's neck, and the maiden led the now docile beast into the city. When the townspeople saw the dragon, they were terrified, but St. George assured them that if they would only believe in Jesus Christ and be baptized, he would slay the beast at once.

After the king and thousands of his subjects converted to Christianity, St. George killed the dragon, and oxcarts transported its body to a safe distance. The king offered St. George the hand of his daughter, but the knight declined. Instead, St. George made four requests to the king, asking him to maintain the churches, honor priests, attend religious services regularly, and show compassion to the poor. Like Moffatt, St. George chose a life of celibacy and promoted Christianity and its works in a strange land with many dangers. In Moffatt's vision of the Charlestown academy, the daughters of the aristocracy would enroll in her school, untouched by popular anti-Catholic sentiment in Boston, and their spotless white dresses and pink sashes would calm the opposition.[46] Girls from her academy would go forth and become Christian mothers who would slay the beast of religious intolerance in New England. But the life of the mythical St. George was not to be without intense suffering, and Moffatt's life contained severe trials as well.

According to Butler's *Lives of the Saints,* as St. George continued to work toward the conversion of heathens, his work fell under the scrutiny of the emperor, who assigned a henchman named Datianus to stop his teaching. Datianus ordered that St. George be beaten with clubs, tortured with red-hot irons, and tossed into prison. But during the night, the saint was miraculously restored to health. The henchman then sent a magician to prepare for St. George a deadly poison—but the drug had no effect on him, and the magician was converted because of the miracle he witnessed. Angrily, Datianus ordered an even crueler physical punishment: St. George was to be crushed between two spiked wheels, then boiled to death in a cauldron of molten lead. Even then he emerged unscathed so Datianus called the executioner to behead him. This proved effective, and St. George died instantly. At the moment of martyrdom, a holy vengeance was wrought, and fire rained down from the heavens, consuming Datianus.

The story of St. George's martyrdom is filled with suffering and dominated by images of destructive fire. It tells of a saint who struggles heroically to save souls in a heathen land, but whose death yields many more conversions. Like St. George, Mary Anne Moffatt withstood many assaults on her property and reputation, fighting bravely as long as she retained the position of superior. But when she was, in effect, "beheaded," removed from her role as superior by Roman Catholic officials in 1835, like the legendary St. George, she was finally vanquished.

M ADAME ST. GEORGE, Mary Anne Moffatt, would have been an extraordinary woman had she been born in any age, but her achievements in early-nineteenth-century America were especially remarkable, given the constraints on women during that historical period. She had a sharp intelligence and was an efficient administrator. Moffatt had developed in herself a cultured refinement, and she was a great lover of music and the arts. She was perfectly bilingual in French and English, and probably had command of other languages as well. As the new mother superior of the Ursuline academy, Moffatt helped transform a day school offering the rudiments of education to Boston's poor immigrants into Charlestown's elegant and flourishing academy, enrolling the daughters of the Boston elite, mainly Harvard-educated Unitarians. From Father Thayer's early vision of a school ministering to poor Catholic girls, Moffatt, together with Bishop Benedict Fenwick, shifted this mission to serve a vastly different clientele.

The bishop saw in the opportunity to build an elegant new boarding school in Charlestown a way of amassing Protestant dollars to incubate his infant Catholic diocese. Moffatt was operating within the tradition of the Quebec Ursuline academy, catering historically to Canada's most elite Catholic and Protestant daughters, where she had herself been schooled and professed. Like her Ursuline sisters in Quebec, Moffatt enjoyed authority within her own community as superior, as well as power in the local community. She moved in Boston's upper social circles, a figure respected by the doctors, lawyers, and military officials whose daughters enrolled in her school. In the antebellum United States, there would have been no other route outside the convent for a woman to achieve a comparable authority.

But the path to social eminence through the cloister was fraught with perils, at least in New England, as Moffatt would ultimately learn.

The very nature of cloistered life, a seclusion from the secular world, in some ways contributed to her own and to her community's undoing. In taking lifetime vows in the Ursuline order, a woman made three binding promises: to live a life of chastity, poverty, and obedience. In abjuring sexuality and personal wealth, and in ceding total authority to one's superiors, women in the Ursuline order made some paradoxical gains. A gold ring pledged them to be the spouse of Christ, but freed them from the demands of childbearing which, in the nineteenth century, was difficult and dangerous. The work the Ursulines did was for the glory and benefit of the community, but within its structure, many nuns had more freedom than the average woman to pursue what in our age might be called careers: teaching, administration, and the arts, including music, painting, sculpture, needlework, and writing. The convent's hierarchical structure promised the opportunity for ever-increasing authority and responsibility. Convent vows that were framed as self-imposed limitations in some ways gave nineteenth-century women their best chance for a life of self-expression and fulfillment.

Ironically, had Moffatt not been as ambitious, capable, and visionary in building Mount Benedict, the school and the Ursuline order might have survived nineteenth-century Boston. Her personal success was in some ways the institution's downfall. When John Buzzell, the ringleader of the convent rioters, characterized Moffatt as "the sauciest woman I ever heard talk," he captured a trait that would so enrage the neighboring brick men that Moffatt became the focus of their animosity. Even after she had returned to Canada, they detested her memory enough to burn her in effigy. The rioters' hatred for Moffatt was exacerbated by her outspokenness, which included penning a reply to Rebecca Reed's best-selling exposé of convent life, *Six Months in a Convent*. Moffatt's book, *Answer to "Six Months in a Convent,"* sold out of its first printing of five thousand almost immediately, and a second printing of the same quantity had to be issued. For many years following the event, Moffatt would remain an object of scorn.

In August 1835, to celebrate the one-year anniversary of the burning of her convent, some of the ruffians who had participated in that riot gathered to mark the day. In colonial Boston, similar gatherings had marked "Pope Day" with parades through the streets, at least until the custom was prohibited by General George Washington. Pope Day, otherwise known as Guy Fawkes Day, had been transplanted from England with the arrival of the first settlers. It commemorated an unsuccessful plot by Catholic conspirators to blow up King James I and the assembled Parliament on November 5, 1605, in revenge for English laws against Roman Catholics. During Pope Day, it was customary to parade effigies of the Pope through the streets. To mark the first anniversary of the Ursuline convent's destruction, the party focused on a different icon. In this anniversary parade, marchers carried an effigy of Mary Anne Moffatt, the mother superior, which was first used as a shooting target, and then burned as a fitting commemoration of the fire that had taken just about all she and her community owned.[47]

Even after she was forced by Roman Catholic authorities to leave Boston and return to Quebec in May 1835, fascination with Moffatt continued. Rumors about her origins and fate abounded in both anti-Catholic and Catholic sources. One of the most interesting rumors involved speculations that she had entered the convent to hide her true identity. Some nineteenth-century sources charge that her name was not Mary Anne Moffatt, but Sarah Burroughs. The first rumors that she had purposely assumed a false identity appear in an anti-Catholic source in 1835, shortly after Moffatt walked out of the doors of the Quebec monastery for the last time and seemingly off the pages of history. Both here and in a later Canadian source, Moffatt's father is said to be named Burroughs or "Lord Burleigh." In Rebecca Reed's *Supplement to "Six Months in a Convent"* (1835) and in an appendix of Maria Monk's anti-Catholic book about a Montreal convent, *Awful Disclosures of the Hotel Dieu Nunnery,* the second edition of which was published in July 1836, Sister St. George is alleged to be Sarah Burroughs, the daughter of a notorious New Hampshire rake named Stephen Burroughs. Burroughs had gained a degree of fame by writing a best-selling book about his adventures as a forger and counterfeiter. Monk called Moffatt the "late Lady Superior of the Charlestown Nunnery" and claimed that she and St. George had spoken together in the Hotel Dieu Nunnery in Montreal. In context, the word "late" here must mean "recent" because her text continues, "Saint Mary St. George [*sic*] as she called herself, or Sarah Burroughs, daughter of the notorious Stephen Burroughs, as is her real name, removed to Canada at the latter end of May, 1835."[48] Moffatt in fact returned to Canada in May

1835, and stayed for a few weeks at Montreal's Hotel Dieu Nunnery before returning to Quebec.

The allegation that Moffatt was the daughter of Stephen Burroughs found its way into Catholic sources, and is repeated in Isaac Frye's monograph about the convent riot published in 1870. Frye suggests three surnames for Moffatt: Burroughs, Burley, and O'Boyle.[49] In Byrne's *History of the Catholic Church in New England* (1899), William Leahy, in his chapter on "The Burning of the Convent," says her name was Grace O'Boyle and that her sister, Sister Mary St. Henry, succumbed to tuberculosis after the riot.[50] The Burroughs hypothesis appears to have been taken less seriously in the twentieth century, but following the media glare cast upon her as a major character in the Charlestown riot, rumors and misinformation about her identity have remained. Looking at these accounts today, it becomes clear that the hypothesis that St. George was a member of the Burroughs family is plausible, though ultimately false. Like Moffatt, Burroughs led an interesting life, cultivated various identities, and wrote a best-selling book. Burroughs was, according to one source, "a splendid liar and a master of sophistry, in addition to his talents as an imposter, a thief, a counterfeiter, a seducer and a reflective moralist."[51] In his youth, according to his published autobiography, he confessed to being the worst boy in town. Later, he became a good parent and, like Moffatt, entered the field of education, serving as headmaster of an elite boys school in Trois Rivières. At the end of his life, Burroughs became a devout Catholic.[52]

Like Burroughs, Moffatt shaped her own identity as a colorful nineteenth-century personality. Described in contemporary sources as "a woman of masculine appearance and character, high-tempered, resolute, defiant, with stubborn, imperious will," Sister St. George had been born Mary Anne Moffatt in Montreal on August 28, 1793 of a Protestant family.[53] Her parents were William Moffatt and Genevieve Barbe Turkington (variations of her mother's name appear as Tarkington and Surkington). Moffatt's dominant role in the Ursuline convent tragedy becomes even more compelling given the adversity she faced prior to entering the order.

The downward path of her life following the convent burning, that is, from a high social and economic position to being rendered penniless and a pariah, is foreshadowed in the vicissitudes of fortune she experienced during her earliest years, even before the age of seventeen. The first years of her life, like those following her strange and troubling disappearance in 1836 from the Quebec monastery, have been shrouded in mystery for two centuries. But now a slim historical record has come to light, allowing us to confirm her family name and piece together a partial picture of those formative years.

There are very few solid facts to build on. A small fiche in the Ursuline monastery in Quebec lists Mary Anne Moffatt's birth date and the names of her parents, but the spelling of both parents' names, first and last, appear with many variations even in convent documents. Records of the boarding school affirm that Moffatt was enrolled as a student in the Quebec academy for three or four months during 1805, her tuition paid by her father, and again from 1807 to 1810, with the costs paid by her mother. One published letter, which is probably a translation from French, gives a few more details, mainly that she is the daughter of a British officer who died before May 1810, and that Moffatt, her mother, and a sickly brother were then living in Halifax, Nova Scotia. There her mother struggled to support the impoverished family by sewing.[54] On June 22, 1810, Mary Anne Moffatt abjured the Protestant faith and became a Roman Catholic in the Chapelle des Congrégationistes in the presence of Mrs. Catherine Bouchaud Wilson, her daughter Flore Wilson, and an M.A. Bouchard (probably Mrs. Wilson's sister).[55]

In addition, three letters of recommendation for Moffatt from Monseignor Edmund Burke of Halifax to the bishop of Quebec are in the collection of the archives of the Archdiocese of Quebec. In one of these letters, Father Burke fondly refers to Mary Anne as "a girl made for heaven," attesting to her faith and goodness. These letters, dated August 13, August 17, and September 9, 1811, seem to be the only documentary evidence about Moffatt's life before she entered the Ursuline monastery in Quebec in 1811. Consequently, a narrative of her early years must be based upon a hypothesis about her identity, drawn from compelling, but still circumstantial, historical evidence. This evidence has emerged from sifting through hundreds of Canadian land grant applications, land transfers, and the records of Canadian notaries.

Only one William Moffatt appears in these documents for the correct place and time in the Montreal district where Mary Anne was born in 1793. A couple of key facts support the hypothesis that this man is her father. First, a William Moffatt was living in a boarding house in Quebec City during the same period Mary Anne was enrolled in the Ursuline academy there, from roughly 1806 to 1809.[56] Second, the name of Mary Anne Moffatt's baptismal sponsor's husband, Thomas Wilson, appears in some of the same documents detailing William's business dealings. Wilson, who announced his engagement to Catherine Bouchaud in 1793, the year of Mary Anne's birth, had business dealings in Caldwell's Manor, south of Montreal near the Vermont border, during the time that William Moffatt lived and worked there.[57] Thomas Wilson's name also appears on the same land grant petition, August 4, 1792, as William Moffatt's.[58] That both Mary Anne and William lived in Quebec City at the same time, along with at least an eighteen-year connection with the Wilson family, strongly suggests that William Moffatt of the Eastern Townships is Mary Anne's father. The strongest evidence that he was *not* her father is that this same William married a woman named Jane and lived with her in Albany, New York. But this evidence is tempered by the fact that the name Jane in French Canada is often *Genevieve,* the name French Catholic records list for Mary Anne's mother.

When the American colonies went to war against Great Britain, a number of colonists remained loyal to the British. Many of these Loyalists were well-established businessmen whose economic success was tied to the current system of government, and who were not anxious to test their financial well-being under a new revolutionary system. A number of upper-class Loyalists were Anglicans by faith, and their strong loyalty to the ruler and obedience to law were not only political but religious tenets.[59] William Moffatt was a successful merchant and a manufacturer of potash, a fertilizer made from wood ashes. He owned a house in White Creek, Albany County and lived there with his wife Jane and a son Robert, born around 1773.[60] According to his own affidavit, he owned "a valuable Farm and a variety of personal property amounting to Two Thousand Seven hundred pounds New York Money."[61]

In 1777, William Moffatt joined the British Army under Lieutenant General Burgoyne, at Fort Edward, and served until his capture by Revolutionary soldiers. Moffatt wrote in an 1802 petition for compensation, that he "went into the service of the Government under Majr Keene . . . and continued in His Majesty's service until he was taken a prisoner by the Americans and carried in irons . . . and thrown into an ignominious Gaol."[62] Moffatt was a prisoner of the Americans for two years, before he made a dramatic escape from jail. He fled to Canada and joined a Loyalist regiment under the command of Major Edward Jessup, in whose corps, Jessup's Rangers, he served until the general reduction of the British troops in 1783.[63] On July 14, 1783, the same year he finished his military service with the British government, all of Moffatt's property was seized by the State of New York, on account of his adhering, with force and arms, "to the Enemies of this State, against the Peace of the People of the State of New York and their Dignity."[64]

Moffatt's decision to remain loyal to the Crown was both economically and personally costly. His wife Jane took the opposite side in the conflict, supporting the Revolutionaries. Thirteen years later the couple was still separated. The 1790 Vermont census lists William Moffatt as living alone in the island town of South Hero, Vermont, in Lake Champlain, near the Canadian border. Jane Moffatt is listed as Head of Family, in Albany County, New York, in the 1790 census, along with one free white male under sixteen years, probably her son Robert. In the surviving historical record, we can see themes that foreshadow some of the experiences and traits of Mary Anne Moffatt. It is not surprising that Moffatt, as Sister St. George, Canadian Ursuline, was not anxious to move to the United States when requested to do so in 1824. After all, the Yankees had imprisoned and probably mistreated her father. The seizing of his property in the name of American democracy may even seem to foreshadow the events of 1834, in which an ungoverned American mob took the law into their own hands and destroyed all she owned in the Charlestown convent. Moffatt's strong personality may well have been inherited from her mother Jane, who defied her husband's political beliefs by refusing to take an oath of loyalty to the British. Even after she apparently rejoined her husband in Canada, some time after 1790, Jane Moffatt continued to refuse to take that oath for another decade and a half. And with a substantial grant of 1,200 acres of land as her inducement, Mrs. Moffatt apparently refused to renounce her loyalty to the Americans.[65]

One year before Mary Anne's birth in Montreal, her father was in Quebec applying for compensation for his losses during the war. The British government had offered Loyalists an opportunity to apply for grants in what was called "the Waste Lands of the Crown." Loyalists and their dependents were typically offered two hundred acres each in areas the government wished to see settled as English townships. One such area was Chateaugay, lying directly across the St. Lawrence River from Montreal, and that is where, on July 7, 1792, "William Moffitt late of Jessup's Rangers for himself & Son" applied for two hundred acres of land.[66] During the same year, he also filed several other land grant applications. He took out a mortgage on a property on the island of South Hero (Grand Island) in Lake Champlain, where he had been living alone in 1790, from a farmer named Jesse Heath.[67] In 1794, the family was most likely living in Missisquoi Bay, on Lake Champlain in the town of St. Armand, near the Vermont border, not far from Grand Island. All of William Moffatt's petitions for these various substantial land grants were ultimately unsuccessful, mainly because the contested border between the United States and Canada during this period, as well as the mountainous terrain, made it impossible for the British government to guarantee such a grant.[68]

Between 1794 and 1804, Mary Anne's father spent periods of time, sometimes alone, at Caldwell's Manor, working for the wealthy Henry Caldwell, who was the lord, or seigneur, of a large estate. Today, the Caldwell's Manor area is the Canadian border town of Henryville, on the Richelieu River that connects to Alburgh, Vermont, in the general vicinity of St. Armand. While it is certain William Moffatt lived in Caldwell's Manor during the 1790s, the family seems to have moved away, since there are no records of Moffatts in the Anglican Church which opened there in 1815. The name Griggs, that of Moffatt's business partner, appears often in the Anglican records after 1815. In August 1795, Moffatt's petition for land in Chateaugay was granted, and he was given four hundred acres in the town, two hundred for himself and two hundred for his son. This area was incorporated as the Township of Godmanchester.[69]

By September 1795, Major Moffatt had sufficiently recovered from his losses in the American Revolution to loan a fellow Loyalist, Moses Cowen, the enormous sum of two thousand pounds. A notarized document in the hand of M. LeGuay, a Canadian notary public, hints of a troubled business deal into which Mary Anne's father and his partner, Major John Griggs, from Alburgh, Vermont, entered into with Cowen.

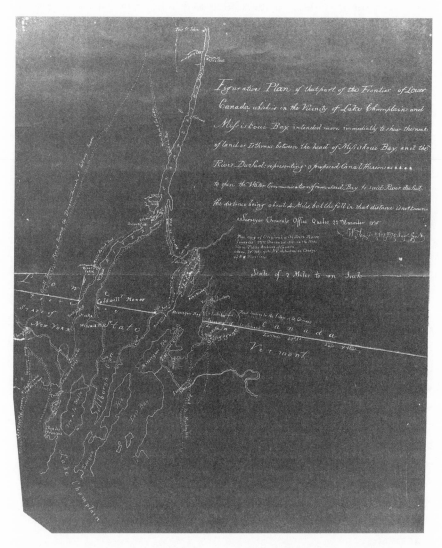

*Map of the frontier of Lower Canada, 1815, showing Caldwell's Manor,
St. Armand, and other locations where William Moffatt resided.*

At the time this deal was signed, Mary Anne would have been a toddler. In 1797, the Canadian notary LeGuay recorded and deposited the original deed, before witnesses and bearing the signature Wm. Moffitt.[70] Five years earlier, Moses Cowen had successfully applied to the British Government of Canada for a land grant in the township of Stoke, on the River St. François, in the Province of Lower Canada. In building a settlement and a mill, Cowen had run out of money, and had been forced to strike a deal to divide his land with Griggs and Moffatt. In advancing Cowen two thousand pounds, Griggs and Moffatt became partners with him in one-half of the township of Stoke. Moffatt thereby assumed a one-third share in half of the township of Stoke, on the banks on the River St. François, about ninety kilometers from his home on the Vermont border.

He was also successful in obtaining six hundred acres in the township of Shefford, a haven for Loyalists. During 1800–1802, the family remained at St. Armand, and William continued to pursue compensation for his war losses. But by February 1802, William had moved to a farm in Shefford, and sold one of his three two-hundred-acre lots for one thousand pounds.[71] On August 11, 1802, Moffatt finally received word that he would be compensated for his service in the form of 3,600 acres in Ham.[72] Four years later, however, the security of this grant was still uncertain because his wife Jane and a daughter of the same name had not yet taken the oath of loyalty to the king. In fact, it appears that the 2,400 acres were lost, 1,200 each for Jane and his daughter, because they were unavailable or refused to take that oath. Only William, who took the oath, retained 1,200 acres.[73] The existence of these two Janes raises some concerns about the hypothesis that William is Mary Anne's father. No application for land for Mary Anne, to which she would have been entitled as the daughter of a Loyalist, has been uncovered. We have seen that the wife's name might be a variant of the French *Genevieve,* the name listed as Mary Anne's mother in convent records. And very little is known about Mary Anne's siblings, outside of a sickly brother living with Mary Anne and her mother in Halifax in 1810. But two letters from 1835 and 1836 written by Mary Barber, a nun from the Charlestown convent, refer to Mary Anne's two nieces, named Mary Anne and Josephine, though no last name is given. According to Quebec monastery school records from the period, there were no Moffatts enrolled. So it is likely that Mary Anne and Josephine are the daughters of a married sister, possibly Jane Moffatt, who may have refused to compromise her principles to acquire a British land grant.

The refusal of his wife and daughter to take the loyalty oath resulted in legal troubles that would plague William Moffatt for years until his death sometime before 1810 when the family was plunged into poverty. Mary Anne Moffatt had entered the elite Ursuline Academy in Quebec as a boarding student the year before. The evidence for this comes from a letter written by Sister St. James, the Ursuline superior, dated May 24, 1810, to her brother, Jacques Panet, rector of the parish church of L'Islet, near Quebec City.[74] From this letter, we learn that by 1810, William Moffatt, an officer in the British army, had died and left his family in a state of near-poverty. Mother St. James wrote, "Four years ago, her daughter came to our Boarding School, her board being paid by a friend of her mother, on condition that she would not become a Catholic, although she is one secretly. . . ." So we can deduce that while William Moffatt lived in a boarding house in Quebec City, his daughter boarded at the elegant Ursuline academy, with the financial assistance of a family friend. By May 1810, Moffatt's mother, then a widow, was living in Halifax, Nova Scotia "with a sick son who consumes all that she can earn by sewing."

Moffatt's mother consented to Mary Anne's public conversion to Catholicism on June 22, 1810, and her admission to the Quebec monastery as a novice in October 1811, but as the superior of the Quebec monastery lamented, " . . . she possesses nothing." In her letter, St. James appealed to her brother, as a fellow member of the wealthy and powerful Panet family, to grant her request for "The charity which can do all and fears nothing." St. James was in fact asking for her brother's help in contributing to the *dot,* or dowry, which was customarily paid when a young woman entered the prestigious Ursuline community. To strengthen her case, St. James added,

> The demon, jealous of the conversion of souls, employs and will employ everything to hinder her salvation. You can oppose him by your charity, and promise to assist this young lady to her profession, which will be within two years if she still persists in these pious sentiments.

Whether or not Reverend Panet was able to assist, on June 22, 1810 sixteen-year-old Mary Anne Moffatt abjured the Protestant faith and became a Catholic at the Chapelle des Congrégationistes in Quebec City. Because she had already been baptized in the Protestant faith, a second baptism was not administered for conversion, but an abjuration. Permission for the service was given by Genevieve Moffet, her mother and *tutrice* or guardian. The abjuration record, with her signature, "M:A:U: Moffet," is in the Basilica of Notre Dame de Quebec.

Following this life-changing event, Moffatt returned to Halifax, Nova Scotia, presumably to await the arrival of her *dot* from the Reverend Panet. During the year, she was partially supported by the bishop of Nova Scotia, Edmund Burke, and engaged in helping him open a Catholic school. This is mentioned in three letters of recommendation from Monsignor Burke to the bishop of Quebec, found in the collection of the archives of the Archdiocese of Quebec, dated from the late summer of 1811.

In the first, Burke discussed the growing border tensions between Canada and the United States during this period and wrote that he was making preparations to send "*la petite Moffat*" to her convent in Quebec. He described her impatience to depart—and seconded the plan for two reasons. He called her a "*très bonne fille*," a very good girl, that the Quebec community needed, and noted that, although he had his own plans to open a school in Halifax, he dared not think only of that. He continued with his second reason, "*La seconde est quelle me coute de l'argent que je peux employer autrement*," her support was costing him money that he needed to spend elsewhere.

Bishop Burke's letter, along with Mother St. James's plea for assistance with the dowry, highlight the Moffatt family's poverty. But with assistance from Catholic supporters, and from her close relative, a Captain Robinson, aide-de-camp of the governor, the eighteen-year-old anxiously awaited her opportunity. When a boat left Halifax for Quebec around August 17, 1811, Moffatt, however, was not on board. An officer accompanying her relative Captain Robinson had bragged of being an atheist, and the strong-willed teenager refused to share the same boat with him.[75] Her next opportunity to leave was September 9, 1811, when Burke wrote to the bishop of Quebec that *la petite Moffat* finally would make her departure for the monastery in Quebec. Burke said *"elle m'a toujours paru une fille faite pour ciel"*—she had always seemed to him to be a girl made for heaven—and that he was sending her to Quebec to deflect any suspicions that he made her into a religious because he needed her for his own fledgling school.[76]

According to the records of the Ursuline monastery in Quebec, Moffatt entered the Novitiate on October 20, 1811, shortly after her arrival from Halifax. She took the veil on January 25, 1812 and made her profession according to schedule two years later. It was then that Moffatt chose the religious name of the knight St. George, slayer of the fiery dragon, and Christian martyr. All that is known of her life in the cloister for the next ten years is that she rose to the position of mistress of the *demi-pensionnaires,* or day pupils. Her name appears in an 1818 census listing as one of thirty-seven *soeurs de choeur,* or choir nuns, living in the Quebec monastery, but most of her life during this period is shrouded in the veil of time and the cloister.

During the same period that Moffatt left the world behind and entered the convent, border skirmishes broke out between the United States and the British army in Canada. The growing tensions are alluded to in the series of letters from Reverend Edmund Burke in Halifax to the bishop of Quebec. Just a few months after Moffatt's profession as an Ursuline nun, a man named William Moffatt from the same region of Canada, possibly her brother, broke ranks with his regiment and crossed enemy lines to marry a girl, probably an American.[77] That this man bears the same name as Mary Anne's father, and comes from the same region of Canada, where the border tensions were building, strongly suggests he is Moffatt's brother. If indeed he was, instead of taking a step up the social ladder, as she did, with lifetime vows in the elite Ursuline order, he took a step down. His disgrace provides quite a contrast to the station of his sister, who for the next ten years was a rising member of the elite and prestigious Quebec Ursulines.

One week after her community voted to come to Boston's aid by lending her to their New England sisters, Moffatt left her home on March 18, 1824, and boarded a boat for what would turn out to be an unexpectedly long journey.[78] She traveled to various religious houses for shelter, including the Soeurs de la Congregation de Notre Dame at Pointe-aux-Trembles, then to Champlain, then to the Ursulines at Trois Rivières, to the home of a parish priest at Berthier, and then on to

Montreal. In a letter written by her Quebec superior, Mother St. Henry, asking the Ursulines of Trois Rivières to provide her with a night of hospitality, Moffatt is affectionately described by her superior as "half of my soul, the heart of our venerable Mother St. Xavier and the glory of our institute."[79] After nearly a month's stay with the Soeurs Hospitalières in the Hotel Dieu convent, she would board a steamboat for Boston. Moffatt's trip began somewhat inauspiciously, as she was stranded in Montreal by an ice-jam on the St. Lawrence River, from March 23 to April 18, 1824. When she was finally able to depart, she boarded the steamboat *Congress,* which docked at White Hall, New York. Moffatt then boarded a packet boat for the Hudson Canal, headed for Albany, where her parents had lived before the Revolution.

From there, Moffatt wished to travel by land to Boston, but was told it was not practical. During the early 1820s, the best route to Boston was considered to be a steamboat to New York. On the steamboat *Richmond,* dressed as a lay woman, Moffatt traveled down the Hudson River to Long Island Sound, and stayed in New York with the Sisters of Charity. From New York, she took Captain Bunker's sailing boat, *Connecticut,* for a rough trip through Long Island Sound to Providence, arriving in Boston on April 30, 1824, forty-four days after her departure from Quebec.

The next day, on May 1, Moffatt joined a community grieving the death of their superior, Mary Ryan. She comforted them in their sorrow, they elected her superior, and she took immediate charge. The Reverend Taylor was very enthusiastic about the choice of St. George, since he had specifically requested a nun who spoke English. In a letter to Bishop Plessis of Quebec, Taylor wrote, "In selecting for us Madam St. George your Lordship could not have made a more happy choice; she is remarkably well calculated for the meridian of this city; and I am certain, with God's assistance, she will be a valuable acquisition to our infant but rapidly increasing establishment."[80] He repeats this sentiment in several other letters as well, praising her as a "saintly woman."[81]

Taylor also wrote frequently to alleviate anxiety in Quebec about Moffatt's well-being in the tuberculosis-ridden Boston convent. When the bishop of Quebec expressed deep concern for the health of St. George because of the recent deaths of the three Irish nuns, Taylor replied that the problem was not really the confined convent at all. A physician of celebrity, he wrote, pronounced the Ryans' complaint "a hereditary consumption" and said that the "contracted scale on which the convent is erected can not be, even remotely, influential in generating the disease of which the Ladies died."[82] Despite Taylor's assurances, however, cloistered life in Boston, with its lack of fresh air and no area for exercise, was clearly hazardous to the health of the sisters, and they needed a more wholesome location for the convent school. With the administrative talent that had marked her ascendancy in the Quebec monastery, Moffatt began planning the move. Within two years of her arrival, the Boston nuns were packing up their belongings and moving everything to a small farmhouse in Charlestown. At the center of the first Mass celebrated in the modest but freshly painted structure was the silver ciborium that would be desecrated on the night of the convent fire.

Moffatt herself described her pivotal role in the decision to move to Charlestown in the petition for indemnification from the State of Massachusetts after the fire. She wrote, "[I]n the year 1826, I, being Superior of this Community, with the approbation of its members, sold this property, in Franklin street, to Bishop Fenwick, for eight thousand dollars, and delivered into his hands, between seventeen and eighteen thousand dollars, the proceeds of sales of the stocks, (which sum was quite unconnected with the eight thousand before specified,) for the purpose of purchasing Mount Benedict, and building the convent."[83] Furthermore, after 1824, when Moffatt arrived in Boston, the fortunes of her family continued to improve. In the same petition for indemnification Moffatt added this note about the financial standing of her relatives during her years in Charlestown: "The property of the Community, has been increased every year, by liberal donations of *my* relations and friends, of *at least,* $600 or more, each year."[84] Apparently, the fortunes of the Moffatt family had risen along with those of Mary Anne as she rose to prominence in the Ursuline order.

INSCRIBED ON THE BASE of the battered but lovely ciborium, the vessel for holding the consecrated host, are the words "Marine de Brest." This silver vessel was forged in the seacoast town of Brest in French Brittany during the late eighteenth century. According to Ursuline legend, it was still lying on the anvil, and the branding iron had just impressed on the foot the crest of its birthplace, when a naval officer named DeGrasse entered the craftsman's shop.

> "The French monarch," announced DeGrasse to the silversmith, "has resolved to dispatch a military force to aid the American Colonies in just rebellion against the Mother Country. Count Rochambeau, who has today been appointed Lieutenant-General and placed in command of about 6,000 men, mostly all Catholics, has obtained a chaplain for his regiment and I am to provide the sacred vessels for the divine service." With an approving glance at the just minted chalice, DeGrasse saluted the shopman and departed. The modeler at once plunged the brass cup into a bath of purest silver, then lined it with gold.[85]

Later, after Count Rochambeau addressed his troops as they prepared for their departure to the colonies, the ciborium served as sacred vessel in a Mass for the success of their enterprise. It glittered in the sunlight during Mass out in full ocean, with the army chaplain whispering over the soldiers' bowed heads, *"Hoc est enim Corpus meum!"* Convent legend tells us it was part of the "divine morning repast" spread out on the shores of Newport, Rhode Island, where the French troops assembled before battle, to assist the Americans in the patriot's cause. The story continues that after "victory twined double garlands around the banners of France and America," Rochambeau remained in America, keeping with him the silver ciborium that had inspired such courage in his troops.[86]

Convent lore also tells us that Rochambeau, who died in 1807, visited an unnamed Ursuline convent with the ciborium he intended to bestow as a gift. According to this account, twelve nuns formed a circle around their friendly visitor. As one of the Canadian nuns regaled him with the tale of the burial of the French general Montcalm in the Ursuline Chapel in Quebec, his face glowed with patriotic gratitude. He stood erect and presenting the ciborium to the prioress he declared:

> This has been to me a most sacred amulet ever since I received the title of Lieutenant General. In the name of France I present it to you as an evidence of our appreciation of the Ursulines.[87]

Despite the legend, it is unlikely that Rochambeau gave the ciborium directly to an Ursuline convent—since the convent in Boston was not established until thirteen years after his death. Rochambeau might have presented the ciborium to Bishop Cheverus, who had arrived in the city of Boston on October 3, 1796—eleven years before the death of the general—and had been appointed bishop in 1808.[88] But the most likely scenario is that the ciborium was in the possession of Abbé de la Poterie, the chaplain who had served the French fleet in the West Indies.

In the summer of 1788, the fleet, under the command of Marquis de Sainneville, cruised to northern waters to avoid tropical hurricanes. The French ships anchored in Boston on August 28.[89] There the troops were warmly welcomed, attending a festive dinner given by Governor Hancock and a ball in which the elite of Boston mixed with French officers. When the French fleet sailed out of Boston Harbor on September 28, 1788, Abbé de la Poterie deserted and remained in Boston.[90]

Historian John E. Sexton believes that de la Poterie, the first resident priest of Boston, celebrated Mass on November 2, 1788 using an altar stone, sacred vessels, and vestments in the service that had been part of his navy chaplain kit.[91] La Poterie, whose real name was Claude Florent Bouchard, departed for New York and then to Quebec eight months later, on July 3, 1789.[92] Though he left Boston under a cloud of disgrace, the Cathedral of the Holy Cross in Boston was so named because de la Poterie was a Knight of the Order of the Holy Sepulchre of Jerusalem, and he had obtained a relic of the cross in Rome. In de la Poterie's original mahogany box with brass ornaments, that relic—said to be a piece of the true cross—still lies in the cathedral.[93] When de la Poterie left this relic behind, it is possible that with it, he also left the ciborium. The clergyman quit Boston in haste after being suspended from the ministry because of his bad character. His offenses included running up large debts and exploiting Boston's gratitude to the French king to line his own pockets.[94] If the ciborium remained behind, it would have been used by la Poterie's successors, Father Louis de Rousselet and Father John Thayer, who left all his property to the Ursulines.

But if it had been given to Bishop Cheverus by Rochambeau, perhaps the bishop, before his departure to France in 1823, would have bestowed this gift upon the Ursulines in recognition of their community's care of the French General Montcalm, following his mortal wounds in

*The Mount Benedict ciborium thrown away on the night of the fire
by Henry Creesy, who later committed suicide.*

battle on Quebec's Plains of Abraham.[95] Evidence for this surfaced during the testimony of the rioters. During the trial, descriptions were given of the some of the sacred vessels lost on the night of the fire, and the damaged ciborium may have even been introduced as evidence in court. Mary Anne Moffatt testified that "there were silver ornaments [a piece of silver was produced]. It was presented to the institution by the Archbishop of Bordeaux (Cheverus). This piece of plate was on a small altar—there was a cross on it formerly."[96] If this is the same ciborium, its cross may have been repaired following the trials. Whether the ciborium came to the Ursulines from Father Thayer or from Bishop Cheverus, once in the possession of the Ursulines, it was the very center of the key event at daily Mass, the consecration and transubstantiation of the Host.

On the night the convent was attacked, two sisters raced to the chapel to remove the tabernacle, and hid it in a bush in the convent garden. One of the nuns in the convent, Mother O'Keefe of Saint-Joseph, told a version of the ciborium story which was recorded by a sister at Trois Rivières. With the rioters at the door, said Mother O'Keefe, "Sister Saint Ursula came to my aid, and together we carried the whole tabernacle, for it was not yet fastened solidly to the altar. While we worked to save our most precious treasure, the broken panes of glass covered the carpet of the sanctuary and we had hardly time to leave the chapel, when a crowd of ragamuffins invaded the holy place." She went on to say that the tabernacle was hidden, as she recalled, "in a clump of asparagus which must have been three feet high. . . . [O]ur intention was to ask a priest to remove the holy articles when the mob should have gone away."[97] In Charlestown, it is likely that consecrated host from this valuable ciborium spiritually comforted the Loyalist's daughter, Mary Anne Moffatt, as she renewed her covenant with her adopted church, in her adopted land.

## CHAPTER TWO

# MOUNT BENEDICT BLOOMS

## *Convent Secrets and the Early Years*

*I remember the convent before there was any trouble. As a young fellow, I
used to hop on the provision wagons that were going up the hill and
through the gates. I could see how the place looked inside, and could see
the lady superior and the rest of them there. Everything was quiet then,
but it didn't last very long.*

—JOHN C. TENNEY, Somerville resident

O
N A JUNE MORNING IN 1826, a company of young girls
walking to school passed the newly established Ursuline convent in Charlestown, Massachusetts. The property had just
been purchased and the Ursulines were preparing to expand their
school for young ladies in this more spacious location. Turning to her
friends, one of the girls asked how they should like to become nuns.
Among her listeners was quiet thirteen-year-old Rebecca Reed, destined to become the Charlestown convent's most famous escaped nun.
The young girl who had posed the question, a Roman Catholic, described the life of cloistered nuns, and the spiritual inducements that led
to their taking the veil.

"I should like it well," declared Rebecca, intrigued with her friend's
picture of a holy and secluded life. Five years later, she would flee the
convent and tell sensational stories of her life in a cloister that would
fuel the convent's destruction.

The Ursuline sisters who were the property's new owners had not yet taken possession of the renovated farmhouse standing at the base of the rocky hill that had served as a fortification during the Revolutionary War. For most of the fifty years after the war, this drumlin, known as Ploughed Hill, had stood a rough and broken wasteland, despite its magnificent views of Boston's harbor islands. In the years before the purchase, a small farm had been established. A few weeks after their conversation, the schoolgirls could look out of their classroom windows at Mount Benedict, newly renamed in honor of Boston's bishop, Benedict Fenwick, who himself paid several visits to the new property. And the girls watched the Ursulines' hired men as they began their steady improvement of the nunnery grounds.

The long black veils worn by the nuns, their black robes and starched white aprons struck the girls as both solemn and romantic. These new neighbors fascinated the girls and were the subject of lively discussion and speculation among them. What would it be like to live in a convent? Do nuns spend the whole day praying? The girls dreamed of hearing the beautiful singing of the convent choir. When one of the scholars remarked that the women were Roman Catholics, and that her parents disapproved of their beliefs, the girl who had asked how they should like to become nuns burst into tears. She begged the girls to refrain from such comments, insisting that the nuns were truly *saints* and *God's people*. Rebecca Reed and her friends listened intently to the Catholic girl's passionate defense of the community and the nuns' secluded holy life. The idea of a quiet and cloistered life appealed deeply to Reed. A few months later, Rebecca approached her parents to ask if she could join the convent as a novice.

The Reeds at first thought their daughter was going through a passing phase. When Rebecca's health appeared to decline a little, and she had apparently not lost interest in the convent, her parents decided to send her to New Hampshire for an extended visit with friends. This rural setting, though, only whetted the girl's appetite for a life of seclusion, and five summers later, at age eighteen, Rebecca would enter Mount Benedict. In a narrative written after her six months' stay as a novice there in 1831, she recalled her teenage fascination with the cloister, especially during her summer in New Hampshire, when she imagined she would spend "hours of retirement and happiness."[1] During the summer

Reed's fantasy was born, the hired men, possibly some of those who would later turn against and destroy the community, steadily improved the property for its exotic new owners.

I N HER DETERMINATION to relocate the Ursulines, Mary Anne Moffatt found a ready ally in Boston's new bishop, the Right Reverend Benedict Fenwick, who had arrived there on November 1, 1825. Fenwick was a native of Maryland, born September 3, 1782. He was a patrician descendant of one of the first two hundred families that originally came over from England under the charter of Lord Baltimore to settle the state.[2] Fenwick had been educated at Georgetown, became a Jesuit and taught for a while on the faculty there, and served as the college's president.[3]

Unlike his slight and delicate predecessor, Bishop Cheverus, Fenwick was vigorous and amply built. In his later years, he is said to have weighed three hundred pounds. According to Robert H. Lord, "his complexion was so swarthy and his hair and eyes so dark, as with other members of his family, that among Georgetown students the quite improbable story circulated that there was a strain of Indian blood in the Fenwicks."[4] He was at once a southern gentleman, a scholar, a practical man of business, and a missionary devoted to the spread of Catholicism. Of Fenwick's intellectual powers, Orestes A. Brownson, a well-known nineteenth-century writer and convert to Catholicism, said,

> He seemed to have read everything, and to have retained all he read. No matter what the subject, however obscure or remote from his professional studies, on which you sought information, he could either give it or direct you at once to the source whence you could obtain it. He left on us the impression of a man of rare natural powers, of varied and profound learning, and of being the best informed man we have ever had the honor of meeting.[5]

Having proved himself a successful administrator, Fenwick was sent to Boston, where he had one assistant, the Reverend Patrick Byrne. The Catholic population was growing, and at the end of his first three years in Boston, it numbered over seven thousand, a tenfold increase from the

*Portrait of Bishop Benedict Fenwick, circa 1831, by James Bowman, who also painted a missing portrait of Mary Anne Moffatt.*

date of Bishop Cheverus's arrival in 1796.[6] By 1829, a second church was needed to handle the increasing numbers of Catholics in the Boston vicinity, and Charlestown was selected for the site. St. Mary's Church was dedicated in 1829. One of the chief attractions of Charlestown was that together Moffatt and Bishop Fenwick had established the Ursuline convent there in 1826.

Immediately upon his arrival, Bishop Fenwick had attributed the Ursulines' "sickly and infirm state" to the fact that they were "extremely confined . . . unable to take any exercise or enjoy the pure air."[7] In the first entry of the multi-volume diary he kept for more than twenty years, the bishop recorded his surprise that the location adjacent to the Cathedral of the Holy Cross should ever have been selected for the establishment of a nunnery. The drawbacks were obvious. It was located in "the immediate neighbourhood of a Theatre, confined & contracted & withall exposed to the observation of all those inhabiting the opposite houses." There was no room for the cloistered nuns to exercise, and consequently, the six nuns seemed to "drag out a lingering existence."[8]

Mary Anne Moffatt may have at first been surprised that Bishop Fenwick was such an enthusiastic advocate for the Ursulines. She had favored another successor. When Bishop Cheverus's seat had become available, Moffatt, like Cheverus himself, had hoped that the bishop would be succeeded by the Reverend William Taylor, whom Cheverus had appointed vicar-general. Like the superior, Father Taylor had been born of a Protestant family and converted to Catholicism. His birth and solid education in Ireland rendered him sympathetic to liberal Protestants, and he was an intelligent and articulate speaker, well-mannered and eager to unite Catholic with non-Catholic.[9] But Rome decided against offering the bishopric to Taylor, even though Cheverus and Bishop England of Charleston, South Carolina had supported him.[10] Taylor's support among the other U.S. bishops was limited. Taylor himself was extremely disappointed to have not been offered the position, and permanently left the country for France after preaching a bitter sermon in Baltimore on the topic of episcopal appointments.[11]

Mary Anne Moffatt, the subject of many admiring letters by the Reverend Taylor to Quebec, reacted with indignation when he was passed over. In fact, in her anger, she turned against one of Father Taylor's closest supporters, Bishop England, inexplicably blaming him for the turn of events. In a letter to Bishop England, dated February 6, 1826, she apologized for her unfriendly reception of him, probably during his visit for the induction of Bishop Fenwick:

> Let me now apologize for the cool reception which I gave your Lordship—When I think of it, I am quite confused; and am tempted to regret, that your visit to this quarter did not take place at some other time; for, on that occasion, I felt so sensibly the approaching departure of my sincere friend and brother in Christ, the Rev. Mr. Taylor, that it was almost impossible for me to act otherwise . . . [12]

Moffatt's letter clearly demonstrates her headstrong quality—and certainly a lack of submissiveness before a bishop, which would lead to her own departure a decade later. Whether, upon looking back, she truly regretted the behavior or simply recognized that it was not politic is hard to tell. In the same letter, she asked Bishop England to extend a welcome to the Ursuline order for establishment in Charleston, South Carolina. Ten years later, Ursulines opened their third convent in the United States in England's diocese—close to the time that Moffatt's convent was reduced to a heap of smoldering ruins. On this and other occasions to follow, Moffatt may have found herself regretting that she had reacted in haste.

Within six weeks of writing her apology to Bishop England for expressing her dismay over the choice of Fenwick, she wrote to the Reverend Panet, now Bishop of Quebec, asking for financial assistance to aid Fenwick's plans for expanding the Ursuline school. In this letter, she refers to Fenwick as *notre cher évêque,* our dear bishop, who is very zealous for the glory of God, and who is building for the community a new monastery.[13] On April 21, 1826 she received a negative response to her request. The former bishop had left a large debt, and it was unlikely that any of the Canadian parishes could spare their thin resources for the Boston mission. Mary Anne Moffatt, then, had to depend almost entirely on the help of her new bishop in Boston, Benedict Fenwick.

Moffatt was able to work very effectively with Fenwick and in the early years of establishing the Charlestown academy they enjoyed a collegial relationship. Both shared an ambition to found an institution of a different sort than had originally been intended by Father Thayer. Mount Benedict would not be a school for poor Irish girls—but an elegant academy that would attract the daughters of Boston's and other cities' elite. It would be a high-priced school that would use Protestant money to help build the Roman Catholic mission in the area. The refined Ursulines would improve the image of the Church Fenwick was anxious to mainstream, and the girls graduating from Mount Benedict would influence their husbands and sons to look benevolently on a growing Catholic presence. When the mission shifted is not precisely clear—but it certainly began with bringing Mary Anne Moffatt from Quebec to lead the institution. That she and Fenwick shared a common vision helped the institution flourish during these early years.

The Ryans, attracted by the charismatic Father Thayer and his passionate devotion to the poor, had shared his desire to work with the immigrant classes in Boston. While they studied and took their vows at Trois Rivières, the Ryans never officially entered that community. The Canadian convent served only as training ground for religious life and rule. There, the foundresses focused exclusively on spiritual training, manual work, and mastering the Rules and Constitutions.[14] Ursuline monasteries in this era were autonomous and a woman entering a convent did not take lifetime vows in the order; instead, she pledged her life to a specific monastic community. The Ryans, entering at Trois Rivières, were intent on founding their own group with a specific mission—to educate the poor Catholic girls in Boston.

Historically, the community of Trois Rivières has served a more diverse community than that of Quebec. The sisters there ran both a school and a hospital. They were a spinoff community from the Quebec Ursulines—but once removed from the cosmopolitan setting of Quebec City, the mission became more diversified. Seventeenth-century Trois Rivières was a trade outpost for fur, wood, and commerce with the Amerindians along the St. Lawrence River that would evolve into a bustling town.[15] The mission of the Ursulines of Quebec was traditionally directed to the education of the urban elite, but Trois Rivières began accepting boarders only in 1836.[16] When Mary Anne Moffatt came on loan from Quebec to the struggling Boston community, she brought with her a vision of an elegant boarding academy, for which the Ursulines of Quebec had long been famous.

Within six months of his arrival in Boston, Fenwick had located a suitable property for sale and had figured out how to make the deal work financially. With part of the Ursulines' proceeds from the sale of the Boston convent, he purchased ten acres in Charlestown along the Medford Road on May 18, 1826. The property was an old farm that had excellent rich soil, and for $3,300, the sisters became its new owners. The trustees of Mount Benedict were four Americans: Fenwick and three Ursulines, Catherine Wiseman, Elizabeth Harrison, and Mary Barber. With his own purchase of the convent next to the church for $8,000, Fenwick was able to secure the cathedral on one side from troublesome, annoying neighbors, who might have purchased the convent themselves and "converted the house into a drum shop & the yard into a nine pin alley."[17] He planned to use this property as a residence for himself and his clergy.[18] The day after he signed the agreement, a carpenter was engaged to do needed repairs to the Charlestown farmhouse and to add two wings to the structure, one for a chapel and the other for a kitchen. To preserve the sisters' cloistered life, Fenwick immediately had an acre and a half fenced as an enclosure.[19] By June 1826, when Rebecca Reed and her friends watched with interest the doings on the property, Fenwick had contracted for a new road, dug a new well, and decided that on the prospect of the hill, he would build an elegant monastery.

In his diary of June 21, 1826, Fenwick recorded his obvious pleasure in this new acquisition, seemingly oblivious to the local curiosity about the community:

> Here they can exercise & enjoy the pure air without being inspected by or exposed to the observation of neighbours; here they have a property sufficiently spacious for any desirable purpose for a farm, for pasture, for a garden, for a vineyard; for large & spacious walks; for an orchard, in short, for anything whether of utility or comfort; here they can have an abundance of every kind of vegetables not only for their own consumption, but likewise for market; here they can keep their own cows, raise their own pigs, their own poultry, & much of their own provisions . . . here they possess in fee simple a landed estate which will encrease in value in proportion to the encrease & improvement of the

town near where it is situated, & which, in its natural soil, will always afford a sufficiency of the necessaries of life for even a numerous family. God be praised, it is theirs![20]

The bishop, unfortunately, was not always a perceptive reader of the social and political climate. Throughout his years of involvement with the convent, Fenwick tended to underestimate the level of hostility that a Catholic presence was generating.

On July 31, 1826, the six nuns left Boston at four o'clock in the morning to avoid the stares of their neighbors, and moved into the enlarged farmhouse at the foot of the hill. The next day, the bishop gave the sisters a tour of their new property and they were, he notes, "enchanted with the prospect from the hill, the site of their future house." During their walk, Fenwick outlined how he envisioned developing the property, with its extensive gardens and orchards:

Here . . . is your Monastery to be built. The front shall face Bunker hill there. Behind shall be your garden. It shall occupy two acres of land. There on the declivity of the hill towards the north your orchard shall be—further on between the orchard & the canal shall be laid out in a meadow—all that side next to the Medford Road shall be appropriated for a vineyard. There at the brow of the hill extending all along said brow shall a fence run till it meets your enclosure—the same on the other side—the space enclosed between shall be your garden . . ."[21]

Fenwick's dream was to be fully realized in the tastefully arranged gardens and elegant brick building that were to rise on the site. In the front, extensive gravel walks were to be shaded by forest trees including elm, horse-chestnut, and sycamore planted by the bishop himself. Along the canal ran more than two acres of lush meadowland, of clover and alfalfa. On the steeply descending south side, terraces were laid where a vineyard of the choicest grapes was planted, through which shady walks could be made.[22] The convent faced east, and from its front windows, Boston, with its beautiful State House and dome towering over the urban scene, was visible, as was the large harbor with sailing vessels entering and departing, and the green harbor islands beyond. Closer, tall masts bobbed in Charlestown's United States Navy Yard, and the sites of Revolutionary battles, Bunker and Breed's hills, rose nearby. To the left of the convent building, the growing towns of Chelsea and Malden, connected to Charlestown by two bridges over the Mystic River, bustled in the distance, behind which beautiful hills rose with a gentle slope. Here, gorgeous sunsets could be enjoyed from the convent windows as the eye ranged over verdant fields and cottages, gardens and orchards spreading to the west. The Middlesex Canal wound through the hills until its waters once more mingled with the Charles River. To the right, the estates of Roxbury and Brookline could be seen, as well as picturesque hills skirting the horizon in the direction of Dorchester. And beneath, traffic streamed over the Charles River bridges connecting East Cambridge with Boston.[23] It was a spectacular acquisition. The school's *Prospectus* described the nuns' new property in glowing terms: "This beautiful and extensive establishment about two and a half miles from Boston . . . commands one of the most beautiful prospects in the United States." Moreover, as the bishop had noted, it was theirs entirely, for during the trial of one of the convent rioters, John R. Buzzell, Moffatt testified "that the community owed nothing for the lands or buildings at Charlestown."[24] The Ursulines could be proudly independent from their neighbors and, to some degree, from the diocese of Boston.

But not everyone shared the superior's pleasure. One of the Charlestown selectmen, John Runey, whose gossip may have helped goad the mob into attacking the convent, had for his own reasons wished to take down the farmhouse into which the nuns were moving. Perhaps he had plans for the land himself. In a letter written after the convent burning, Moffatt said of Runey's jealousy, "he himself told me, after we removed to Mount Benedict, that it had been his intention to come with thirty men and tear down the house situated at the lower part of the hill. . . . [I]n the mean time, we resided in the house which Mr. Runey contemplated demolishing, the first night that we spent under its roof: he was deterred from putting his design in execution by seeing me walk out on the hill that morning, and all the community doing so the next day."[25] Furthermore, she continued, "All of the men whom we employed at Mount Benedict were unanimous in saying, that Mr. Runey had no good feelings toward our institution; that he said it would never prosper, and that it would one day be destroyed."[26]

Toiling away at the foot of Mount Benedict in the brickyards that lay at the outskirts of urban Charlestown, brick makers, mainly Presbyterian Scots from New Hampshire, daily gazed up at this flourishing community. These men were largely of the same ethnic stock as Mary Anne Moffatt and had come south to labor for a pittance, having failed at growing grass crops on overworked New Hampshire farms. In the brickyards that surrounded the area of Mount Benedict, they earned a scant three to four dollars a week, and the relatively opulent life style of their new Roman Catholic neighbors, foreigners and—worse—*women,* was a source of irritation. From outside its gates, Rebecca Reed and her teenage friends subjected the convent's inhabitants to intense scrutiny and gossip.

The cloister's inhabitants, meanwhile, were making plans to build their elaborate brick edifice on Mount Benedict, spacious enough to receive what they hoped would be many new pupils. With subsequent purchases totaling about $6,000, the nuns ultimately had twenty-four acres in an area of Charlestown known as "beyond the neck," referring to a peninsula connecting Charlestown to its western portions. Work began shortly afterward on the magnificent brick building on the hill's summit, to be completed within two years. By January 27, 1827, the 150,000 bricks that would make up the main part of the new convent were delivered, representing a substantial contract for the local brickyards. In April, the bishop was overseeing the planting of forty apple trees in the convent orchard[27] and cherry trees along the front driveway.[28] While he gently patted the dirt around the tender trunks of the new trees, he looked up to see the workmen pouring the foundations. The bishop contracted with Bell & Vaughn, local carpenters, for the work, for which he agreed to pay $4,400.

The masonry firm of Stowel, Murphy, Carroll & Co. was hired at the rate of one dollar and a half per perch for the stone work to build the double-faced brick wall. The masons would provide the laborers and scaffolding, and the bishop would provide the stone, brick, lime, and sand.[29] The foundation stone for the new convent was laid on May 8, 1827. Fenwick saw plans for his school, which he intended to "put on the most respectable footing," progressing apace, and he hoped it would be ready to welcome students in September 1827. Bishop Fenwick faithfully drove the two and a half miles to Charlestown twice a week to say Mass for the Sisters. He expected to be able to appoint a chaplain to the Ursulines—but for the next seven years, the duty fell mainly to him. Fenwick and Moffatt were the main links that connected this insular community of women to the outside world.

MARY ANNE MOFFATT was a competent businesswoman and could be charming in the company of her boarders' parents. Because of her outspoken and abrupt manner, however, the superior did not make close friends easily. When she arrived from Quebec in May 1824, she found in the last of the Irish foundresses an intimate companion. Margaret Ryan, who had learned French from Father John Thayer in Ireland, was Moffatt's assistant superior. From all accounts she appears to have had a very different personality. Where Moffatt had a secular and executive mind, Ryan was intensely spiritual and artistic. Each of Ryan's three sisters had become Ursuline nuns, and all were deeply religious women. Moffatt's expertise was administration, but Ryan was an artist—a talented musician and composer. These traits engendered deep admiration and love from her superior. The women became inseparable, with Ryan serving as Moffatt's closest confidante. It appears that this relationship with Margaret Ryan was one of the few deep relationships in Mary Anne Moffatt's life. It was reciprocal and evident to the other members of the community that the two women shared an intense and deep affection.

The happiness of the new inhabitants in their spacious property, especially that of Mary Anne Moffatt, was dimmed by the continuously failing health of this much loved figure. Sister Mary Augustine was a gifted woman—an able administrator, an exceptional teacher, and a talented musician. For St. Patrick's Day in 1827, a beautiful hymn that she had written in honor of the saint had been sung, and it continued to be sung for their March 17 celebrations in years to come.[30] As mother assistant, Ryan was a crucial member of the community, and her personal piety was a model for others. Her illness and death would be personally devastating to Moffatt.

Sadly, the move from the suffocating accommodations in Boston to the clean air of Charlestown could not save this beloved companion from the scourge of tuberculosis. When Ryan began manifesting symp-

*The distinctive signature of Madame St. George,*
*the convent's mother superior.*

toms of the disease, the bishop needed to offer words of consolation not only to her, but to Moffatt.[31] The sisters living in the convent at that time believed the change of location was fatal to her health, although she must have been suffering from the early stages of tuberculosis before the move. As Elizabeth Harrison, Sister Mary John, wrote, "the sudden change from a close confined house to this delightful situation, where the atmosphere is so remarkably salubrious, has been detrimental to her delicate constitution."[32]

On May 8, 1827, the same day the foundation stone was laid for the new convent, Ryan began vomiting blood. When she suffered another episode two days later, the doctor was called and he prescribed blood letting. After this she seemed improved, and Moffatt and the other sisters were encouraged. But on May 31, 1827, the feast of Ursuline foundress St. Angela Merici, the last surviving foundress of the community had a terrible relapse. The physician, hastily summoned, gave Moffatt the devastating news: her dear Margaret would not recover.

After Bishop Fenwick visited Ryan's sick room on June 8, 1827, he described her condition in his diary (referring to himself in the third person, as was his practice).

> She seems far gone in a consumption. He is greatly afraid she will never recover from it, though her usefulness is such that he cannot but entertain the hope God may yet spare her for the Convent—her talents being great and her piety being most exemplary.

In the whitewashed convent infirmary, Fenwick recommended that Ryan pray for patience in her suffering. He then told her he would be leaving the next day for a visit to the Catholics in the state of Maine. Ryan asked how long he would be absent. When he replied, six weeks—she said, with quiet resignation, "You will not on your return find me alive."[33] The bishop offered words of consolation "addressed as much to the other religious as to her" and returned to Boston to prepare for his journey. Ryan's prophecy, it turned out, was true. She died August 11, 1827, seven years to the day before the beautiful convent, now nearing completion, would meet its fiery destruction at the hands of an angry mob.

With Fenwick away, and Ryan's condition worsening, the convent was plunged into a frantic ritual of prayer and sacrifice. The Last Sacraments were administered, and Ryan "answered all the prayers with an admirable presence of mind."[34] Elizabeth Harrison, writing to Trois Rivières on behalf of Moffatt, who herself was too overwhelmed or distraught for the task, described the demanding course of prayer and sacrifice followed by members of the community in an attempt to stave off the certain death predicted by the doctors. Significantly, Harrison, whose own mental illness caused her to flee the convent during the summer of 1834, sparking the convent riot, outlined the desperate measures taken. In her letter from 1827, Harrison narrated the frantic rituals that might have seemed to outsiders a form of communal madness. Had the Protestant parents who entrusted their daughters to the decorous Ursulines been aware of these measures, they might have concluded that the Catholics were indeed susceptible to dangerous superstitions. At Moffatt's direction, the community was plunged into a desperate attempt to manifest a miraculous cure of Margaret Ryan, with the aid of a mysterious miracle worker named Prince Alexander Leopold Hohenlohe-Waldenburg-Shillingsfürst, titular Bishop of Sardica, and a member of a Germanic princely family of the Holy Roman Empire.

Hohenlohe was born August 17, 1794 at Kupferzell in Würtemberg. Ordained a priest in 1815, his miracle working began in 1821, when he cured the eight-year paralysis of Princess Mathilda von Schwarzenberg. The prince is reported to have effected several cures of the terminally ill in Europe, nearly all of them women. Three years earlier, on March 10,

1824, Prince Hohenlohe, then in Bamburg, Bavaria, had offered to pray for people outside of Europe, and had reportedly effected the cure of the sister of the mayor of Washington, D.C. At 9:00 A.M., which corresponded to 3:00 A.M. in the District of Columbia, the mayor's sister, Mrs. Ann Mattingly, who had been suffering from cancer, was miraculously cured of a variety of devastating symptoms. According to the watch of the officiating priest, Mrs. Mattingly's restoration took place at 3:45 A.M. Roman Catholic believers in this case thought this time frame was proof of Hohenlohe's efficacy, but skeptics sneered that "a miss was as good as a mile." Furthermore, they contended, only three cases in Europe actually contained evidence of cures, "and those *all of females*."[35]

Between 1824 and 1838, at least seventeen miraculous cures took place in Maryland, Kentucky, and the District of Columbia, most of which were attributed to Hohenlohe. Mrs. Mattingly was again cured—this time of a sprained ankle in 1831, and thirteen other women were healed, ten of whom were nuns. Six cures occurred in the Convent of the Visitation in Georgetown, three at St. Joseph's, Emmitsburg, two among the Sisters of Charity of Nazareth in Kentucky, and one in the Carmelite monastery at Portobacco, Maryland.[36] In summer 1827, while Boston's Bishop Benedict Fenwick was away on his six-week mission to the Indians, the prince was invited to intervene in the illness of Margaret Ryan. Harrison's letter to the Ursuline superior at Trois Rivières describes Ryan's death from the disease, despite Hohenlohe's officiating at a series of Masses on her behalf, and the nuns' round-the-clock novenas stretching for a period of almost two weeks. Prince Hohenlohe had a chequered reputation in the decades that followed until his death in 1849, near Vienna. The frenetic rituals connected with this failed cure are one of the real secrets of the Charlestown convent:

> We made two novenas in unison with the prince but our prayers were not heard, the Almighty in his infinite wisdom, having other designs in her regard. Though her recovery was not effected, our hopes did not fail, we attributed it to the prince's not saying Mass on that day. August approaching and seeing that she still survived, we commenced another novena, animated with much confidence and trusting that on the 10th (the day on which Prince Hohenlohe would pray for that intention) she would be restored to

perfect health. The day arrived, and the holy Sacrifice was offered at three o'clock, after which, the holy Communion was administered to her, but the miracle not being effected, resignation to the Divine Will became our only resource.

Rather than bowing to divine will, however, Moffatt pressed on. As Prince Hohenlohe's hoped-for miracle had not occurred, another round of prayer was ordered by the Superior. Even when Ryan herself recognized that the end was near, Moffatt could not accept it:

Seeing now, that she had only death to expect, she awaited its approach with a serenity and calmness which indicated the sweet assurance and composure of her heart. We, however, did not despair of her cure, to obtain which we commenced a novena to St. Joseph on the same day. She answered the prayers with us in a distinct tone of voice, after which she composed some verses, addressed to our dear Reverend Mother Superior, to the religious, and one also to our dear bishop, who was then absent, being on a mission to the Indians. On the preceding day, the physician had found her so much better, that he thought she might yet live one or two months, but the hour of her dissolution had arrived. . . . [O]ur Lord would not prolong her banishment, but hastened to welcome her to those regions of bliss where he had prepared for her a recompense adequate to her merit. On the same evening, about eight o'clock we perceived a great rattling in her throat; which, increased before ten o'clock. It was then she took about a spoonful of arrowroot, but could afterwards swallow nothing else until 12 o'clock, when being told that it had been our Reverend mother's intention, for her to take some drink, it seemed that obedience gave her additional strength, for though extremely weak, and visibly seized by death, she took the glass in her hand and drank the whole. Shortly after she spoke to me, but afterwards remained silent. About three quarters after twelve, I spoke to her but she made no answer, soon after I did the same again, but she still continued to make no answer. I then felt her hand which was covered with a cold sweat & I perceived that the blood had settled in her fingers and feet, which were quite stiff and cold. Perceiving all the symptoms of the rapid approach of death, I called our Reverend mother who saw immediately that she was dying. She repeated the names of Jesus, Mary and Joseph telling her if she heard her, to press her hand. She did so, and repeated after her those sacred names. When she could no longer repeat them she continued to press our mother's hand, and made a sign intimating that she could repeat them in her heart. About five minutes after she calmly expired, having a sweet smile on her countenance. She was a bright example of every religious virtue, and a consolation to our Reverend and dear superior, who feels most sensibly the loss we have sustained.[37]

Mary Anne Moffatt herself could only pen a short note in French at the end of Harrison's long letter, expressing Ryan's tenderness for the community at Trois Rivières. Harrison summed up the convent's resignation at the failure of Prince Hohenlohe's miracle by saying, "doubtless, the Almighty has his own designs which differ very widely from our weak conceptions."[38]

Ryan's body, according to the regulations of the order, was dressed in a starched habit, and in her hands was placed the parchment containing her vows, which she had signed on the day of her solemn religious profession, together with a crucifix. Her head and bust were elevated, so that she appeared to be only reclining, with her hands joined before her breast. The sisters took consolation from the look of joy on her countenance, that seemed as if in contemplation of the well-kept vows and of the emblem of redemption. On the day of her funeral, the body was placed in a coffin, and the usual rites performed in the presence of her afflicted community. The coffin was sealed and carried by a black horse-drawn hearse to the cemetery of St. Augustine in South Boston.[39]

When the bishop returned from his journey on August 23, 1827, the community was in deep mourning at the loss of this valuable member, but none more so than Mary Anne Moffatt. In his diary of August 23, 1827, Fenwick wrote that he went to Charlestown to pay a visit to the Ursulines

to condole with them for the very great loss they have sustained by the late death of Sister Mary Austin. He finds the good Religious deeply afflicted, especially the worthy Superior, having lost, in her, her assistant, her counsellor, her constant friend, to whom she had been particularly united & to whom she had always looked for consolation in her trials and pains. The *B'p* feels for her situation, & says everything to console her; but fears for her health & that of some others of the religious . . .

Worried about the community, the bishop encouraged the sisters to rest and restore their health, endangered by the exhausting vigil over Margaret Ryan. He urged them to "relax in some degree their usual austerity" to try recover from this blow. While the community did go on to thrive, with new novices entering, it appears that Mary Anne Moffatt never really recovered from this loss. Following the death of her beloved friend, whose gentle spirituality was a marked contrast to Moffatt's more secular ambitions, the superior virtually withdrew from other close connections. She seems never to have found anyone to take the intimate place of Margaret Ryan in her life.

One summer night following Ryan's death, Moffatt collapsed in a drunken stupor behind the barn and had to be helped back to her room. This information is found in a confidential letter from Mary Barber to Fenwick in which she complained that the lay Sister Mary Claire had "more confidence placed in her than in any of the *choir nuns*." The reason for this "stroke of policy" on the part of Sister St. George was that "no one but Sr. M. Claire ever entered the pantry to see how much wine or brandy she took. Besides, Sr. M. Claire used regularly, twice a day, to take a *dram* for St. George to her own room; and she *saw* her, even when we were in the lower establishment, stretched out by our barn, dead drunk. St. George knew that she was in her power, and fearing she might betray her, treated her with as much regard & confidence as if she had been *Mother Assistant*."[40] From this period on, Moffatt seems to have developed a dependency on alcohol that remained with her throughout her time in Charlestown, and possibly for the rest of her life. Even more so once she was in the new convent, Moffatt was able to isolate herself from the surveillance of most of the community, and could drown her sorrows in the privacy of the superior's quarters.

Like the round-the-clock rituals performed by the sisters to stave off Margaret Ryan's death, Moffatt's use of alcohol was hidden from Protestant eyes. In an era when the temperance movement was gathering influence, an accusation that someone was a secret drinker could shatter a reputation. Only after the convent had been destroyed and Moffatt had disappeared did this allegation surface at all, and then only in confidential correspondence from Mary Barber to the bishop. Had the parents of the Mount Benedict Academy students known of such excesses, both of belief and alcohol abuse, they might have been less confident in entrusting their daughters to the Charlestown sisters. And had the wider Yankee community gotten wind of these doings, they might not have had to invent stories of imprisoned nuns to raise an alarm.

A FEW MONTHS AFTER the death of Margaret Ryan, the work on the brick convent building was completed, and the community moved into their new home. Among them were six professed sisters and one novice. In addition to Mary Anne Moffatt, the group included two accomplished women, Catherine Wiseman, daughter of the English consul, and Elizabeth Harrison of Philadelphia.[41] Mary Barber was a new novice in the convent, making her profession the following year. To Moffatt and the other inhabitants, the new surroundings offered a standard of living that could be considered opulent compared to the lives of most Charlestown residents. During a time when a Catholic school in Lowell charged six cents a week[42] and the bishop's own day school for boys, two dollars a quarter, the Charlestown boarding school planned to charge many times more than that. At $160 per year, with additional costs for music, dancing, and ornamental work, the Charlestown institution would clearly be catering to a different class of student.

In discussing his boys' academy in his diary, Fenwick wrote, "The price is put low, that Parents in the most moderate circumstances may have an opportunity of sending their children."[43] The bishop's day school would allow a cross-section of boys from various social classes to benefit from an education. Just as public schools stressed the education of boys, so Church authorities believed that Catholic boys needed to read and write in order to prosper in the changing nineteenth-century economy. With the elegant Mount Benedict Academy under construction, as Fenwick noted, a school was being created that would be on a very different footing, for wealthy girls whose families wanted the benefits of a "finishing school" to make their daughters more marriageable. The combination of a strong academic program which also emphasized the feminine graces, and the protection afforded the young ladies by confinement in a cloister for their school years, appealed strongly to families who could afford the luxury of learning for girls.

During the fall of 1827, another smaller building was begun near the convent under construction. Mr. Murphy, a mason, was contracted to build a small tomb, with a tiny chapel over it specifically for Masses for the dead. In just over a week, the brick work for the mausoleum was complete. Like the convent school, still waiting to welcome its occupants, the tomb stood waiting. On December 22, 1827, the bodies of the deceased Ursulines in the burying ground at St. Augustine's in South Boston were transferred to the new tomb at the convent in Charlestown. Margaret Ryan, her cousin, and her two sisters, the original Irish foundresses, were interred on Mount Benedict. There they would sleep undisturbed until the men who attacked the convent seven years later desecrated their tombs. By the end of 1827, the new building was complete, and notwithstanding the loss of Margaret Ryan, the community had increased by four sisters: two new postulants, or candidates for admission to the order, and two new lay sisters, typically lower-class or less educated women who tended to the domestic duties of the convent.

The New Year of 1828 began with a festive ceremony that included the blessing of the Ursulines' domestic chapel, which Bishop Fenwick dedicated to St. Joseph. Afterward, he walked through the whole house, blessing every room with holy water. Perhaps inspired by the memory of Margaret Ryan, the choir nuns performed a high Mass by a composer named Dumont. At communion, several pieces of sacred vocal music were performed, accompanied by harp and piano. Finally, the bishop led the nuns and two visiting priests, Father Fitton and Father Tyler, through the doors for a blessing of the convent's gardens and fields. With a light snow covering the walks, the procession issued through the western door, and passed around "the garden to the little chapel, thence returns thro' the main walk to the house."[44]

In late January 1828, the bishop published the school's prospectus in a Boston newspaper, the first advertisement for boarders. The document also appeared in New York's *Truth Teller* and the *Catholic Miscellany* of

Charleston, South Carolina. Bishop Fenwick hoped to add quickly to the eight girls already enrolled in the convent school.[45] During this period, Fenwick continued to faithfully arrive at the convent to say early Mass, and celebrate religious holidays. On the Feast of Purification, he appeared at the gate to perform the blessing of the candles for the sisters. But the porter, through mistake or forgetfulness, left the outward gate of the convent shut. Fenwick knocked and shouted for the porter, but was unable to obtain entrance on a cold February morning.[46] Though Fenwick had his own house on the grounds on Mount Benedict, he apparently did not have a key to the front gate.

By later that month, another boarder had enrolled in the school, as well as a few day students.[47] The winter passed, and Fenwick was able to decline a (to him) unappealing St. Patrick's Day celebration in Boston, and spend the day at his beloved Mount Benedict.[48] On April 10, 1828, the bishop added to the growing establishment at Mount Benedict two and a quarter acres, adjoining the convent lot. For the cost of an additional $450, the Ursulines' land now extended to the canal. The following week, he employed the carpenters Bell & Vaughn to extend the fencing around the new acreage.[49] In May 1828, Mr. Bruce, the slater, replaced the leaky shingle roof on the new convent with a slate roof, costing the nuns an additional $250.[50] Mary Anne Moffatt well approved of these improvements to her property, and had the pleasure of knowing that her sisters in the Quebec monastery would soon hear about her thriving property firsthand. In July, Bishop Fenwick left for a journey to Canada, especially anticipating visiting the Quebec monastery, where Moffatt told him she had made her start.[51]

Upon his return, the bishop presented letters of greeting from Quebec to the Charlestown Ursulines and prepared for the ceremony of giving the black veil to Mary Barber, who would become Sister Mary Benedict on August 15, 1828, the Feast of the Assumption. Barber had completed the requisite two-year probation period, during which a white veil is worn by the candidate.[52] Daughter of an eccentric family (both her parents converted to Catholicism and entered celibate religious life despite the fact that they had five young children to care for), Barber ultimately became "mistress of the senior division" and was described by colleagues as "accomplished and amiable."[53] After Moffatt's departure from the order, Barber would assume the position of superior when the academy reopened in Boston in 1838. Her veiling was to be a public ceremony, to which the superior had invited "a number of respectable Protestant Ladies" who had "expressed a great desire to be present at it." The Protestants were treated to a ceremony that the bishop described as solemn and that "drew tears from the eyes of almost every stranger present."[54]

Before a rapt audience, the nuns assembled in the chapel, clad in their choir mantles, each bearing in her hand a lighted taper. Mary Barber, dressed in a beautiful lace dress like a wedding gown, with a filmy veil setting off her lovely dark hair, placed herself between the superior and her newly named assistant, Elizabeth Harrison. Barber kneeled to ask Moffatt's blessing, and pronounced her new religious name, Sister Mary Benedict, chosen in honor of the bishop. From this day forward, she would bear this name and a new identity as an Ursuline nun. Each sister, whether a lay sister or a choir nun, chose a name at her veiling to follow the shared first name Mary. The second name, which could honor either a male or a female saint, distinguished the nuns from one another. Their secular names could continue to be used after the vows if they chose.

The sacristan opened the choir–gate and returned to the choir, the grated area to the side of the altar. At Moffatt's signal, Elizabeth Harrison began the hymn, *O gloriosa Virginum,* and all the choir nuns joined in. This Latin hymn translates

> *Mary! Whilst thy maker blest,*
> *Is nourished at thy virgin breast,*
> *Such glory shines, that stars less bright*
> *Behold thy face, and lose their light.*

As the hymn was sung, the cross bearer passed through the gate and entered the choir, followed by the novices and professed nuns, each according to their rank, two by two. They genuflected in the middle of the room, and arranged themselves in the back seats, with the eldest nearest the grate. Barber, Harrison, and Moffatt approached the grate, and the cross bearer placed the cross on the step behind them. Moffatt entered last, holding the postulant Barber's hand, flanked by Harrison, the mother assistant. Before she stepped inside the grate for life, the postulant made a low curtsy before the Blessed Sacrament, and knelt down with her hands joined. Another prayer was said, and the bishop pronounced a blessing on her candle. After sprinkling it with incense and holy water, Fenwick approached the grate, and presented the lighted candle to Sister Mary Benedict, the convent's newest choir nun, who would sing at Mass and chant prayers called "the offices" three times a day. Following his sermon, the superior raised Sister Mary Benedict from her seat, and presented her to the bishop for questioning at the grate.

"My child," he asked kindly, "what do you demand?"

In a clear voice, audible to the Protestants filling the chapel, Sister Mary Benedict replied, "The mercy of God, the holy habit of religion, the charity of the order, and the society of the mother and sisters."

"Is it with your free will and consent you demand the habit of religion?"

"Yes, my reverend father."

Turning to Moffatt, Fenwick asked, "Reverend mother, have you inquired into the other points necessary to be known, for those who enter into religion, and are you fully satisfied?"

Moffatt answered in the affirmative, and the bishop once more turned to the postulant. "My dear child," he said, "have you a firm intention to persevere in religion to the end of your life; and do you think you have sufficient strength to bear constantly the sweet yoke of our Lord Jesus Christ, for the love and fear of God alone?"

Sister Mary Benedict issued her definitive reply. "Relying on the mercy of God and on the prayers of the mother and sisters, I hope to be able to do so." She then curtsied and knelt before the bishop. "What God has commenced in you," he said, "may He himself make perfect." After the blessing, Sister Mary Benedict rose, curtsied once more, and retired with the other sisters to change her lovely gown to plain religious dress. The Bishop had blessed the nun's clothing before the postulant dressed herself in it. In her new habit, but unveiled, Barber returned to the grate, and genuflected. After singing another hymn, the bishop sprinkled Sister Mary Benedict with holy water. Elizabeth Harrison stepped forward to raise her up, and both genuflected before the altar. The mother assistant then conducted her to the superior, before whom

Sister Benedict kneeled. Lifting her up and embracing her, Moffatt directed Sister Benedict to embrace all the sisters, commencing with the elders on the left. The postulant made a little bow before and after embracing each nun. The mother assistant then accompanied her back to the grate where she again knelt, holding her candle. A processional hymn began, and the nuns filed out of the choir. Before the altar Sister Benedict covered her head with the veil, then prostrated herself before the altar, her arms extended in the form of a cross, until the completion of the ceremony shortly afterward. Many Protestants in the audience were disappointed to learn that Barber's flowing dark hair would not be cut until after the ceremony.

With the invitation to the veiling ceremony, Moffatt indulged Protestant curiosity about the interior life of her convent—but only to the degree she chose. Giving upper-class Protestants a taste of the exotic rituals of the Ursulines contributed to their sense that Mount Benedict was a *foreign* institution, and in some ways may have undermined Fenwick's plan to mainstream Catholicism into the high culture of Boston. The men who lived in the surrounding brickyard barracks, of course, had the added irritation of seeing their social betters fraternizing with the Roman Catholics at mysterious rites, the content of which they could only guess.

WITH THE VEILING OF Mary Barber, the community now had four professed choir nuns (Moffatt, Barber, Harrison, and Wiseman), two professed lay sisters (Rebecca DeCosta and Elizabeth Bennett), and two novices, women in the first stage of entering religious life. Caroline Alden was preparing to become a choir nun and Grace O'Boyle a lay sister. In the late summer, the bishop employed carpenters to build a small house at the convent for the chaplain—this likely was the bishop's cottage, since during most of the time the convent was in existence, the bishop himself served as its chaplain.[55]

On October 3, 1828 another important ceremony took place in Charlestown—the laying of the cornerstone for the second Catholic church in the diocese of Boston: St. Mary's. This new acquisition and the purchase of land for a cemetery in Charlestown marked a growing Catholic presence in the community. The town, as we have seen, had been a Yankee stronghold, and the increasing visibility of Catholic institutions was regarded by some of the locals with alarm. While the upper-class Protestants at Mary Barber's veiling ceremony may have found it diverting, the working-class citizens of Charlestown saw this increasing Catholic presence as a threat, although for a time this was not readily apparent to Bishop Fenwick and the Mount Benedict community.

Just after the first anniversary of her friend Margaret Ryan's death, Mary Anne Moffatt received news of another loss—the death of William Taylor, the former vicar-general of the Boston diocese, in Paris.[56] Toward the end of that same year, she may have been informed of the death of a relative, Robert Moffatt, in the township of Stoke, where her father had once had part ownership.[57] On the heels of this sad personal news came another emergency at the convent. Sister Mary Frances (Catherine Wiseman) was taken ill with a discharge of blood and was diagnosed with full-blown tuberculosis, the disease that had killed the foundresses. This was a tremendous setback for the community, as she was one of the sisters principally employed in the school and a trustee of the institution. Doctors advised that Wiseman be sent to a southern climate to recover, but this was never arranged.[58]

Mary Anne Moffatt made an emergency application to the Quebec monastery for two additional novices, one most likely being a niece of Mary Louise McLaughlin, Mother St. Henry, superior of the Quebec Ursulines.[59] Moffatt sent Grace O'Boyle, a candidate for the white veil, a lay sister-in-training, to Quebec to present the petition. O'Boyle returned with a denial saying that the bishop of Quebec believed the needs of the Quebec monastery were too pressing to spare any novices.[60] This was at least Moffatt's second unsuccessful appeal to Quebec for assistance, and laid the foundation for later friction. In earlier letters, the previous bishop of Quebec had expressed concern and anxiety about the rampant consumption that plagued the Boston Ursulines. But Moffatt must have felt somewhat abandoned by the next, Bishop Panet, and her home community, hundreds of miles to the north, who continually refused her petitions.

These difficulties, however, were only asides in Bishop Fenwick's year-end review of the convent's accomplishments through 1828. Already, he had conceived of adding two wings to the large brick structure proudly seated at the top of Mount Benedict. In his year-end summary for 1828, Fenwick recorded his obvious pleasure in the progress of Mount Benedict, as about twenty additional students had been added:

> Hitherto that Establishment, so far as relates to the School, has flourished beyond his most sanguine expectations; & continues still to enjoy every prospect of becoming a most useful Establishment. The number of Professed Nuns including the Superior is four; of Novice, one, of Postulants, one; of Lay Sisters, two, of Scholars in the School Department, twenty eight. It is not the least of the Blessings, that during the whole of this year just past, the peace of the Church has not been in the least interrupted.

Snow fell heavily on New Year's Day in 1829. Bishop Fenwick, looking out his window in the darkness of the winter storm, sent for a chaise to carry him to say his usual early Mass on Mount Benedict. But his serving man returned with the news that no chaise was to be had. With resignation, the bishop donned a heavy coat and boots and set out through the storm to walk the two and a half miles to Charlestown. When he reached the main gate of the convent, the sky had lightened a little although snow continued to fall under a heavy cloud cover throughout the day.

For New Year's Day, the community planned a modest celebration that reflected the bishop's buoyant and optimistic mood about the convent's progress. In the community room of the new building, the ladies assembled with the children to present the bishop with kind wishes on the occasion of the day. Little Maria Fay, daughter of Judge Fay of Cambridgeport, who remained a staunch supporter of the convent after it was attacked, was selected to give the main address. The Bishop reported himself impressed with the pretty way she comported herself. In all, twenty-six girls stepped forward with a curtsy and greetings for their honored guest. In turn, the bishop congratulated the community on their wonderful progress during the year, and praised the girls for their good behavior. The girls were rewarded with a day to be spent with their families, and the bishop himself retired to his little cottage while the snow fell outside until evening.[61]

January 1829 was a festive month at the convent, despite the unusual cold snap that gripped New England. But the cold was kept at bay by cheerful warmth in the fireplaces, and kind gifts from some of Boston's resident priests. Father Wiley sent the sisters a jar of fresh grapes costing five dollars, the equivalent of two days' wages for a laborer. Father Fitton brought some fancy cheese and a handsome paint box as a present to the sisters. And the end of the month brought a new postulant—a French woman, Claudine Olagnier—to join the community.[62] But this accession to the ranks was short-lived and she departed a week later.[63]

During this especially severe winter, the snow was piled so high at the convent gates that planks had to be laid so that it would be possible to walk up the hill.[64] By mid-February 1829, the snow topped the fences. During this difficult season, the health of Sister Mary Frances Wiseman continued to decline. In his diary, Fenwick noted,

> The good Sister Mary Frances grows every day weak & weaker. It is supposed that this week will prove the last. A swelling has taken place in her frame which Physicians say forebodes an approaching dissolution.[65]

On March 25, 1829, the bishop performed extreme unction and other ceremonies for the gravely ill sister. At about the same time he also began to negotiate the purchase of seven acres of land adjacent to the property. Mary Anne Moffatt likely encouraged him to pursue this deal, as Fenwick recorded that

> The Nuns are extremely anxious to obtain possession of this Lot, as it will forever remove neighbors & at the same time secure to them the enjoyment of a beautiful prospect in the direction of Bunker Hill & Charlestown.[66]

This would be the third separate purchase of land for the convent, and the additional seven acres would have stretched the property to the east, toward the center of Charlestown. However, the bishop was unable to make the deal work, and he agreed to rent the land for a year at the rate of $30.[67] On April 7, 1829, Sister Mary Frances Wiseman, one of the convent's most proficient teachers and a trustee of the property, expired after a lingering illness of nearly six months. Preparations were made for hers to become the fifth body interred in the convent tomb.[68] Wiseman's funeral took place on April 9, 1829, and Fenwick described it as follows:

> The *B'p* repairs to the Convent with Rev'd Mr. Tyler for the Funeral of Sister Mary Frances appointed for 7 1/2 OC'k. In a little time the Carriage drives up containing the Clergy who are to assist in the ceremony, viz. Rev'd Mr. Wiley, Rev'd Mr. Fitton, Mr. O'Flaherty. These were attended by two Boys who had been accustomed to serve in the Sanctuary. At the appointed time the *B'p* commences a solemn Mass for the Dead with Deacon & Subdeacon. This is sung by the Clergy attending, the good Nuns assisting together with the Children of their school amounting to thirty two. After Mass the service is performed over the Corpse in the Choir. A Procession is then formed to the Tomb at the bottom of the garden with great decency & order where the remainder of the service is sung. After which the Corpse is committed to the tomb, & all return again to the Chapel in the same order. The whole could not but be highly impressive.

But Providence seemingly wished to repair this loss, for in the same entry, Fenwick recorded that, "In the afternoon of this day a lady arrives from New York, a Postulant for the Convent." And on April 23, 1829, work commenced on the planned two additional wings. By now, the number of children at the academy had blossomed to thirty-six.[69] During this same period in which he was facilitating expansion at the convent, the bishop also decided to establish a Catholic cemetery in Charlestown.

The bishop's pleasure in the progress of the convent school was dimmed in late May 1829, when he received news of the death of his mother. Mrs. Fenwick had raised her own children, plus, for a time, the two youngest of Virgil and Jerusha Barber, the parents of Mary Barber. Fenwick was greatly saddened by her loss. He departed immediately for Washington. In Georgetown, he visited with the family of Elizabeth Harrison, the choir nun who wrote so movingly of the death of Margaret Ryan. Ever mindful of the needs of the convent for personnel, the bishop convinced Elizabeth's sister Mary to return north with him to enter the convent as a postulant. Mary did not take to life in the convent—she remained only a week before returning to Georgetown.[70] But on the day of her departure, another novice, Miss Sarah Chase, later Sister Ursula, from New Hampshire arrived to take her place. The following week, Miss Woodley from Rhode Island also joined, but the candidate named Mary Brown returned to New York.[71] Despite its success in attracting boarders, the convent's inability to add to and retain personnel would cripple its progress. Ultimately, overwork led to the breakdown of Elizabeth Harrison, whose flight from the convent in the summer of 1834 was a key factor in the riot. Though Mary Anne Moffatt was an able administrator, she seems to have lacked some of the personal warmth that would bind a young girl's affection to her community.

WITH THE BRICKWORK on the wings nearing completion, it seemed that Providence once again smiled favorably upon Mount Benedict. On June 25, 1829, Bishop Fenwick was finally able to arrange the purchase of nine adjoining acres along the side and the front of the convent.

> This lot now perfects their establishment & secures the good religious on every side from Intruders to say nothing of the Prospect. The whole of their landed property now amounts to 24 acres—all excellent land.[72]

With their additional land, and the accession of two additional nuns, Miss Chase and Miss Woodley, an air of celebration reigned at the habiting of the nuns. Mary Anne Moffatt again invited the best Protestant families to come and view Miss Woodley's veiling on August 20, 1829:

> Miss Woodley, the sister of the Rev'd Mr. Woodley this day receives the holy habit of religion in the Ursuline Convent on Mount Benedict. The B'p with five of the Rev'd Clergy & three Acolytes attend on the occasion. The ceremony is performed in an unusually solemn manner. A number of the most respectable families of Boston & Charlestown are invited to be present at it.

A very elaborate & impressive Sermon is delivered by the Rev'd
Dr. O'Flaherty which is the first delivered by him since his being
ordained Deacon, & must have made a due impression upon the
audience.

Fenwick was pleased with the decorous ceremony and the warm reception the Mount Benedict community seemed to be receiving.


I N EARLY 1830, Mary Anne Moffatt's agreed upon term as superior
was nearing an end. She had been loaned from Quebec for six years.
Bishop Fenwick wrote a letter to Bishop Panet that began: "The time allowed by your Lordship's illustrious Predecessor for the pious and excellent Madame St. George to reside amongst us as superior of the Ursuline
convent established formerly in our city of Boston but now in
Charlestown has nearly expired." He requested an extension of her obedience for six more years, until 1836. He stated that the departure of St.
George would mean "the utter destruction of the establishment, as only
two would be left & they in extremely delicate health."[73] Bernard Claude
Panet, of the Panet family who originally paid Moffatt's *dot,* wrote back
with an extension of four more years, until 1834.[74] For this he received a
gracious, calligraphied letter of thanks from the Ursuline Community of
Mount Benedict.[75] Again in 1833, a year before the expiration of Moffatt's term, Bishop Fenwick wrote to Panet anxiously asking for another
extension of the loan of Moffatt. The letter clearly demonstrates Fenwick's utmost confidence in St. George's administrative abilities:

In proportion as the time advances for Mad. St. George to return
to Quebec the more apprehensive I become for the stability &
permanency of our infant Institution. Only one year more remains, as she informs me, when her time expires agreably to the
permission which your Lordship was kind enough to extend to
four years after the lapse of the first six. . . . I need not acquaint
your Lordship with the difficulties religious houses have to contend against in their formation especially in a country drowned
in heresy & overrun with prejudice. Hitherto ours, through the
superior management of Mad. St. George acquainted as she is

with the genius of our Republican Institutions & a government peculiarly Protestant, has succeeded beyond expectation. Although highly prosperous so far as relates to the commanding the attention & confidence of Protestant parents who with difficulty entrust their children to the care of the Establishment for their education, yet it has not progressed with the same rapidity in the formation of members of the Community. Giving to deaths & the scarcity of candidates, the house possesses as yet only four professed religious—but great hopes are entertained, if your Lordship will but consent to allow this excellent Lady to abide in the Community six years more, now that the principal difficulties are happily removed so far as related to the prejudices of Protestants against institutions of this nature, that this Ursuline Establishment will have attained by that time such an accession of strength as to render its stability no longer doubtful. May I then hope that your Lordship will not refuse me this request. We are indeed already indebted much to your Lordship's indulgence & hope that this will not be asking too much when the extension of the kingdom of our divine redeemer is concerned, & on the granting of the request our hopes of the future prosperity of this little community principally and mainly rest.[76]

Fenwick's letter praised Moffatt for her ease in associating with the Protestants—a trait Roman Catholic officials would eventually have cause to regret when her close friendship with Protestants proved an obstacle to her removal. And while Moffatt was quite successful in attracting the confidence of Protestant families, she clearly did not inspire the same confidence in novices who could staff her school. Still, Fenwick's letter persuasively argued for the retention of Moffatt, though his view that Protestant prejudice had been "happily removed" was naïve. The new bishop, Joseph Signay, issued a favorable reply, extending the obedience, as requested, for six more years—until 1840. But in 1835, this obedience would be revoked—and Moffatt forced to return to Quebec against her will.

Despite the obstacles with staffing the school, it continued to attract students. At the start of 1830, the pupils in the convent numbered forty-two. By mid-April Bishop Fenwick laid out the lawn and planted a number of trees, in anticipation of the upcoming celebration of the distribution of the premiums, prizes given annually to the best pupils. In October, the Ursulines gained the important addition of the two O'Keefe sisters from Cork. By the end of 1830, the bishop could report in his diary four new candidates for the black veil and one for the white. There were now sixty-four boarders enrolled in the school,[77] its highest number of students during its eight-year existence.

A T THE START OF 1831, Mount Benedict seemed to have weathered a series of crises due to the deaths of key personnel because of illness, although the scourge of tuberculosis remained a constant threat to the cloistered community. The accession of the O'Keefe sisters suggested a potential new source of personnel from Ireland, and the convent community remained hopeful it would be able to attract more American candidates. The academy's student population, mainly consisting of daughters of prominent Protestant families, was growing rapidly. Protestants of the better classes, some of whom had been invited to view the dramatic veiling ceremonies of Mary Barber and Miss Woodley, seemed satisfied in their curiosity about life in an Ursuline convent, and pleased with the education their daughters were receiving. They remained blissfully unaware of some of the more questionable aspects of life at Mount Benedict, including Prince Hohenlohe's attempt at a miraculous cure, and Moffatt's dependency on alcohol. Moffatt, as Sister St. George, impressed both the parents and the bishop with her capable leadership. To the relief of the bishop and the Ursulines, the question of her continued tenure as superior of the Charlestown convent was settled by 1833. Seemingly oblivious to the storm clouds gathering in the community surrounding the convent walls, the residents of Mount Benedict focused on a bright future within its whitewashed interiors.

## CHAPTER THREE

# CHARLESTOWN IN FULL FLOWER

## *Education and Convent Life*

*Shall we send our blooming daughters to Ursuline Cloisters to be properly
taught how to behave in the world, and fulfil the relations of wives and
mothers, by the precepts and examples of female recluses, who have immured themselves by a vow in their infancy, and solemnly forsworn,
as a grievous sin, every endearing tie on earth!*

—Supplement to "Six Months in a Convent"

I
N A LARGE RECEPTION ROOM at the Mount Benedict Academy
for girls, the scholars were assembling. Pre-teenage girls mostly,
some young enough that their laughter still showed missing baby
teeth, some budding into early womanhood. They filed in quietly in
their slate gray jumpers under the watchful eye of Sister Mary Benedict.
As they passed through the door, the young mistress marked attendance
in her register. Sister Mary Benedict, who had been born Mary Barber,
was the beautiful and articulate class mistress for academy seniors, and
the girls were a little in awe of her. In stolen moments, they whispered
stories about her unusual upbringing. Daughter of Virgil and Jerusha
Barber, she had been raised in a convent along with her four siblings after her Anglican parents converted to Roman Catholicism and took up
separate lives as celibate Roman Catholic monastics. Barber had entered
Mount Benedict as a sixteen-year-old novice at its foundation in 1826,
and her veiling ceremony had fascinated invited Protestant guests. By
her early twenties she had gained her supervising position.

The nun's black veil and layered habit only added to the mysterious and arresting beauty of her face and figure. A contemporary publication described her dress and that of the other Charlestown Ursulines:

> The teachers are very tastefully dressed in black, and are decorated with a splendid cross suspended by a surplice to a great length, and are very frequently reading prayers, probably in the Latin language. Their veils hang from the forehead, and are thrown over the head or in front, as occasion requires. While associating with the "Community," they are unveiled, but on walking out to enjoy the air, the veil is drawn over their eyes, to signify their exclusion from the world.[1]

To the young girls in the boarding school, the costumes of the Ursulines added to their authority an imposing foreign quality, and enhanced the beauty of Sister Mary Benedict's stunning porcelain face.

As mistress of the senior division, Barber assisted Mary Anne Moffatt in a managerial capacity, overseeing teachers and students and devoting herself to full supervision of the classroom. Her duties had been spelled out in detail in the twenty-seven specific articles on classroom management in the centuries-old Ursuline Rule, and Mary Barber ruled this space, taking attendance, replenishing supplies, and making recommendations to the superior on meting out punishments and rewards. She attended to the spiritual growth of her charges, and oversaw the specialists teaching reading, arithmetic, writing, and needlework.[2]

Earlier in the day, Barber had presided over the toilette of the senior boarders in the dormitory, seen to their morning prayers, taken them to Mass, then to breakfast before shepherding them in to their lessons.[3] The junior class was supervised by Sister Mary Austin (a.k.a. Augustine) one of the O'Keefe sisters from Cork, who, according to convent custom, had taken the name, with its variants, of the deceased Margaret Ryan. The school was divided into two classes, senior and junior, occupying separate apartments and having for the most part a different set of teachers. Except on general recreation days, or by special permission, there was very little interaction between the two.

Ursuline rule required that the mistresses of the divisions live with the children as true spiritual mothers. The sisters assigned to this duty slept in the same room as the boarders. The beds, each enclosed with linen curtains for privacy, were lined up in large dormitories—but provided opportunities for twenty-four-hour surveillance. One student, Louisa Whitney, described the Mount Benedict facilities this way:

> There were no *rooms* in that part of the building devoted to the pupils—rooms are for a few, *halls* for many—and we inhabited halls exclusively. Each dormitory was occupied by sixteen girls; there were eight windows on each side, and room for a little white bed between every two. The floor was carpetless, the windows curtainless—each girl's trunk was placed at the foot of her bed.[4]

In the morning ritual of dressing, rich and poor alike followed the same regimen—what one scholar called a 'hardening process' that would have delighted that philosopher of childhood, John Locke. The girls rose early in unheated apartments; washed on the porch where the water frequently froze in the basins; and partook of a frugal breakfast of rye and carrot coffee and dry bread.[5] Louisa Whitney remembered,

> Dry bread, though excellent of its kind, and a mugful of milk for breakfast; dry bread and a bit of butter, with a glass of water for supper—[for noon dinner we] usually had but one course . . . soup made with vegetables one day, soup-meat mixed with vegetables on the next. Salt-fish ditto, or hasty-pudding and molasses, or rice-milk on Fridays and fast-days which seemed to me to be very frequent at that time.[6]

Another former pupil, Lucy Thaxter, described a typical day in the convent this way:

> The hour of rising was six in winter, and in summer five o'clock. Half an hour was allowed for the duties of the toilet, we then descended to the school room where the morning prayer was read by the young lady whose turn it was. After prayers there was half an hour of silence, that is, we were not allowed to run around and talk; but studied the lessons for the day. Then came breakfast, after

that, half an hour's recreation, usually passed out of doors in the garden, or walking in front of the establishment. When we returned to the house, we entered upon the regular school exercises for the day.[7]

The small number of sisters in the Charlestown convent meant that each nun carried a heavy workload, and this was especially true of the assistant superior and music instructor, Sister Mary John, or Elizabeth Harrison. In 1834, Harrison would suffer a breakdown precipitated by overwork, and her escape over the convent wall would have disastrous consequences for the convent. As assistant superior, Harrison reported to Moffatt, who assumed ultimate responsibility for the school, deciding on admissions and administering the curriculum and personnel based upon Harrison's reports. Moffatt presided over exhibitions given by the pupils as well as faculty and staff meetings. The superior also oversaw the training of young religious, which paralleled the training of the students in the academy.

At the start of the school day, the murmuring of Latin prayer blended with the clanging of the convent's bronze bell, which before its installation here had tolled the arrival and departure of trains on the nation's spreading network of rails. Now it pealed in the open air of the convent tower, calling the girls to their classes. Two by two, in they marched, each class separately, five pairs at a time, dressed in the puritan dress of the academy.[8] An older girl who had been honored with a supervisory role over the ten, walked behind. As the children passed, they silently curtsied to the nuns who opened the door, and then, curtsying again to the class mistress, they took their respective places on a wooden bench. The whitewashed walls of the classroom had been sparsely decorated with religious pictures and statues, and the scholars began, as they did every day, with a morning prayer, which the older girls took turns in leading. All rose for the prayer, curtsied again to Sister Mary Barber at its completion, then resumed their seats to begin the morning lessons,[9] which lasted for three and a half hours, followed by a break for industrial work and study.[10]

According to Lucy Thaxter's account of the school day, written nine years after the convent burning,

Each lesson had its appointed hour for recitation. The music lessons and hours for practicing, being so arranged as not to interfere with the other lessons—eleven o'clock was the dinner hour. Then followed an hour's recreation, sometimes as an indulgence lengthened into two; then school again until five, when we went to tea. After tea, recreation again for an hour or so; then evening prayers. At seven in the winter and dusk in the summer, we went to bed. Wednesday and Saturday afternoons were given us for recreation. In summer time, we often took our work and sat out under the trees, while one of the young ladies read to us, or sometimes the Nuns would invent stories for our amusement.[11]

The older girl who was charged with supervising the five pairs of girls was called a *dixanière* and it was her duty to assist the teachers in the classwork and in the maintenance of discipline. Each *dixanière* was responsible for *dix* or ten pupils, hence the name, and these were a standard feature in many French-style academies such as Ursuline day schools. Generally this position rotated every two or three months.[12] According to one scholar, it was the duty of the *dixanière* "to assist in hearing the Catechism lesson and drilling the pupils, to take care of and to distribute the school books . . . and to marshal the ranks in groups of ten. . . . She was to keep account of the children, noting all disputes or any tearing of clothes, or playing naughty games . . . [or] being noisy in the school hall or disorderly in rank."[13]

The reading lesson began with the *dixanière* unlocking the cupboard that held the books, including Murray's *Grammar and Exercises,* Jamieson's *Rhetoric and Logic,* and *Walker's Dictionary.*[14] Frequently, reading was taught from the same books that served for handwriting instruction. The *dixanière* handed a book to the waiting group on the bench, and the lesson proceeded with each child reading in turn. Sister Mary Austin gave the easiest reading to the beginners, teaching them to recognize the letters, reading a few words at a time, and trying to tease out their meaning from the context. Then, with impeccable pronunciation and with careful attention to pauses and accents, Sister Austin read a page. The girls followed in their own books, reading out loud in a low tone, word for word with the teacher. Next, a pupil was appointed to read the same passage in a loud voice, with the rest of the group quietly reading along. When a girl stammered over a passage, the teacher patiently corrected her, and once everyone had had her chance to read, the lesson was complete. The same method for learning to read in English served as the basis of learning other languages, each offered at Mount Benedict for an extra charge of $24 per year: French, Latin, Spanish, and Italian.[15]

Following this, there might be a time of quiet sewing as the girls tackled its manual intricacies. Learning needlework began with the simplest tasks, making a plain seam or a hem, on canvas or linen. The aspiring seamstress would move on to other kinds of work, such as embroidering flowers, embroidering in gold and silver, and making French and English lace, a specialty of the Ursuline nuns.[16] At other times, students were given instruction in mathematics. To supplement the material in Smith's *Arithmetic,* the textbook used in the Charlestown academy, math lessons were also conducted using small disks made from ivory or metal, called *jetons.* The beads were given to the pupils in quantities, and the girls arranged them in a vertical scale on the table. These *jetons* were manipulated in a manner similar to the balls on an abacus. Older students worked on practical problems involving buying and selling, measuring, and other familiar experiences.[17] Mathematics instruction was known in academy parlance as "casting accounts."[18]

"What would be the cost of fifteen yards of cloth at six shillings a yard?" Sister would ask.

The girls would then need to find the price, working out the figures on paper, with quill pens.[19] The Ursulines were attempting to frame the problems, according to one scholar, "in terms familiar to the pupil's experience . . . basing calculations on the things girls would buy, working them out in money . . . the little girls would be likely to use."[20] Students at the Mount Benedict Academy worked in both Roman and Arabic figures.[21] When the writing teacher called them for the lesson, the girls rose, curtsied to the class mistress, and filed out to the writing room.[22] At numerous points during the day, the students would assemble to say a series of prayers, with Catechism lessons interspersed.[23]

For every subject taught at the Ursuline Academy, a specific pedagogy had been devised which dated back almost three centuries. Though an approach for each subject taught in Ursuline academies was

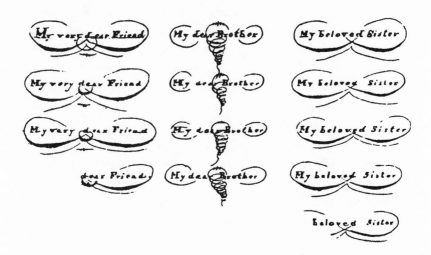

*Penmanship sample from the writing book of Maria Cotting.*

clearly articulated, it was not necessarily mandated. The *Règlements,* or Rules, of this ancient order state:

> This method has been proved by experience to be the best, nevertheless it is not desired to restrict the teacher to it, so that she may not make any changes in it, if she judges proper.[24]

The "best" method of handwriting instruction, for example, was found to take place in the dining room, where girls could sit at a spacious table. Let us follow young Maria W. Cotting, who won the junior medal for excellence in 1830, through her round of lessons.

Several teachers were in the room to help with the instruction of writing, offering special guidance, especially during the first six weeks of the term.[25] Maria and her friends sat up straight at the table, and small girls who were not tall enough would not be confined to the task for very long. Before the class began, Sister Mary Austin prepared models for the lesson, of a single line, two lines, or short verses, and these would be distributed to the pupils.[26] One scholar paints a scene of the writing lesson, imagining "long rows of children sitting very straight, their quills grasped just so with three fingers, as they meticulously copy the model placed before them; the room in perfect silence; the nun bent over the slower ones carefully guiding rebellious fingers across the page."[27] Sometimes Sister Mary Austin wrote on Maria's paper, modeling the letters and correcting faults. The basic classes began with how to form *O* and *I*, then moved on to *A, U, M*, and *N*, not going on to the next letter until Maria knew how to form each one well. After that followed *b, d, l, f, g, h*, and the rest, with the easier letters practiced first. Combinations followed: *um, mm, mn*. Words that had no consonants were practiced before words that had them, in both Roman style and Arabic.[28] At the end of the hour-long lesson, Maria's paper, along with her classmates' work, their names clearly written, were placed in a cupboard for safekeeping.[29] Any letters home that Maria wrote to her parents were corrected for style and spelling with the same vigilance. In keeping with the convent's philosophy of rewarding excellence, the girls with the most beautiful handwriting were permitted to write the class notices for saints' days.[30] Maria was chosen for this honor, and this series of little successes culminated in her receiving the coveted crown for best student during the examination period in the long days of June.

Spelling followed writing, and stressed word perception, practice, and review for groups of eight to ten children. Maria and the others were handed a sheet of white paper. Sister Mary Austin, in her clear and distinct voice with just a hint of brogue remaining, began the dictation of two or three lines from the spelling book, and Maria wrote it down, word by word. The *dixanière* then assisted in passing out copies of the spelling book to all the children, and Maria consulted it to correct her own spelling, writing the correction above the mistake. Sister Austin asked the girls to close their books and Maria placed her book over the top of the page to cover what she wrote before. The same lines were read again, followed by the system of checking and correcting mistakes. At the close of the hour's lesson, Maria and the rest of the children marched in formation back to their classroom, to read and await the bell's dismissal for the noontime meal. The next day, on a fresh sheet of paper, Maria wote the same few lines, and her lesson would not be changed until she could write it perfectly.[31]

During the noon break, students walked in the convent gardens. The nuns joined the girls in games such as battledore and shuttlecock, or a game of chess. They were never, however, allowed any such "highly improper game as card playing."[32] Walking was by far the favorite means of relaxation, and on weekends, it extended beyond the convent grounds, when the young ladies, accompanied by fully veiled nuns, marched decorously along the streets of Charlestown, two by two.

Following lunch, the students assembled in their places as before. After prayer, the afternoon lessons began with a second lesson in reading. Then the different groups were called out to the math lesson in the same way they had earlier been called out for writing. The afternoon session, which lasted about two hours, ended with a prayer before the pupils were dismissed for the day.[33] During the afternoon, the girls would add to their studies courses such as history, French, and geography.[34] Students in the Ursuline Academy studied nearly year round, with a six-week vacation from July 1 to August 15. Some academies desired to keep the young ladies during the holiday season in order to train them to a profitable use of their leisure time, which they spent engaged in embroidery, mending their clothes, and enjoying simple picnics and games.[35] It was just a few days before the end of this summer vacation that the convent was attacked and burned, and the large number of students in residence, about fifty, suggests that not many of the boarders took even this short vacation.

The Ursulines at Mount Benedict followed an alternate system to our modern arrangement of semesters and grades. While the students were grouped according to age, the small classes allowed intensive individual instruction, so that each student's mastery of the material was expected before she could move on in her studies. Promotion depended on industry and progress, hence the attainment of a place in the higher classes was, according to one scholar, "pretty sure to be a criterion of real scholarship."[36] Throughout the year, the students could expect regular visits from the convent's superior, Mary Anne Moffatt, who examined the pupils and decided upon promotions and the distribution of awards.

The *Règlements* are very clear on the code of conduct expected of the girls. They must complete their work and not eat in the classrooms. If they were neglectful of their work, or disrespectful, Ursuline Rules called for them to be subjected to " . . . some little embarrassment before the rest, such as going to the foot of the class, or to another part of the room, or standing up while the others are seated, and the like."[37] Lucy Thaxter recalled the method of discipline in the Mount Benedict Academy, adding that "Punishments of any sort were very rare."

> When the ordinary discipline of the school-room was insufficient to insure order and obedience, the unruly one was taken to the Superior to receive a private reprimand from her. If this failed, the delinquent was placed on the pyramid, a small flight of steps, where she sat in view of all the class until sufficiently repentant to return to her duty.[38]

Another nineteenth-century graduate of a different convent school attributed her excellent vocabulary to the form of discipline at her school that involved committing to memory a column in the dictionary for each violation of the regulations: " . . . as I was frequently among the delinquents," said Mrs. Logan, "I had learned much of the dictionary by heart."[39]

The *Règlements* of the Ursulines are quite clear about keeping the punishments in the academy mild:

> Take care never to use compulsion, which should never be used but in extreme necessity, and with prudent regard for time and place, as well as the disposition of the person addressed. God hath made us all free-willed, and to no one's free will doth he do violence. He leads them to obey Him by show of reason, by inviting motives and by gentle persuasion.[40]

Mary Anne Moffatt herself handled serious misdemeanors; she alone could inflict corporal punishment on girls younger than twelve.[41] As a later incident will show, Moffatt could be swift and effective in her punishments of the girls' offenses. But there did not seem to be many occasions on which such drastic measures had to be taken. Both the curriculum and the regulations about behavior were based on "principles of order, self-control, and consideration for others, leading to an intelligent womanhood."[42]

Prospective *pensionnaires* were required to present themselves at Theodore Baker's clothing shop, at No. 223 Washington Street in Boston, to procure the requisite academy uniforms: dark slate-colored pongee dresses in summer, and black Circassian wool frocks in winter.[43] The girls who came to the convent brought with them a few simple necessities. Along with her uniforms, a boarder at the academy would pack her trunk with two white dresses, eight pairs of hose (four black, four white), five aprons (four of them in black, two of bombazett, two of silk, and one other to wear for gardening), a light blue satin cape and sash, a blue belt, a slate-colored garden bonnet to match the pongee uniform, and her "Leghorn," a broad-brimmed straw hat trimmed with blue ribbon. In the cold Charlestown winters, the girls wore a dark blue merino cloak and silk hood over their black dresses. Besides her clothing, every student was asked to bring six napkins, six towels, one knife and fork, one silver goblet, one silver dessert and tea spoon, and two pairs of sheets and pillowcases. As the lawsuits filed for indemnification after the convent was burned illustrate, however, many of the students also brought their own musical instruments and other property, including jewelry.

Students admitted to the convent ranged in age between six and fourteen years. The tuition and board were about $40 per quarter, and the curriculum included, for an extra charge, the fashionable lady's pursuits of the French language, the fine arts, painting, embroidery, music on the piano forte and harp. An Italian dancing master was engaged to give dance instruction, and it was not unusual to hire practicing artists for further instruction.[44] One artist who probably offered drawing and painting instruction at Mount Benedict before leaving for Canada was the American James Bowman (1793–1842), who painted the only known portrait of Mary Anne Moffatt. The superior's portrait, like so much other information about her, has mysteriously vanished.

An entry in the Ursuline annals of 1832 confirms that the oil painting was done in Boston at the same time as Bowman painted a portrait of Benedict Fenwick, probably the year before. The occasion for the Quebec notation was Bowman's arrival at the Quebec monastery to offer instruction in painting. The annals say that Bowman, an excellent American painter and a good Catholic, was sent there by Fenwick, who asked the artist to present the Quebec Ursulines with two paintings: one of Fenwick and one of *notre chère soeur St. Georges,* our dear Sister St. George. In Quebec, Bowman's four pupils were the nieces of Mère St. Henry, the Quebec superior.[45]

In September 1831, Madame St. Henry had herself sat for Bowman at the behest of a priest named Abbé L-J Desjardins, who noted that to sit for such a painting required special permission, in order to avoid censure. Perhaps that explains why, in his letter encouraging St. Henry to view the Moffatt painting, Desjardins refers to Moffatt somewhat disparagingly as *la suave Mre St. George.*[46] No record exists of Moffatt asking for Quebec's permission to sit for the artist. Though Moffatt's sitting for a portrait may have privately raised eyebrows in Quebec, her 1836 dispute with the academy's dancing teacher, Mrs. Barrymore, was much more public. But for the most part, Mount Benedict's interactions with lay teachers seemed to run smoothly.

The institution's report card shows the curriculum extended well beyond the typical "finishing" school of the day, and included academic subjects such as poetry, geography, chronology, history, mythology, astronomy, philosophy, and languages,[47] a challenging and serious curriculum for nineteenth-century young women. Between 1750 and 1865, the female academy was the prevailing type of institution for women's education in the United States.[48] Girls had been admitted to public schools in Boston in 1789, and then for only six months of the year. They were not permitted to attend public school year round until 1828, and even then were probably limited to attending during those hours when boys were not in school.[49] At the start of the nineteenth century, a small number of private academies for girls had emerged: at Pittsfield, Massachusetts in 1807, Catherine Fiske's at Keene, New Hampshire in 1814, and George B. Emerson's private secondary school for girls in Boston, which opened in 1823.[50] Often these female seminaries were short-lived.[51]

By the early 1830s, the Charlestown school had attracted fifty to sixty boarders, many the children of Unitarians who had moved into positions of social power during the early nineteenth century. The Unitarians were more liberal in their views on religious tolerance than the conservative Congregationalists they had displaced on the social ladder. That men of property should choose a European-style convent education for their daughters was not all that surprising. Options for higher education of young women were limited during the antebellum period. Upper-class families were willing to send their daughters great distances, to be separated from them for long periods, and to put aside their religious prejudices knowing the girls would return home fully prepared to take their place in the society in which they were to move.[52] The stated aim of the Mount Benedict Academy was, by precept and example, to develop the ideal Christian woman, and the young ladies and their families would not have interacted socially with the classes that were more open in their hostility to the Catholic community.

In the *Prospectus* for the Mount Benedict School for Girls, the educational philosophy is described as: "extensive; comprehending all those attainments which may be found necessary, useful, and ornamental in society." Their teachers, dedicated to the education of young girls by the mission of the Ursuline order, were pledged to adorn students' minds with "useful knowledge, and . . . to form their hearts to virtue." The Ursuline constitution stated their primary objective as being "to give a good and solid education to young persons, according to their condition." To this end, "all the teaching religious ought to prepare themselves in the sciences and arts, so as to be always capable of meeting the exigencies of the times and to thoroughly master all they may be called on to teach."[53]

No one could have foreseen that the growing tensions in Charlestown between the Protestant and Catholic communities would stretch the convent's personnel in ways they were not prepared for—no matter how they strived to be "capable of meeting the exigencies of the times." During this period of relative quiet before the storm, the sisters went about making improvements to their extensive property and continued to develop their school for girls in a way that they believed honored the legend of St. Ursula, and according to the rule of the foundress, Angela Merici.

T HE URSULINES' CENTURIES-OLD emphasis on women actually originated in the dramatic legend of their namesake, St. Ursula and her eleven thousand virgins. In the liturgical calendar, the feast of St. Ursula is celebrated on May 31, but the legend long predates the Christian era. St. Ursula, most scholars agree, was not a historical figure, but a mythological hybrid of the Saxon goddess Ursel, the "Ercel" of Thomas Rhymer's *Erceldoune,* and the Greek goddess Artemis. Ursel means "She-Bear" and is associated with the constellation of the Great Bear (Ursa Major), otherwise known as the Big Dipper. The legend's ancient roots are also connected with the virgin huntress and Moon goddess Artemis, whom the ancients said ruled all the stars until Zeus usurped her place.[54]

A ninth-century tale provides cultural context for the events in Charlestown a millenium later, connecting primeval tensions to events surrounding a community of women dedicated to virginity. According to church legend, St. Ursula was a fifth-century Breton princess betrothed to Conon, prince of England. Ursula agreed to marry her suitor on these conditions: his conversion and a postponement of the wedding while the two of them and eleven thousand virgin attendants embarked on a three-year holy pilgrimage. In Cologne, West Germany, the caravan encountered the Huns, who slaughtered Conon and the eleven thousand virgins. Ursula was offered a reprieve if she would marry the leader. Refusing his hand, she was shot through the heart with three arrows. The fact that Ursula used her virginity to convert her future husband and obtain a three-year reprieve from marriage and motherhood is one illustration of the way celibacy accorded women a degree of power not possible within traditional cultural roles, and it was this power that celibate nuns also enjoyed.

According to church historians, Ursula's pilgrimage to Rome originated as a spiritual journey to plead for heavenly intercession against the pending invasion of Western Europe by the Huns. The Huns invaded France in 450, sweeping through the cities of Gaul, Trèves, Metz, Soissons, Paris, Troyes, and Orléans. At Châlons-sur-Marne, the Huns were checked by the Romans and the Goths, and driven westward. The invaders turned in their fury against Cologne, conquering, sacking, and destroying the city. On the plains to the north, a band of British women was chained along with other female captives from France and Belgium, where they were to serve the appetites of their captors, or die a violent death. The bones of the virgins at Cologne, according to church historians, "show traces of a frightful martyrdom: many of the skulls have been cleft by sharp instruments, and traces of hair and of blood are preserved; many of the breast bones are incontestably broken; in many the arrows are still embedded; many arms, feet, skulls, jaw bones are shattered."[55] The Virgin Islands, discovered by Christopher Columbus, are named in honor of St. Ursula's entourage.

The shrine of St. Ursula at Cologne, where the skulls of the virgins were adorned with decorative caps, became a popular stop on the European excursions of nineteenth-century American tourists. Archeological evidence suggests that these skulls are largely Breton, Celtic type, and that they belonged to young robust women. Out of a hundred skulls, there are about fifteen males.[56] Twenty years after the Reverend Lyman Beecher's anti-Catholic preaching helped incite the mob that burned the Charlestown convent, his more famous daughter, the writer Harriet Beecher Stowe, visited the shrine. Stowe, in her staunchly Protestant way, mocks Catholic preoccupation with preserving bodies of saints for aesthetic display. Describing her trip to the shrine in *Sunny Memories of Foreign Lands* (1854), she writes,

> I was much amused. . . . A sort of cupboard door half opened showed the shelves all full of skulls, adorned with little satin caps, coronets, and tinsel jewelry; which skulls, we were informed, were the original head-pieces of the same redoutable females. "Dere," said the priest, opening an ivory box, in which was about a quart of *teeth* of different sizes, "dere is de teeth of the eleven thousand."[57]

To Stowe and to many nineteenth-century Protestants, Catholicism appeared to revel in strange and exotic rituals, and a cupboard full of saint's skulls wearing pretty hats and decorative ivory boxes of teeth was just another telling example.

The Ursulines, dedicated to the memory of St. Ursula, were founded in Brescia, Italy about 1535 by St. Angela Merici.[58] Suspicion about the interior life of Ursuline convents was a burden borne by its members long before Aldous Huxley's peek inside diabolical Ursuline convent walls in *The Devils of Loudun*. Some sources suggest that at its very founding, this order was regarded with suspicion—even by prominent members of the Roman Catholic hierarchy. One Pope, Calixtus III, just fifty years before, had described Merici's hometown of Brescia as a hotbed of witches.[59] And Merici's spiritual leanings in some ways seem more occult than conventionally Christian. The saint's first religious vision came to her not in a church, but in an open field under the moon. She was gifted during her lifetime with numerous charisms, or divinely conferred powers, including the gift of tongues, infused theological knowledge, interpretation of Scriptures, the gift of prophecy, and the reading of consciences.[60] Official confirmation of her order did not come until 1544, four years after her death and more than half a century after her vision.[61] Her original group of twelve sisters had their first assembly in 1534, exactly three hundred years before the convent in Charlestown was destroyed. Significantly, these Ursulines made their first devotion in a church dedicated to another transmogrified goddess, St. Aphra. As happened with many saints of mythic origins, Christians converted a local cult dedicated to Aphrodite, goddess of love, into followers of a born-again Christian St. Aphra.[62] The popular nineteenth-century suspicion that Catholic communities of women ostensibly dedicated to celibacy in fact worshiped at the temple of love is, in this case, connected quite literally to the foundation of the Ursuline order. St. Angela Merici was canonized in 1807, only three decades before the Charlestown convent was destroyed. In the investigations surrounding her sainthood, it was affirmed that her body lay unburied for thirty days after her death, and emitted a sweet floral fragrance.[63] Her body, still "intact and uncorrupt" when it was last officially examined in 1774, lies in a glass coffin at St. Aphra's shrine in Brescia.[64]

From the earliest ages of the Roman Catholic Church, women have consecrated themselves to various forms of religious life, individually or in communities of virgins. But it was not until 1535, when St. Angela Merici first assembled her Ursuline Order, that they united the practice of evangelical counsels to the work of educating youth.[65] One scholar calls the teaching institute founded by Merici "probably the very first Christian organization on record in history for the education of young girls."[66] Merici was born in northern Italy in 1474, nine years earlier than Martin Luther. Her philosophy drew its inspiration from the active interest in pedagogy that thrived during the northern Italian Renaissance.[67] But the influence of the Humanists, with the Classical concept of woman's position in the home, had also begun to erode the place of women in Italian society. The Roman notion of *Paterna Potesta,* Father-Direction, began to receive emphasis in this Humanist conception of society, and one scholar argues that "consciously or unconsciously, Angela Merici's movement in Brescia was a reactionary reform against the pagan ideals imported through the Humanists into the education of girls. Her movement may be clearly defined as a reaction in which the

Mother-idea according to Christian tradition was to be reemphasized and made workable."[68] The formation of Merici's army to improve the education of women was contemporaneous with the spiritual militia organized by St. Ignatius Loyola: the Company of Jesus, or the Jesuits,[69] Bishop Fenwick's order.

Angela Merici first articulated her vision of women's education in 1535, and it was further expounded by Frances de Bermond in 1610.[70] This vision, which came to her literally as a heavenly inspiration, is called the Vision of Brudazzo. Along the road that skirted beautiful Lake Garda, connecting the sixteenth-century Italian towns of Desenzano and Salo, a teenage Angela kneeled to pray during the season of harvest. Suddenly, she was immersed in heavenly light, and her soul was flooded with ecstasy. From where she kneeled, a luminous ladder extended up-ward into the heavens. Upon its rungs, ascending and descending, were richly dressed maidens in jeweled crowns.[71] They sang as they climbed, with singing so beautiful that it rivaled the fabled heavenly choirs over Bethlehem. Angels accompanied the voices with golden instruments, and Angela was transported with joy at the sight of her recently de-ceased sister among them. The music stopped, and her sister spoke from the chaste multitude, "Angela! Angela, know that God has shown you this vision to signify that before you die, you are to found in Brescia, a company like these virgins."[72]

As a result of this vision, Angela believed she was called to organize some special work in Brescia for the benefit of her sex.[73] The goals of her community, as she stated them, were spiritual as well as educational. Angela had founded her order "not only for the salvation and perfection of its members, but also that these may help and serve their neighbor by the instruction of young girls."[74] This twofold object could be attained by religious instruction which emphasized the girls' Christian duty "to-wards their God, their parents, and superiors; towards other members of society, and towards themselves."[75] From the beginning, the order's em-phasis on training the child, not only intellectually, but as a moral being, found its "fountain spring in the Middle Ages."[76] Merici's original vision of her order, the Company of St. Ursula, was of a group of uncloistered virgins, canonically protected by the Church, formed to improve the condition of women.[77]

After Brescia, the Ursulines established a house in Milan during the mid-century, and then expanded to Parma and Rome. The uncloistered sisterhood with their good works began attracting attention in other countries. In 1596, Frances de Bermond established the first Ursuline community in southern France, near Avignon.[78] By 1610, the Ursuline order had spread to northern France, and in Paris in 1612, they were cloistered.[79] The French order of Ursulines added to the three usual vows of religious (poverty, chastity, and charity) a fourth commitment— the instruction of young girls.[80] Within a hundred years of their estab- lishment in France, there were 360 Ursuline convents[81] (two-thirds of these would be destroyed during the French Revolution).[82] The Que- bec monastery, where Mary Anne Moffatt entered religious life, was founded in 1639, a progeny of a house at Tours, descended from the mother house at Paris.[83]

Frances de Bermond amplified Merici's original Rule, which con- tained prescriptions for leading the life of an Ursuline sister as well as dictating the society's organization. Bermond's pedagogical supplement added detailed descriptions for how Angela's daughters were to comply with the task of training youth.[84] The most important attribute of this training was faith. Bermond wrote, "Just as coal that is scarcely warm will not inflame another coal like one that is on fire, so people who are but little afire with the love of God will rarely, and with great difficulty, inspire others with that love."[85] The *Règlements* were designed to shape teachers who would foster both spiritual and intellectual strength in their charges.

The relationship between teachers and pupils in an Ursuline setting was to be personal—the sisters were to understand, nourish, and cherish the individuality of each girl, as a mother would do, bearing in mind "each one in particular, her quality, her natural disposition, her inclina- tion and habits."[86] Merici outlined the essence of the teaching relation- ship as love and charity. In the *Règlements,* she wrote:

> We see that if mothers according to nature had a thousand chil-
> dren they would find room for them in their hearts and think of
> each separately for thus works love. . . . With still more reason
> spiritual mothers can and should act thus, since spiritual love is
> beyond comparison more powerful than human love.[87]

And to fully develop this maternal model of teaching, she advised her followers: "Charity will teach discernment and discretion will judge when to be indulgent and when severe." But most importantly, the teachers "should study to display a conduct full of sweetness and charity, of prudence, discretion, motherly foresight, full of kindness and not too exacting."[88]

The Mount Benedict *Prospectus* underlined this maternal role in its description of the sisters who administered the school:

> The Ladies who preside over this Establishment, are scrupulously careful to supply those who, placed under their care, with abundant and wholesome food; and to watch over their health, as well as their morals, *with all the solicitude of maternal tenderness* [my italics].—Cleanliness and neatness are rigorously attended to.

For their part, the students were encouraged to develop a filial devotion to the nuns, taking those who taught them "for their mothers, since they hold the place of a mother."[89]

This maternal tenderness was promoted, at least in the ideal, by a small teacher-to-student ratio. As we have seen, de Bermond's amplifications gave specific instruction for the pedagogical approach to teaching many different subjects. Most scholars believe that early academies, both Catholic and non-Catholic, relied on both inductive and deductive methods of teaching, with drill, practice, and review playing an important role.[90] The Ursuline emphasis on small class size and individual instruction also suggests attention to what contemporary educators call "critical thinking."

Like other nineteenth-century schools, the Ursulines' anticipated today's advocates of collaborative learning and multi-age grouping in their employment of *dixanières,* the honorary pupil-teachers whose duty it was to assist the teachers in the classwork and in the maintenance of discipline.[91] By this use of exemplary pupils as scholar-teachers and by their emphasis on fostering a maternal model of teaching, the sisters at Mount Benedict placed great value on teaching girls by good example. The *Règlements* emphasized that "their pupils shall learn from them virtuous habits as well as the knowledge of their religion. The first means for training others must be the mistress's own exemplary life."[92]

This exemplary living, however, was not necessarily to form the students into future nuns, but followed the explicit Ursuline mandate to shape girls into "virtuous Christian women who live honorably in the world."[93] In fact, the Ursuline Rule for the instruction of students differs from the tradition of monastic academies in warning *against* initiation of girls to religious life. Take care, the *Règlements* advise, "not to introduce anything that belongs to the religious life, either by talking or in any other way, and [do] not try to attract them to it in words or by any tacit means."[94] If a young girl were to conceive of entering religious life, she should do it on her own initiative. This philosophy, of course, directly contradicts the complaints made by Rebecca Reed, the Canadian Maria Monk, and other escaped nuns—that their confinement in Roman Catholic convents was enforced.

T HE ADMINISTRATIVE STRUCTURE of most Catholic girls' academies in the nineteenth century was modeled after the French, as was Mount Benedict's practice of awarding points weekly, with oral examinations at the end of each session, and the solemn distribution of prizes at the end of each year.[95] According to the Mount Benedict *Prospectus,* the difference between the junior and senior departments was a question of proficiency and sophistication. In the junior department, the scholars were taught the common branches of education, as well as geography and ancient and modern history. They were also taught plain and fancy needlework "and the Extra Branches, if required." The Extra Branches, that carried extra charges, included music, drawing, painting, dancing, and japanning, the art of coating surfaces with lacquer in the Japanese style. Girls were promoted on the basis of their accomplishments in specific areas.

In the senior department, girls continued their work in many of the areas described above, but also studied mythology, astronomy, logic, philosophy, chemistry, geometry, and botany among other subjects. A part of Ursuline education has always been vocational,[96] and at Mount Benedict, cooking was offered for an additional $20 per year. As noted earlier, the academy's tuition before these extra charges was $160 per year, during a time when six cents a week was charged at the Catholic

Day School in Lowell, Massachusetts. In most nineteenth-century Roman Catholic academies, girls were also taught sewing, mending, embroidery, dressmaking, knitting, and lace-making.[97] They learned how to construct artificial flowers from paper and silk, an art which the nuns had mastered as a means of altar-decoration during the winter months when their cutting gardens were covered in snow. While the pupils were busy at work under the supervision of one of the sisters, "another sister would read some interesting sketch or story so that their minds would be nourished at the same time that their fingers became more nimble."[98] Three times a year, there was a public exhibition of this "industrial" work of the students, with prizes for those who excelled.

Though the Ursulines brought with them a formulaic plan of study—the *Règlements* of the Ursulines—the curriculum in Charlestown was clearly influenced by American culture. It was American parents who demanded a broad curriculum, and placed a strong emphasis on music.[99] One nineteenth-century superior, Mother Guerin of the Sisters of Providence of St. Mary-of-the-Woods, writing twenty years after the founding of the Charlestown convent, described the curriculum offered at a girls' school in Frederick, Maryland, run by the Sisters of Charity:

> They teach the various sciences scarcely known in our French schools, but they excel in music, which is an indispensable thing in this country, even for the poor. No piano, no pupils! Such is the spirit of this country—Music and Steam! At Frederick, of the five Sisters, three teach piano and guitar.[100]

In order for a girls' academy to be profitable, then, it was necessary to offer a strong arts curriculum since the greatest source of income was often private lessons in music and art.[101] At Mount Benedict, dancing instruction by Mrs. Barrymore, a specially qualified instructor, was offered to develop poise and grace of movement and to prepare the young ladies for social life.[102]

Overall, a great deal of attention was paid to the "finishing" aspect of convent education. Though the learning of course content was a combination of memorization and individual instruction, when it came to the acquisition of fine manners the method was "learning by doing":

Girls had to walk the whole length of the study hall to learn how to approach the teacher gracefully and to salute her respectfully. Furthermore, they were trained to make a most profound curtsy to their classmates as they entered or left the classroom. Before going to the parlor the young lady was made to practice the manner of entering the room gracefully, of saluting her guests politely, and of withdrawing without embarrassment.[103]

A letter from Mary Barber corroborates that the Ursuline Academy was concerned with instilling grace in the pupils, noting that "At Mt. Benedict, the young ladies were obliged to make a courtesy [sic] each time they entered or left an apartment, before & after each class, and every time they handed or received anything from a mistress." She also related anecdotes that suggest that this training in good manners made Mt. Benedict pupils immediately recognizable:"Entering a store to purchase something, often was the question asked"—relates Barber, "'Are you one of the convent pupils?' and upon an answer in the affirmative, the gentleman replied, 'I thought so; the young ladies of the convent are so polite.'" She added, "At Mt. Benedict, the children, during studies, at the refectory, in the dormitory, were so silent that you might hear a pin drop on the floor. In the refectory, they never raised their eyes; in the dormitory, they never left the side of their bed esccept [sic] to be combed, and never left the school-room without permission. The nuns observed the rules and knew how to govern their pupils as religious ought to do."[104]

Another French feature of Catholic academies was the frequent coexistence within the same institution of an *école payante* and an *école gratuite* (free, or charity schools, for the poorer classes).[105] When Rebecca Reed entered the Mount Benedict Academy in 1831, it was as a charity scholar. This democracy of education was another important innovation of Angela Merici's. The *Constitution of the Ursulines* stipulates that Angela's daughters should "rejoice in the Lord and take a special pleasure in teaching poor girls, honoring therein the mission of our Divine Savior, sent to evangelize the poor."[106] For poor as well as wealthy girls, the convent academies offered some of the best education for women available at the time. It was difficult for Protestant girls' schools to compete with

Catholic academies, according to one expert, because they "had no religious body of women who could give their lives to the education of youth."[107] Though convent school education was seen by affluent families as one of the best available for women, many Protestants remained ambivalent about the practice of educating Protestant children in Roman Catholic nunneries. Even as strong a supporter of women's education as Sarah Josepha Hale, the editor of the influential *Ladies Magazine,* averred, "We certainly should not select a Catholic seminary as the place of education for our own daughters; yet candor obliges us to say, that from all we can learn of the system pursued at the Ursuline Convent, we think it offers, when compared with 'Young Ladies' Seminaries, in general, its fair proportion of advantages."[108] And the *Christian Register* magazine published in Boston on May 8, 1830 issued this warning about the dangers of a Catholic education, focusing on the careful scrutiny given the girls:

> All letters or communications that are sent to these young ladies from parents or friends must be inspected by the *Lady Superior,* and whatever information they may wish to forward to their friends must also pass under the inquisition of this Lady. How cautious are the managers of this Institution to guard against *"evil communications!"* The principles of the Nunnery might be exposed to the minds of those who are capable of understanding the philosophy of its machinery by the letters of the scholars. May the time soon arrive when Protestant parents will open their eyes, and examine well the moral and religious tendency of every Academy to which they send their children.

For some parents, however, one of the strongest selling points of the convent was the careful overseeing of their daughter's behavior it promised. Louisa Whitney, in her narrative, *The Burning of the Convent,* recalls:

> The conventual school-system had great attractions for parents brought up under stern Puritan regulations, against which their daughters were beginning to rebel; but it was an odd idea to call in Catholic discipline as a substitute for Puritan restraints which they could enforce no longer.[109]

And in at least two existing letters, Mrs. Lydia Russell, mother of two of the Academy's students, wrote to the superior about the bad influences of society on her daughters and the Ursuline convent's good discipline. "I cannot conceive a more fortunate protection for my children than yours, nor can I wish other advantages for them than the high qualities of the Ladies of that Community" as a counter to the "prices of handkerchiefs which has diseased the imaginations of my children" for which she blames the "indulgences of home."[110]

Many academies, such as Mount Benedict, offered this surveillance twenty-four hours a day, as the sisters slept in the same room as the boarders. And of course "Catholic discipline" included close supervision, detailed this way in the Mount Benedict *Prospectus:*

> Parents being ever sensible to the happiness and welfare of their children, and anxious to know, even the smallest details of what concerns them, every three months, Bulletins will be issued, relating to their health, the extent of their application, and their progress in study.—Care will be likewise taken that their children write to them the 15th of each month.

The pupils were expected to live up to an "exact compliance with every rule and the form of polite deportment." They were so closely supervised that they could not go "beyond the reach of a watchful but maternal superintendence, whose vigilance secures the preservation of morals, and the willing obedience of rules."[111] While working in the garden, the students were required to wear gloves, their gardening aprons, and straw hats. The farm stretched for twenty-four acres, and students were allowed to take their recreational walks throughout, though the Mount Benedict *Propectus* notes, "always, however, under the immediate superintendence of one, or more of the Ladies."

In a description of the contemporaneous Convent of the Visitation in Georgetown, D.C. published in 1830, Ignatius Loyola Robertson writes:

> There is no espionage; no making use of one to find out the faults of another; but their care and watchfulness are so sisterly and maternal, that the pupil is naturally moulded, not drilled, to

good manners. Discipline is constantly going on even in those hours of relaxation in which girls left to themselves often acquire an awkwardness of manners that cleave to them for the whole course of their lives. Such schools are rare. The Ursulines have just opened one on the same plan, near Boston, which is flourishing under an accomplished superior.[112]

At both the Visitation Academy and Charlestown there was a strong emphasis on character education, which they believed close surveillance helped to achieve. All students had to attend morning and evening prayers daily, and divine services on Sundays, since that was the only way the girls could be continually supervised.[113] Lucy Thaxter noted that at Mount Benedict,

> On Sabbath days, we attended service in the morning. The Protestant pupils were required to take their own Bibles or Prayer books into the Chapel, and to read them during the service. In the afternoon, we attended Vespers, the evening service recited by the nuns, with the same requirement to take our Bibles or some other religious book for our own reading. During the day we had much the same hours of silence as on other days, to be passed in reading of a moral or religious nature. We were also required to commit to memory and recite a chapter or part of a chapter from the New Testament. The Catholic pupils had lessons or instructions apart from us with which we had nothing to do.[114]

This close supervision, probably an echo of the French Jansenist influence, was one of the marked differences between non-Catholic and Catholic academies of the day.[115] While nineteenth-century Protestant academies like Lyman Beecher's daughter Catherine's experimented with democratic government within the academy structure, Catholic academies subjected the daily interactions of the girls to authoritarian scrutiny.[116]

The official report of those investigating the institution after the convent burning, however, asserted that this supervision was not in the name of conversion:

No means were taken to influence or affect their religious opinions; their attendance upon the services in the chapel was voluntary, never exacted. The only religious services, forming a part of
the system, were morning and evening prayers, common to all
christians, and discourses by the bishop, on Sundays, upon the
practical truths and religious duties which are peculiar to no sect.
*Nor can it be ascertained that any pupil placed under their charge for the
purposes of education, has been converted from any other to the Catholic
faith, or induced to become a member of the community.*[117]

Still, some of the students attested to the romanticizing of the monastic
way of life as seen through Protestant eyes:

After tea there was another hour of profound silence enjoined
while the Nuns were at the Vesper service. My soul thrills as I recall the melancholy beauty of that hour. Motionless, I watched
the slow setting of the sun, lighting up the broad summer land-
scape with a golden glow and darkening it with purple shadows;
and when the sun had dropped behind the distant hills, and the
changing opal sky was fading into dull gray, the voices of the Sisters rose solemnly from the Chapel below, and the faint scent of
incense mingled with the breath of the white roses trained against
its walls, and floated into the open window on the evening air.[118]

Louisa Whitney's lush description details the "foreign quality" of the institution that made a deep impression on Rebecca Reed, and many others. Like the veiling ceremony and other convent events to which
Protestants were invited, the Roman Catholic Mass, as evoked by Whitney, had a powerful effect on the girls who were simply supposed to be
reading their Bibles.

During High Mass on Sunday, the nuns were concealed from the
scholars behind heavy crimson curtains: But, though unseen,
their exquisite singing ravished the ear,—so ravished my childish
senses that I should not have been surprised had a troop of angels
swooped out upon us from between the parted curtains, with

white wings brushing the crimson, looking perhaps like the beautiful St. Ursula over the altar.[119]

Protestant children at the Charlestown academy were often included in prayer sessions and in celebrating religious feasts:

Thus they were brought up on the Liturgy, and were taught to love their share in that great voice of praise by which the Church hymns the Creator during the ceaseless round of the Christian year.[120]

While some critics of Mount Benedict charged that this active practice in following the feasts of the Christian year contradicted the order's stated philosophy of not enticing children into religious life, the Ursulines believed that this practice reached beyond monastic rule:

to train the young to see the meanings and purpose of such a worship which in their age and country could be heard resounding in any cathedral or collegiate church, a service to which the general faithful went as to a feast of the soul, voiced in music, art, and dignified ceremonial; the object was, in short, not to incline young girls to monasticism, as this was expressly forbidden by the Ursuline rule whose real objective was the influencing of the Christian home, but to make them as Christian women, lovers and participants in of the life which is everybody's Christianity.[121]

Ultimately, the primary impression that the Ursulines seem to have made on their young charges was one of kindness and affection. The official report of the committee appointed to investigate the riot found that

of the truly maternal kindness with which the children were uniformly treated, and of their filial affection to the ladies of the establishment, and of the entire confidence and respect to which they are entitled, the Committee have the fullest assurances both from children and parents. Nor can it be believed that, if undue severity had been exercised upon the pupils; or harshness, or cruelty had been inflicted upon any member of the community; or if anything inconsistent with purity of deportment had existed, it could have escaped the scrutinizing observation of so many inquisitive and active minds; or could fail to be communicated to their friends; and still less can it be believed, that upon a disclosure of this sort, a father or mother could be found who would suffer a daughter to remain under their roof.[122]

Contrary to Rebecca Reed's charges of cruelty to its inmates, the convent community, it seems, was for the most part serene, happy, and tranquil.

Despite close living quarters, many aspects of the lives of the nuns were obscured from the pupils—with the deep privacy stemming largely from the institution of cloister. The daily routine of sisters teaching and administering a day and boarding school was full and demanding. In addition to those who ran the school, other sisters were needed for the domestic duties of the convent. Lay sisters, usually lower class and less educated, generally fulfilled these roles of providing clothing, caring for the household, and cooking the meals. Though the life of a girl in the Mount Benedict Academy was carefully structured to support her social, intellectual, and spiritual development, life in the cloister was even more regimented.

Each hour was accounted for and the *horarium,* or hourly schedule, carefully followed. The sisters rose before sunrise, at half past five, washing and dressing themselves within a half hour. From six to seven, some sisters said a series of prayers and studied Christian Doctrine, while others supervised the toilette of the girls. In the full morning light at seven o'clock, they would breakfast before classes began at eight. Lessons would run until noon, including the time the nuns spent teaching industrial work. Following a two-hour break, during which time the girls would eat and take walks through the convent gardens, classes would resume. The afternoon of a lay sister would be devoted to cleaning, cooking, and laundry. Classes ran until five o'clock, when the sisters would release the scholars. A quiet period of needlework and study followed until dinner at half past six.[123] After Mary Anne Moffatt gave her final blessing for the day, the bell in the convent tower would sound a peal for bedtime.[124]

The large amount of prayer blended into the life of members of the convent community, including the classroom instructors as their duties permitted, demonstrates how the center of the life was a truly spiritual one. It was a community "in which the spiritual fabric was made up of individual parts each in its way contributing to the entirety of effect; the nun who swept the kitchen being at once contributor and recipient in the general benefactions, through the great work of education."[125] While the "exigencies of the times" during the nineteenth century demanded sophistication in learning on the part of the teachers, the curriculum in convent schools was still chiefly Christian doctrine, and necessitated the most study. But scholars of convent life aptly observe that this study of Christian doctrine "was linked up with the religious life of the teachers in such a way that the essence of their own best teaching actually was an outgrowth of their own individual lives, action springing from contemplation."[126]

As SUPERIOR, Mary Anne Moffatt oversaw all aspects of life in her convent, both practical and spiritual. The teachers in the school reported to her, as did the lay sisters. She was responsible for both the administration of the academy and the spiritual life of the nuns in the convent. In addition, Moffatt had a small crew of men doing repairs, upkeep, and gardening. Irish groundskeepers lived within the walled compound, and saw to day-to-day maintenance. With this help, Moffatt took an active interest in developing the convent grounds. In March 1831, for example, Moffatt wrote to Levi Thaxter, the father of one of the pupils, asking for his assistance in procuring more fruit trees. She asked him to select from a nursery in Watertown, Massachusetts fifty apple trees, fifty plum trees, thirty quinces, and six snowballs. She herself set the terms for the transaction: two shillings a piece for the apple trees, and fifty cents for the plum trees, adding, "I shall deem it a great favor if you will have the kindness to make the bargain as if it were for yourself." She signed this letter as she signed many others to those outside the Church's hierarchy, *The Superior,* with a large flourish.[127] Part of the timing of this letter in March would be for preparation for the institution's grand festival day. Held annually at the end of June, the day demanded enormous preparation from the teachers, who drilled their students' performances to perfection. The floors and furniture gleamed with new polish, and the gardeners brought the grounds, especially the roses and other flowers, to new horticultural heights.

In 1830, Miss Maria W. Cotting, with her beautiful handwriting and other accomplishments, was awarded the silver medal at Coronation Day on Mount Benedict. A hundred years later this medal was in the possession of her daughter, Miss Sarah E. Holmes, a Somerville, Massachusetts resident.[128] Just as the Ursulines prepared extensively for the event, for weeks beforehand the girls, too, were engaged in making white dresses, practicing poetry recitations and musical selections, rehearsing plays, and revising essays to be read not by the writer, but by the bishop. Sister Mary John, Elizabeth Harrison, in addition to her regular lessons, had the extra stress and responsibility for all the musical performances. The lay sisters, too, scrubbed themselves to exhaustion, scouring every corner in preparation for the influx of visitors, clergy, relatives, and friends of the students, who often traveled great distances to be present. They assembled in the rose-filled convent garden, often under a large tent raised for the day. The various programs would last several hours, leading up to the awarding of prizes and the bestowal of the crown. Samples of the girls' penmanship, drawing, painting, plain sewing, and fancy work were arranged for viewing. Public examinations were held, with the girls being quizzed by priests and prominent laymen.[129] For the teachers, pupils, and their families, Coronation Day was the single most important event of academy life.

This major event was preceded by many smaller recognition ceremonies throughout the year. Regular reports apprised parents of the students' academic progress, application, health, and deportment. The Mount Benedict *Prospectus* offered a rationale for the system, designed to "accelerate the advancement of the Young Ladies in their respective classes: distinction of places; daily marks; weekly repetitions; privileges granted to application and merit; honorable mention, made every month, of those, whose assiduity in their studies, and excellency in good conduct, deserve approbation; premiums distributed at the end of the year, &c."

Once a month, the superior assembled the Mount Benedict teachers in the great hall to hear from them an account of the various merits and demerits of their pupils. The most deserving were promoted to a higher rank in the class, while the less accomplished took lower stations. Occa-

Lucretia Beckford's report card, signed by the superior, shows the
challenging curriculum offered at the Mount Benedict Academy.

sionally small premiums, or prizes, were distributed. Convents seem to
have supplied each other with articles to be used for awards. In one letter to the superior at Trois Rivières, Mary Anne Moffatt responded to
that convent's offer to send *l'oeuvres en écorce*, prizes made out of wood
or bark. These were to be given as recompense to the girls—but the superior was concerned they were too costly. She wrote that she would
rather be sent less expensive embroidered prizes—already made and
ready to be distributed.[130]

But by far, the most joyous and festive event of the year at the Charlestown academy was the festival in late June that marked the completion of the school year. Former students Lucy Thaxter and Louisa Whitney recall the event vividly, and the journals of Bishop Benedict Fenwick contain frequent references to Coronation Day. Lucy Thaxter wrote this remembrance:

> We danced, we sang, we played all manner of games, the superior and nuns looking on, as happy in witnessing our enjoyment, as we ourselves. The bishop gave us a feast; and then we bade adieu to our kind teachers, to return home for a six weeks vacation.[131]

Whitney too details the event, highlighting its quality as a "foreign custom . . . which fascinated plain Protestants by its novelty."

> On that day only, parents and guardians passed the limit of the parlor, and were allowed admission to the school-rooms. The music and dancing rooms were prettily decorated, and furnished with rows of seats, which were crowded with delighted elders, who forgot the heat of a July day in admiring the proficiency of the pupils in the accomplishments taught in the convent. There were performances on the harp and guitar, as well as on the piano, by curled darlings, dressed in the prescribed white frocks and pink sashes. Drawings, landscapes in India-ink, and fancy-work were handed about, and high art was represented by theorem-paintings, Grecian ditto, and painting on velvet. There were part-songs, recitations, and little drama performed; the results of the yearly examinations were made public; and, last of all, there was a grand mustering of the white frocks and pink sashes on the platform, from the midst of whom a queen was chosen, not by her schoolmates, but by the Nuns, who led her forward to the front of the platform, and presented her to the public as the prize scholar of the year, averaging first both in lessons and deportment. As it was never known beforehand on whom the choice would fall, this was a moment of great excitement to the pupils, and to the queen herself perhaps the proudest moment of her life. Then there was a Coronation,—a crown of beautiful white

artificial flowers, made by the Nuns, was put upon the queen's curls, she was led to her throne, which was, after a while, transferred to the head of a long table in the Refectory, on which a magnificent collation was spread. The meagre diet of a year was forgotten in the splendor of this repast, wherein figured every indigestible delicacy that French confectioners could devise to tempt the palates of the children. Some of the Nuns were accomplished confectioners,—Paris-trained, as the school legends ran,—and it was a wonder that they did not forget an art practiced only once a year."[132]

Even Bishop Fenwick, who was habitually more restrained in his journals, could not refrain from waxing eloquent about this memorable day. His description of Coronation Day in 1829 corroborates what might at first be seen as fanciful in Louise Whitney's. Fenwick writes of the "sumptuously decorated" hall, at the end of which two "thrones" are placed, one for the bishop and one for the superior. At the other end of the hall, sat two "richly decorated" chairs, for the young ladies to be honored. With the speeches and music concluded, "Miss Mead is introduced by the Superior to the throne of the *B'p,* who places a crown of roses on her head at the same time complimenting her on her proficiency & the satisfaction she had given to her teachers."[133] Following the crowning of Maria Fay of Cambridgeport, daughter of a prominent judge, the premiums were distributed among those of the young ladies who had given general satisfaction. The ceremony ended with selections performed on the piano, harp, & flute.

In a description of a different year's event, Fenwick provides a few additional details. The guests were first treated to "a variety of airs executed on the Piano, the Harp & the Guitar." The Bishop then addressed the students, "commending their application & speaking in high terms of the visible improvement they had made since the last examination & . . . expressing his wish that they would continue to afford the same satisfaction to their teachers on their return to the convent after their short vacation." Next, two girls were presented to him for the honor, and he placed wreaths of roses on their heads: "on the 1st (Miss Thompson of Charlestown) a wreath of white giving her at the same time a gold Medal; and on the 2d (Miss Cotting) a wreath of red, with a medal of silver. They are then conducted to the throne & an appropriate Song is sung by all the others accompanied by the Harp & Piano." The students and their families enjoyed "a sumptuous repast provided by the good Superior," which was followed by further distribution of "premiums . . . consisting of a great variety of fancy articles. During which the Italian Musicians performed in the yard to the great delight of all, a great variety of airs." After this lovely day at Mount Benedict, the girls left with their families to return home.[134]

When a second order of nuns, the Sisters of Charity, arrived in Boston from Emmitsburg, Maryland in May 1832 to open an orphanage and a school for poor Catholic children, the three pioneers of this order were also invited to the feast at the convent. Sister Ann Alexis Shorb, Sister Loyola Ritchies, and Sister Blandina Davaux wore white veils and blue dresses, and dramatic white cornettes on their heads that the priests affectionately referred to as "the flying geese." The visiting nuns rode in carriages to partake of the festivities, and were treated to a tour and performances in their honor by convent students clad in the traditional pink and white.

The arrival of the Sisters of Charity marked a growing Catholic presence in the diocese of Boston, and the mood of the convent feast of 1832 was further enhanced by the celebration of this new ministry. Bishop Benedict Fenwick's ambitious plans for expanding Catholicism in New England were progressing apace, as he welcomed this new group of religious women to his diocese. Eventually these women would care for nearly three hundred children in their orphanage on Hamilton Street, many of them orphans of cholera victims, and operate a benevolent, or free, day school.[135] The merriment of Coronation Day seemed an especially fitting way to celebrate. With song, dance, and pretty poems addressed to the Sisters of Charity, the girls of the Ursuline academy welcomed the newcomers to Boston, and Mount Benedict once again rang with the joy of the feast.[136]

The citizens of Charlestown, however, did not find in this sign of the growing presence of Catholicism, or in the convent festivals, anything to celebrate. Just as the discipline and simplicity of daily monastic life seemed to watching Protestant eyes an overregimentation that curtailed the basic American principle of freedom, so the lavish festivals at the convent came to signify Roman Catholic excess. At its heart, the

*Sister Ann Alexis, the superior of the Sisters of Charity, opened her convent to the Ursulines for two months following the fire.*

Catholic principles of penance and fasting manifested in daily depriva-
tions, such as no meat on Friday and during the season of Lent, were
counter to Protestant notions of moderation in all things. The heart of
monastic celibate life, curbing the appetite and desires of the body, was,
in this view, unhealthy, and resulted in diseases, like tuberculosis, and
madness, to which the women in the Charlestown convent seemed particularly susceptible. The constant surveillance of the girls and the nuns
by convent authorities, both in the monastery's passion for order and
close scrutiny of every aspect of daily life, to outsiders looked antidemocratic. For Protestants, this intrusiveness was exemplified most vividly in
the sacrament of confession, where Catholic authorities had unre-
stricted access to the penitent's mind.

Catholicism has always operated on a more extreme pendulum than
Protestantism, with its days of penance veering into almost riotous celebration, such as Christmas and the Easter season. For Catholics, this
pendulum represents the essential notion of delayed gratification upon
which the faith is founded. Man and woman suffer this vale of tears
with patience in the faith that reward awaits them in heaven. The
Catholic calendar of penance giving way to feast is a metaphor for this
central belief. Therefore, the logic of producing a Coronation Day after
a year's hard labor in the classrooms at Mount Benedict went beyond a
mere pedagogical strategy as it was presented in the school's *Prospectus.*
At its core, the feast was essentially a Roman Catholic metaphor for the
Heavenly Reward. The lavishly decorated thrones of the bishop and superior were symbols of the seats of those divine rulers, God himself and
Mary the Virgin, and the music and feasting the celebrations of the angels and saints. This swinging pendulum of penance to feast is ultimately
what struck Louise Whitney and other Protestant observers as "foreign"
about the veiling ceremonies and festival days at Mount Benedict. And
while invited Protestant guests, the respectable, educated families who
attended the events, found this foreignness to be quaint and old-worldly,
the men who worked in the surrounding brickyards were less than
charmed. Their enforced monastic existence, in the dirty and crowded
male dormitories, far from their wives and families, was an economic
imposition, not a chosen path of spiritual perfection.

So when strains of music and girlish laughter floated down the hill
from under the white tent at Coronation Day, and the brickmen looked

up from their labors to see stately carriages drawn by fine horses standing in the wide drive before the convent door, something tightened inside them. A glimpse of girls in white dresses, their slim waists wrapped
with pink sashes, stepping into those carriages to return to their luxuri-
ous homes at the end of the day, further coiled the men's frustration.
And the sight of a new order of Roman Catholic nuns visiting the convent, who looked even more outlandish than the Ursulines in their
strange costumes, hardened their wills against this foreign imposition.
What was becoming of their fledgling republic? Where was *their* "shin-
ing city on a hill"?

## CHAPTER FOUR

# A DEADLY MIASMA

## *Cemeteries, Cholera, and Catholicism*

MARY ANNE MOFFATT stood at the front door and watched the last of the carriages depart from Coronation Day at the convent. As it wound down the hill, she reviewed with satisfaction the performances of the children, the delicacies that the lay sisters had served for dinner, and the impression that her convent had made on the other newly arrived religious group in Boston, the Sisters of Charity. Their planned orphanage and school for poor children would be financed by the profits of Bishop Fenwick's new newspaper, *The Jesuit,* begun in 1829. The sisters had enjoyed a delightful day of song and dance, expertly performed by the boarders. Moffatt turned to make her way into the kitchen where Sister Mary Claire was straightening up the last of the day's dishes. The nun looked up with her broad smile, and reached to take the pantry key out of her pocket.

"Would you like a glass of wine to celebrate the day, Reverend Mother?" she asked. "It was a great success."

"In a moment, Sister Mary Claire."

Just then the women heard some scratching and a slight whimper at the kitchen door.

"That must be the dog," said Moffatt, referring to the convent's pet. "I'll let him in."

Moffatt pushed open the screen door, and saw the animal outstretched on the step, his face away from the house.

"Why, Puppy," she asked with surprise, "what are you doing?"

She reached down to stroke the fur of his flank, but pulled back in shock from its sticky warmth. To her horror, her hand was red with blood. The dog stirred his head a little at her touch, and let out a sigh. His eyes had a glazed look that at that moment settled into a stare. Before she could respond, he was dead.

"Sister Mary Claire," she said, struggling to get her voice under control. "Call the caretaker," referring to the Irishman who lived at the bottom of the hill. "Someone has killed this poor dog."

THE SHOOTING OF the convent dog by "three ruffian Brick-Makers," as Bishop Fenwick termed them, was not the only foreshadowing of violence against the Catholics.[1] In 1829, the year Fenwick founded his newspaper, *The Jesuit,* the houses of Irish Catholics on Broad Street were stoned for three nights in succession.[2] In 1830, as Fenwick established a Catholic cemetery in Charlestown, the convent's stable was burnt to the ground under suspicious circumstances. In 1832, the *Boston Recorder* published an inflammatory report bemoaning the arrival of the Sisters of Charity.[3] And in 1833, during a disturbance between Catholics and Protestants in Lowell, Massachusetts, to the north of Boston, a Catholic constable, Mr. Cumminski, was shot in the arm.[4] In Charlestown, tension between the groups led to the death on Thanksgiving night 1833 of Benjamin Daniells, a Charlestown native. The following night a riot broke out, during which McGowan's pub, an Irish watering hole, was destroyed.[5] These events demonstrated the simmering anger of the Yankees against the Catholic newcomers. The occasional bubbling would boil over into violence in August 1834.

This animosity, especially in Charlestown, was the result of mounting tensions during the early 1830s. The position of the old elite, the staunch Congregationalist Charlestown Yankees, was being eroded on two fronts. Newly wealthy Unitarians were sending their sons to Harvard, and their daughters to Mount Benedict, and gaining prominent social standing in the professional ranks. At the same time, an influx of lower-class working men, both New Hampshire farmers and Irish immigrants, was upsetting the stability and peace of the traditional Charlestown community. These men were increasingly dissatisfied with their working conditions, and labor unions were beginning to gain a foothold of power. To diffuse some of these new tensions within the

Protestant community itself, both religious and economic, it was convenient to unite against a common scapegoat, the Catholics. In old Charlestown, there was more than one form of anti-Catholicism and it served different purposes for different groups.

L ATE IN THE SUMMER OF 1628, Ralph, Richard, and William Sprague, along with a handful of others, arrived from the colony of Salem to establish Charlestown, Massachusetts, a settlement begun before the foundation of Boston. It was only the third settlement in Massachusetts, after Salem and Plymouth Plantation.[6] Two summers later, in 1630, John Winthrop and a band of about one hundred settlers formed a colony in the area. But Charlestown's beginnings were inauspicious— within eighteen months, nearly four fifths of the population was dead. Lack of potable water, a dangerously hot summer, and an epidemic nearly wiped out the colony, which was further threatened by a shortage of food and the fear of a French attack.[7] One of the dispersed inhabitants, William Blackstone, settled on the slopes of what become Boston's Beacon Hill, so that Charlestown, "the mother of Boston," from her vantage point on the north bank of the Charles River, could, as one historian puts it, watch her precocious child grow.[8]

But Charlestown managed to overcome this inauspicious beginning and began to thrive, with a pre-industrial economy that allowed residents to lead what was, in the eighteenth century, a comfortable middle-class existence. This growth was cut short, however, when the British retaliated for the Battle of Bunker Hill by torching every building in town. The residents pulled together and rebuilt their community, helped by their shared values and ancestral origins. The one church in town was Orthodox Congregational, and nearly all of the townspeople were of English descent.[9] James Frothingham Hunnewell, the best-known of the town's chroniclers, wrote that in homogeneous Charlestown, "There was little of the old tory official or fashionable element, only a moderate amount of higher education, and there were few or none of the leisure class, as it is called. . . . The general community was intelligent, thrifty, comfortable; it was orderly and quiet, yet it probably enjoyed itself."[10]

Historian James Gillespie Blaine II points out that Hunnewell may have exaggerated the idea that Charlestown was not subject to the dramatic forces of change that were assaulting the city of Boston just across the river. Still, the myth of old Charlestown as a stable New England town had enduring appeal, especially to its residents in the early part of the nineteenth century as they watched new groups arriving. These towns were built around the central Puritan doctrine of the covenant, and formed their community relations based upon the collective acceptance of traditions, beliefs, and institutions.[11] The arrival of the Catholics in the late 1820s, then, threatened the sense of stability that Charlestown residents had long relied on for comfort.

The citizens of Charlestown prided themselves on their ability to stand together to overcome adversity. By the first three decades of the nineteenth century, Charlestown was the third largest town in the state, exceeded only by Boston and Salem.[12] Its convenient access to the Charles and Mystic rivers, as well as to Boston Harbor and the Atlantic Ocean, quickly helped transform Charlestown into a thriving market center.[13] With the opening of the United States Navy Yard in 1800, Charlestown was poised to prosper from the burgeoning shipping industry throughout the first half of the nineteenth century.

In addition to shipping, Charlestown funneled most overland trade from the north and northwest into Boston, first by ferry and then, after 1786, by the Charles River Bridge. An article in the *Bunker Hill Aurora* in 1828 describes the large volume of traffic:

> The travel across the present bridge is very great, from New Hampshire, Maine, etc. and from the populous counties of Middlesex, Essex, and part of Worcester. Five public roads concentrate in Charlestown, besides the avenue to the Navy Yard. By an estimate made in October last it appeared that 190 stages, 150 chaises, 127 teams, 250 other vehicles, 16 horses, 6 handcarts, and 2230 footpassengers, passed over the bridge, and on another day there were 5551 footpassengers—the average toll was $110.81 per day.[14]

The profitable bridge contrasted with another transportation venture, the Middlesex Canal, which, after taking ten years to complete, had opened in 1803. The canal proved disastrous for investors, paying returns only in the 1820s and early 1830s, when the railroads dealt a death blow to what were at best modest profits.[15] With the advent of the Boston and Lowell railroad, and the Nashua and Lowell railroad, Charlestown became an important terminal, as well as a seaport and teamster center. A growing number of workingmen flocked there to labor in the transportation industry, and frequented the numerous taverns springing up along dock areas and the routes traveled by truckers and carters.[16]

Many of the rural New Hampshire men who helped burn the convent were probably initially attracted to Charlestown because they could hope to find work in its thriving industrial economy. A small village housing the workers sprang up near Breed's Hill and on both sides of Bunker Hill Street known locally as Dog Point. The men, crowded into inexpensive housing, provided the labor force for the brickyards, ropewalks, oil works, tanneries, and a match factory.[17] By 1813, according to statistics compiled by a townsman, 18 million bricks had been manufactured in Charlestown at a value of $650,000. In 1819, Jedidiah Morse, the father of Samuel F. B. Morse, inventor of the telegraph and a notorious anti-Catholic, stated that "the manufacture of morocco leather and of bricks are carried on here on a larger scale, probably, than in any other town in the state."[18] The prosperity of Charlestown is illustrated in its range of businesses in 1830: two banks, an insurance company, twenty-three wharves, and two breweries. The town also boasted seven meeting houses (Congregational, Unitarian, Universalist, Baptist, Methodist, Puritan, and Catholic),[19] five engine houses, nine primary and three reading and writing schools, a library, five physicians, six attorneys, an alms house, an insane asylum, the state prison, and the Ursuline convent.[20]

The friction from the social changes of this increasing urbanization bled into the religious life of the community. Trinitarians were pitted against Unitarians, and the sects splitting off from established Congregationalists competed for recognition. The increased presence of the Catholic Church after the establishment of St. Mary's in 1828 raised strong emotions.[21] The Baptist Church, often viewed as the spiritual home of the lower social classes, established the Charlestown Female Academy in 1830, which was considered socially inferior to the school on Mount Benedict.[22] Rebecca Reed attended it after she left the convent. The 1830 Federal Census records an immigrant population for

Charlestown of 529, or 6 percent of the population, but historian Wilfred Bisson estimates that, by 1834, the population of Irish Catholics was between 1,000 and 1,500.[23] Between 1820 and 1830, the foreign-born population had increased sixfold.[24]

Both the old elite and the day laborers felt that these newcomers undermined their social position. The laboring classes expressed their discontent in union activity, new political parties, and anti-Irish nativism, and joined the Workingmen's Party.[25] Of the selectmen serving in Charlestown when the convent was burned, four were members of this party.[26] In 1833, the *Bunker Hill Aurora* summed up the party's philosophy:

> The Workingmen comprise the middling and laboring classes of society—their task is hard enough at best; they have to contend for existence and to support their families against fearful odds, we know. They are compelled to labor and to labor hard and to labor nearly all the time to gain a respectable livelihood.[27]

The life of a Workingman, then, was at odds with the privileged life led by the denizens of Mount Benedict. In Charlestown, the party gained a stronghold on its nativist platform. In January 1834, an activist named Seth Luther delivered a diatribe against the Catholic Church to the Union Association of Workingmen in the Charlestown Town Hall.[28] His sentiments had originated during a strike in 1832 of ships' carpenters. Management had advertised for replacement workers to cross the picket line, specially targeting Irish immigrants.[29] The strike was successfully crushed during May 1832. Seth Luther went on to give the speech several times, even into early 1834. While union activity was most frequently directed against the owners and management of businesses, in Charlestown, it was redirected against the Catholic newcomers. *The Report of the Committee* investigating the riot hinted that the better classes played a role in the conspiracy against the Ursuline convent. It is conceivable that as labor unions began to agitate for better working conditions, the business sector in Charlestown found ways to align the workers against a more convenient target: the Catholics.

Seth Luther's was only one voice expressing concern about the growing number of Catholics in New England. During the 1830s, a number of Boston newspapers took a decidedly anti-Catholic stance. The *Boston Recorder* had the following to say about the Mount Benedict nunnery, cloaked in descriptive guidebook language, around the time that the ships' carpenters strike was crushed and Mary Anne Moffatt found her dog dead on the kitchen steps:

> There is a rising ground in Charlestown, from which the traveller views the most delightful prospect. He sees the gentle river playing around the foot of "Mount Benedict"; and Boston and Charlestown rise before him, as if they were of small importance compared with the Mounts in this vicinity. If he turns his eye upwards, he views the cerulean sky smiling on all beneath, and the small cloud from which proceeds the gentle rain, falling on the good and the evil. While lingering around this "Mount," his ears are frequently regaled by the syren voice of music proceeding from the harp and the piano within a Convent; and his memory naturally reverts to the time when these hills echoed the cannon's roar, proceeding from Bunker's heights, and speaking terror to the hearts of oppressors, on the day that Warren lost his life, and our country, in principle, gained the battle.[30]

Recalling the Battle of Bunker Hill, and the death there of the Revolutionary hero Dr. Joseph Warren, this passage on the surface seems favorable, yet a closer examination reveals ambiguity—an ambiguity that generally surrounded the reception offered the convent. The travel-book description here foreshadows the transformation of the convent ruins that stood for fifty years after the fire into a romantic spot—a "ruin of our own" that could be visited without travel to Europe. The rendering of Boston and Charlestown as being of "small importance" underlines one of the rioters' chief complaints about the convent's inhabitants, especially the proud mother superior: their perception that she treated them as underlings. The cloud over the convent that mars the cerulean sky lets fall its rain "on the good and the evil" and it is tempting to see the "syren voice" as part of the evil—a reference to the female sirens of Greek legend who lured mariners to destruction with seductive singing. The *Boston Recorder* refers to the fading glory of the American Revolution, when heroic forefathers stood atop the same mount fighting for democracy. What a contrast to see a perceived anti-democratic institution, a Roman Catholic monastery, atop the hallowed ground. The writer then develops this contrast further:

> Here is "Mount Benedict," which, though it does not boast of its deeds of valour; from its banks may yet go forth, with their minds imbued with such principles, which, if embraced by our descendents, will counteract every good for which our fathers fought; and while the traveller treads this Mount, he sighs for the day when all false religion shall be overthrown, and the true religion of Christ pervade the whole world; when the mind will be free as air, unshackled from the vain sophistry of the deceitful world, however insinuating may be their priesthood, or splendid their mode of worship.

Acknowledging the seductiveness of Catholic ritual, the writer goes on to narrate a history of the academy that articulates the popular concerns:

> On the top of this "Mount" stands an Academy, whose proprietors are Roman Catholics, and who have given it the name of the "Ursuline (an order of Nuns) Community on Mount Benedict." (St. Benedict, the founder of the order of Benedictine Monks, was born in Italy, A.D. 480. He was educated at Rome, and afterwards removed to Subiaco, about 40 miles distant, where he confined himself to a cavern, known only to St. Romanus, who, it is said, visited him, by descending a rope to supply him with provisions. The monks of a neighboring monastery discovered him and made him their Abbot. St. Benedict soon disagreed with his associates, and returned to his solitude, whither many persons followed him, and placing themselves under his direction, he in a short time built 12 monasteries. He afterwards retired to Mount Cassino, where he instituted the order which bears his name.)

In fact Mount Benedict was not directly named after St. Benedict, but in honor of Bishop Benedict Fenwick. Picking up on the earlier theme of the noble hill where the fathers bled for the American Revolution, now desecrated by an order of nuns, the writer continues to let his gendered perspective blind him even to the legends about the founding of the Ursuline order by Angela Merici. Within his rendition of the St. Benedict story lie many of the imaginative themes that run through fantasies about the convent on Mount Benedict, including secrecy ("known only to St. Romanus") and the existence of a secret life underground. Extreme isolation and excessive self-deprivation are also darkly alluded to. The *Boston Recorder* continues with the theme of secrecy at Mount Benedict, noting, "But little is known respecting this institution, and it may be a long time before its internal machinery will be sufficiently made public."

Not only were the local teenage girls like Rebecca Reed and the brick makers in Charlestown interested in the exotic nature of monastic life, but so too were the middle-class subscribers of the *Boston Recorder*. These were the same readers who eagerly gobbled up a fictional best-seller called *The Nun,* published in the early 1830s by a British writer named Mrs. Sherwood, which told the story of a convent burning remarkably similar to what actually happened later in Charlestown. After the *Recorder* describes the nuns' abjuring of property and their assuming religious names, some of the internal workings of the convent are detailed, such as the division of labor between those employed in domestic service and those who have the privileges— "Those who bring money with their persons."[31] With sentiments that were echoed on the pulpit by Congregationalist preacher Lyman Beecher, the *Recorder* concluded:

May the time soon arrive when Protestant parents will open their eyes, and examine well the moral and religious tendency of every Academy to which they send their children, and then there may be some good reason for saying that New England has the credit of sending to the Valley of the Mississippi, or some darker region, fewer Nuns than that of any other section of our country! Christians! be not discouraged . . . take a bold stand against infidelity in all its forms, and you will shortly see Babylon and all its demons lie prostrate at your feet, wailing in bitter strains the sad story of its destruction!

REV. LYMAN BEECHER, D. D.

*The Reverend Lyman Beecher, whose anti-Catholic sermons
helped spark the attack against the Ursuline convent.*

At the end of 1830, Bishop Fenwick and the Catholics had a new
adversary to contend with. While Mary Anne Moffatt had invited leading Protestants to sate their curiosity by witnessing the ceremony of
veiling at the convent, the less well-heeled in Boston exhibited a darker
curiosity. On January 9, 1831, Fenwick recorded in his diary:

> The Rev'd Mr. Beacher [*sic*], a Calvinistic minister in this City,
> having a month or six weeks past commenced a course of lec-

tures the object of which was to vilify the Cath. religion, the *B'p* deemed it proper to cause it to be announced in the Cathedral this day that a course of lectures (to begin next Sunday at 6 1/2 OC'k PM) would be also given in the Cath. Church for the purpose of answering the foul aspersions which said Minister has attempted to fasten upon the Cath. religion. . . . The excitement among Catholics, indeed among all classes of citizens, in consequence of Dr. Beecher's aspersions & the expectation of the answer Catholics would give to them, is very great.

Fenwick himself inaugurated the series, with a Dr. O'Flaherty scheduled to give the second lecture. In his journal, Fenwick recorded some of the exciting events that happened during O'Flaherty's lecture, including a false fire alarm:

*"Dr. Brimstone" cartoon from David Claypoole Johnston's* Scraps, *1835, satirized Beecher's conciliatory stance following the riot.*

He had actually spoken two hours when the cry of fire was raised by someone who was actually led to suppose that there was from the steam of breaths which rushed out the windows, which had been opened & which had all the appearance of smoke. For a little while considerable apprehension was excited & some confusion. Yet the Dr. proceeded & concluded his discourse, without further molestation. Some individuals were hurt from jumping out of the windows on the alarms. The Church on this night was if possible more filled than on last Sunday. The curiosity of the Protestant public to hear the lectures is intense.[32]

According to Fenwick's diaries, these lectures were addressed to packed audiences throughout, until Beecher himself gave up. The cathedral is described as "crowded as usual by Protestants almost to suffocation"[33] and again, "an immense audience . . . the greater part Protestants."[34] With a note of triumph, Bishop Fenwick recorded in his diary that on the day of a lecture on celibacy, Dr. Beecher "announced this evening he should discontinue his lectures." Undeterred by Beecher's vanquishment, the Catholics continued their series. On March 27, 1831, Fenwick recorded that the subject of the lecture given in the Catholic Church was whether Catholicism or Calvinism is more favorable to religious liberty—a question that underlies much of the anti-Catholicism of the period. Attending the lectures was not without its perils, though. The weather was unseasonably warm and oppressive, and the church was so crowded that many of those in attendance fainted. During one event, a piece of stucco fell from the ceiling of the cathedral and injured one of the lecture-goers.[35] Except for jumping from the windows to escape imagined fires and injuries sustained from falling ceilings, most of the lecture-goers emerged unscathed. It is tempting to speculate that among the visitors consumed with curiosity about the Catholic religion was Miss Rebecca Reed, who later that year, in September 1831, entered the doors of the monastery.

One of the novices admitted earlier that summer was Miss Ann Janet Kennedy of New York.[36] This young woman, who ultimately left the order to become a Sister of Charity, became Rebecca Reed's confidante. But with each new gain of personnel, the convent seemed to lose important members. While Fenwick does not mention Reed's entrance in his journal, he does record the administration of the Last Sacraments to another novice, one of the two Miss O'Keefes (Mary Magdalene) who had joined the convent after arriving from Cork.[37] The depiction of the convent inmates' cruel treatment of Mary Magdalene during her illness is one of the most controversial accusations in Rebecca Reed's book.[38]

Part of the reason Fenwick might not have recorded Reed's entrance was that he had just returned from an extended journey to Quebec and that Father Wiley, who had been saying Mass at the convent, was sent on another assignment to Salem and Waltham. On his return from Canada, Fenwick encountered difficulty with customs officials in carrying over the border a set of altar vestments for use at the convent. Fenwick's return after this trip generated much excitement at the convent, with the nuns anxious to hear about Canada and expressing their pleasure at receiving the vestments.[39] The entrance of Reed, the quiet novice, may not have fully attracted Fenwick's attention. He did record the departure of Ann Janet Kennedy on November 13, 1831, a little less than five months after she had taken the veil. In the same entry, he noted that a Catholic Church with the same name as his in Charlestown, St. Mary's in New York, was burned to the ground by arsonists.[40]

ONE MAY MORNING, shortly after Mary Anne Moffatt found the convent's dog expiring on her kitchen steps, the bell at the back gate clanged. Sister Mary Claire admitted a dark-skinned man in ragged clothes, who stood at the kitchen door. In a thick Portuguese accent, the man begged the lay sister to speak with the superior on his behalf to render him some assistance, for he was suffering from terrible poverty. He needed the money, he said, to bring his family from Portugal to this country. Soon Sister Mary Claire returned from the superior's office with a small donation of twelve and a half cents, and sent the beggar on his way.

Within a few weeks, however, the *Catholic Intelligencer* issued the following notice to Catholic and non-Catholic alike, warning against a pair of scam artists "prowling the streets of Boston and its vicinity":

There are two fellows (calling themselves Portuguese) . . . whose object is to enlist the sympathies and wheedle money out of the purses of the credulous and the charitably disposed. These two fellows . . . have lately called upon us. They showed us a printed document in which was set forth the imaginary wretchedness to which they had been reduced. . . . The character of the document and the incoherency of their tale, even in their *outlandish* language, induced us to suspect them, and to put several questions to one in particular. He who had first called upon us, was immediately after the perusal of his document and a few answers we obtained from him, speedily dismissed. . . . The second fellow showed us a list of names of some of the most respectable characters in the city, and the amount of sums supposed, or really given by them to enable him *to bring his wife and children from Portugal to this country.* Among the names and subscriptions of his benefactresses we read the following forgery of the hand writing of the lady Superior of Mount Benedict—viz: *The Ladies of the Ursuline Community*—$1.50." . . . We feel it our duty to caution the Protestant community against such impostors, who may play off their pranks upon unsuspecting goodness, and even upon the *professed enemies* of Catholicity. Our religion tells us to do good to our enemies, and we therefore put them, and all others upon their guard, against such arrant impostors.[41]

Anxious to maintain their respectability, the Catholic newspaper disavowed association with Portuguese vagrants. The Catholics would have done well to take their own warning to heart about Rebecca Reed, a more dangerous impostor, who ingratiated herself into the community at Mount Benedict by presenting her poverty and condition as wretched. Reed claimed to have attracted the sympathy of all members of the convent community. But a fragment of a letter, presumably to Judge Fay and in the hand of Mary Anne Moffatt, refutes this, and asserts that the superior was always opposed to admitting her:

For nine months before Miss Reed was admitted into our Institution, I was repeatedly importuned by her to be received as a member of our Comy. She told me it was her mother's dying injunction on her, to become a catholic and to get into a nunnery. I refused, for I saw she was an ignorant and romantic girl.[42]

Reed persisted, according to the superior, even threatening to kill herself. Only after Bishop Fenwick appealed to Moffatt's sense of charity did she relent and admit Reed as a scholarship pupil in September 1831. The eighteen-year-old was both too old and too uneducated to be admitted to the classroom with the other girls, who ranged in age from six to fourteen. Instead, Reed came into the community as a novice and was offered private instruction.[43] As it turned out, Moffatt's instincts were correct, as Reed betrayed the charity of the Ursulines and the confidence of Bishop Fenwick, who had exhibited a dangerous blindness to her faults.

Reed had been born to what a contemporary source described as "very obscure parentage" and had been brought up as one of several children "amid scenes of poverty and want."[44] Before she was admitted to the Ursuline convent, she had scant education and claimed to have been beaten by her family. William C. Reed, her uneducated father, lived in a poor section of Charlestown named "Milk Row" near Cambridge. Local families occasionally employed the young woman to look after their children, and to perform household tasks. According to the same source, "While her sisters were employed as permanent domestics in respectable families, she was roaming about from one place to another, not content with the quiet routine of domestic life."[45]

When Reed was eighteen, her mother died of cancer, and Rebecca seems to have been left largely to fend for herself. We have seen that from her early teenage years, she had been fascinated with the Ursuline convent, and now probably saw admission as a way of improving her station in life. Once Mary Anne Moffatt had been persuaded to add Reed to the community in September 1831, she supplied her with clothing, books, and other necessities. According to her narrative, *Six Months in a Convent,* published in 1835, Reed was at first happy in her new life. But gradually, the austerities of the convent grew less to her liking, and began to take their toll on her health and morale. In her rebuttal of Reed's exposé, Moffatt speculated about Reed's motivations:

> She came to our Community, doubtless in the belief that she would have nothing to do there, but to read, meditate and join in our prayers. She found that every hour had its employment, and that constant labor was one of the chief traits of our order. The

novelty of the scene wore away, and the hours, she imagined she would spend with so much delight as an inhabitant of a cloister, she found to her sorrow, appropriated to the duties of every day life.[46]

Dissatisfied with her own treatment, and with what she believed was cruel treatment of other nuns in the convent, Reed became convinced that the superior and the bishop were plotting to kidnap her and send her to Canada.

One spring-like day during a January thaw, Bishop Fenwick received a hasty summons to the Ursuline convent. When he arrived, he was informed that Reed had fled from the convent the previous afternoon, January 18, 1832.[47] No one in the convent knew then where she had gone, though it was subsequently revealed she had run first to the home of Mr. Kidder, a toll keeper, and made allegations against the convent and especially against the superior, of when she "spoke highly disrespectfully." She then returned to Milk Row, her old neighborhood, taking refuge with Catholic friends.[48] As Fenwick noted in his journal of January 20, 1832:

> The *B'p* requests the Superior on learning this, to send her without delay her clothes, & to drop at the same time a line to the Lady where she stops, explanatory of her strange proceeding.

Reed herself seemed to have wavered on her decision to leave the Roman Catholic Church, even considering joining another religious community, as a priest from New York wrote,

> After her escape, she wrote to Miss K. [Kennedy] asking for help finding a situation in NY. Miss. K. approached Dr. Varela—a second letter was sent from Reed to Kennedy saying she had given up Popery.[49]

Following the few entries about Rebecca Reed's flight, Fenwick's diaries are silent on her doings—though her own narrative provides other details. His diary does, however, mention that on April 4, 1832, "Rev Mr. Doane, the Church of England Minister, preaches a sermon on the errors of Popery. It is represented as a poor paltry discourse—not more than 50 present." Doane, who had baptized Rebecca Reed, was the best friend and close confidante of the Reverend William Croswell, the rector at Christ Church from 1829 to 1841, who welcomed Reed back to his fold after she fled from the Ursuline convent. Reed rejoined Christ Church (also known as Old North) as a member, and enjoyed the solace of her former Episcopalian religion and of her handsome twenty-eight-year-old pastor William Croswell.

Having consulted with Croswell before making her decision to enter the convent, it was natural that she should now turn to him again in her distress.[50] During the trial of the convent rioters, Reed described her religious affiliation as "Catholic Episcopalian,"[51] a designation that was publicly ridiculed, and misrepresented as "Catholic Protestant," by Judge Samuel P. P. Fay, who had two daughters enrolled in the Mount Benedict Academy.[52] Considering her spiritual advisor's own tendencies toward high church practices, Reed's self-description as "Catholic Episcopalian" was probably an accurate one.

Before coming to Christ Church, William Croswell, along with Doane, who later became bishop of New Jersey and named his first child after Croswell, had edited a newspaper called the *Christian Watchman* from 1827 to 1829, contributing several poems under the pseudonym "Asaph." A cursory examination of them shows Croswell's early "high church" tendencies. On a few of the more hotly contested topics of the late 1820s, such as whether there should be crosses on churches and whether infant baptism should be allowed, Croswell consistently showed his preference for the more high Catholic practice. One such editorial called for the abandonment of the common Episcopalian practice of putting weathervanes on churches instead of crosses.[53] After some controversial exchanges on the propriety of infant baptism, called "pedabaptism," Croswell, writing as Asaph, contributed a poem in favor of the practice.[54]

During this period, the *Christian Watchman* editorialized in favor of retaining the word "catholic" in the Creed—"I believe in one holy catholic church"—another subject of controversy. In 1831, Doane and Croswell jointly edited *The Banner of the Church,* a "neat little folio of four pages"—whose underlying idea was to explain and illustrate the various observances of holy days and Sundays throughout the year—and to combat a newly revived tendency on the part of Episcopalians to oppose Christmas greenery. Doane and Croswell characterized adherents to this movement as "worthy of that gang of canting rogues who broke down the carved work of the sanctuary forgetting that we had bodies as well as spirits."[55] And when an Episcopal bishop passed away, Croswell arranged a memorial service that scandalized some parishioners who thought it was overmagnifying the bishop's office to drape the bishop's chair and organ gallery in black. Croswell himself played funeral airs on the bells during the service.[56]

A classmate at Yale, where Croswell completed his studies in 1822, remembered the eighteen-year-old graduate as a "fair, slender graceful, lighthearted and innocently playful youth" who enjoyed studying the Classics and showed early talent as a poet. But in his later years, Croswell's handsome appearance was distorted by what contemporaries called a "nervous disorder, which showed itself in certain involuntary movements in the muscles of his face."[57] The lighthearted youth had become a man suffering intensely from the stress of embroilment in public controversies during his professional life. Rebecca Reed's return to Episcopal Christ Church, where he was pastor, after her escape from Mount Benedict and the subsequent publication of her narrative, touched his parish with the raging controversy surrounding the burning of the Charlestown convent.

The Reverend William Croswell was born in Hudson, New York, on November 7, 1804. After his graduation from Yale, he entered the General Theological Seminary in New York in 1826,[58] the same year Rebecca Reed and her friends watched with interest as the Ursulines established their convent on Mount Benedict. For a two-year period, he served as editor of the *Christian Watchman*,[59] the religious paper published in Hartford, Connecticut, before being ordained as a deacon in Trinity Church, New Haven, on January 29, 1829, where his father was the rector.[60] On May 21, 1829, at the age of twenty-five, he accepted an offer to become rector of Christ Church in Boston, the historic Old North Church of Revolutionary fame, and he was ordained priest and instituted as its clergyman on June 24, 1829.[61] Later, he would return to Hartford to receive his Doctor of Divinity degree, which was conferred at Trinity College in 1846.[62]

Christ Church in Boston, where Croswell would serve his first ministry, had been for some years in slow decline, despite its historical significance as the church whose belfry shone two lights to warn Paul Revere that the British were making their approach by sea. The building was badly in need of repair, the number of parishioners had fallen, and the church was struggling financially.[63] When Croswell arrived, Old North had to take a loan to pay its bills and to dispense with the services of the church organist.[64] By 1831, the young priest had so revived the church that it underwent needed renovations, but the new debts, accumulated on top of the old, made its financial prospects perilous.[65] During the period Rebecca Reed was living in the Charlestown convent, Christ Church struggled to meet its financial obligations, which were relieved only by a personal loan from Croswell himself.[66] A year after the convent at Charlestown was burned, much-needed repairs to the exterior of Christ Church had been completed, but in 1835, the church was still in poor financial shape. By 1839, the year after the Reverend Croswell had officiated at Rebecca Reed's deathbed, the church's financial condition was improved enough to be described as "fairly sound."[67]

But during the same year, despite the improved economic situation of the church, what one biographer calls "slight disaffections" began to manifest themselves in the parish at Christ Church.[68] The thirty-five-year-old minister was still unmarried and tongues were apparently wagging. Biographer Mary Kent Davey Babcock states that "under the circumstances which surrounded him, he felt that the time had come when he could no longer hesitate as to the expediency and propriety of entering into a matrimonial engagement. His partialities and movements were doubtless closely watched and scrutinized by some who thought they discovered a disposition on his part to make this change in his domestic relations; and he had no difficulty in tracing to their intermeddling the slight disaffections which he experienced."[69] It is uncertain to what these "slight disaffections" refer—but Babcock seems to indicate that the added increase of expenses to support a rector's family would not be welcome to some church members, while others believed they should be consulted as to the best choice of the minister's wife.[70]

The earliest appearance of Croswell's disfiguring facial tic appears to be around 1837, as Rebecca Reed was in her final year of life.[71] This was a difficult year, as an economic recession hit the country and the parish's benefactors themselves experienced financial difficulties. The neighborhood around Old North itself was shifting, as older Yankee families moved away to more upscale locations, and, according to one church historian, "a foreign element mostly Irish was moving in."[72] Interestingly, many of the more established families who left Christ Church went on to join the Church of the Advent when Croswell returned to Boston to be its minister in 1844.[73]

On April 10, 1839, a little more than a year after Rebecca Reed's death at age twenty-six from tuberculosis, Croswell wrote to his father: "My position in the Parish is stronger than ever. But my recent experience convinces me that, like my predecessors, I have some spirits to deal with that are not to be depended on."[74] What could these recent experiences be? Intrigues and speculation about his intentions toward Miss Amanda Tarbell, the church organist? Or were those speculations directed at the nature of his relationship with arguably his most famous parishioner, Rebecca Reed, also unmarried, who had passed away on February 28, 1838? There is some evidence that, at the very least, an aesthetic and spiritual kinship existed between Rebecca Reed and William Croswell, given the strong attraction Roman Catholicism held for them both. Reed's early attraction to Catholicism is well documented in *Six Months in a Convent;* Croswell became a pariah in the Massachusetts Episcopalian Church over his introduction of "Romish" practices in Boston's Church of the Advent during the mid-1840s.

In 1840, when an opportunity arose for Croswell to leave Christ Church to take over the rectorship of St. Peter's Church in Auburn, New York, he wrote to the proprietors in Boston that he had, until this time, believed he would stay at their church for life. He went on to say that "My heart and affections still cling fondly here, and the very vicissitudes of time and *death which have removed so many from us, whose countenance was my chief earthly encouragement* [my italics], have given an endearing consecration to the scene of my past labors."[75] He then refers to "painful information" received from the proprietors that makes him doubt that he remained secure in the affection of all his parishioners.[76] It is interesting that a gifted writer such as William Croswell would err grammatically in the agreement of the plural "removed so many" with the singular "whose countenance was my chief earthly encouragement," especially in an important letter such as this. Croswell seems to be thinking here not of many faces taken by death, but of one in particular.

Was Rebecca Reed, while she lived, the "chief source of his earthly encouragement"?

Despite the strongly professed pleas of the committee for him to remain, he chose to relocate to Auburn, New York. On May 22, 1840, Croswell wrote to his father to announce his betrothal to Miss Tarbell, "a young lady for whom he had formed a strong attachment, who had been for some time organist of the Church."[77] The impending departures of the Reverend Croswell and Miss Tarbell were not the only loss to the congregation of Christ Church. The number of parishioners that Croswell's ministry had attracted was once again on the decline. According to his biographer, "Toward the close of his pastorate . . . because of various reasons, some of which were of the most trifling character, the number of communicants and the congregation became considerably reduced."[78] It is uncertain whether his connection with Miss Reed or a growing marked preference for certain "Romish" practices was the source of the conflict. Episcopal Church historian Mary Kent Davey Babcock cites "many causes of dissention" which left the parish in a "very depressed and disordered state."[79]

But for all his difficulties in his final years at Christ Church, it retained a strong hold on his affections. In a poem published after his death, written during his newlywed years in Auburn, Croswell had composed "A Christmas Eve Pastoral" for his former parishioners.[80] In this ten-stanza poem, his thoughts return to his former home and to the friends he left behind, as in the stanza below:

> *My own dear Church! how can I choose*
> *But turn, in spirit, back to thee?*
> *As, on this hallowed night, I lose*
> *Myself in pensive reverie;*
> *For, in thy courts, a single day*
> *'Tis good, if but in thought, to dwell;*
> *Nor may I tear my heart away*
> *From all that it has loved so well.*

After the speaker proclaims his strong affection for his former parish and its parishioners, he goes on to write eight more descriptive verses of Christmas reverie about Christ Church. The images used here on first glance seem conventional, but Croswell's poetry evokes "Romish" images of crosses, candles, and cloud-veiled angels.

At the end of the poem, he again refers to companions lost to death, writing

> *Though many a friend is dead and gone,*
> *Though many a sainted face we miss,*
> *Long may thy bells, dear Church, ring on,*
> *That call to such a feast as this!*
> *For whence could joy and comfort flow*
> *To aching hearts that bleed for them,*
> *But for His Grace, whose reign below*
> *Began this night in Bethlehem.*

After their marriage on October 1, 1840 and the move to Auburn, Mrs. Croswell's health declined, perhaps due to the birth of their only surviving child, a daughter. References to their matrimonial union in Church of the Advent correspondence and in obituaries are scant, except for an allusion to "private family bereavements."[81] But in the above poem, the Reverend Croswell hardly sounds like a man in the flush of enjoying a new marriage. There is at least one other "sainted face" besides his wife's on his mind this Christmas Eve for whom his heart is aching.

Less than two years after Reed's death from tuberculosis in 1838, Croswell found some happiness in Auburn where he could "preach Catholic doctrine without exciting suspicion as to the soundness of his Protestantism."[82] He returned to Boston in 1844 to establish the controversial Church of the Advent and ironically found himself defending his new church against charges by the Episcopal bishop that the church and its services were too "Romish."

In 1832, Croswell had counseled Reed after her escape from the convent, encouraging her to write down all she could recall about her life in the convent. Reed and Croswell then circulated the manuscript privately, before it made its way to Benjamin Hallett, a Boston newspaper editor, and his Committee of Publication, which brought out the book. Reed discusses the genesis of her manuscript *Six Months in a Con-*

*vent* as originating during a session of spiritual counseling with the Reverend Croswell:

> [I]n applying to the Rev. Mr. C. for readmission to the church, I felt it my duty, in returning as a lost sheep to the fold, to open my whole heart, and disclose all the circumstances that led to my wandering from the truth and embracing the Roman Catholic faith—my introduction to the Ursuline Community—a narrative of my residence there—the circumstances which caused me to doubt the purity of their faith and practice—my consequent elopement from the Convent, and my renunciation of Romanism.[83]

Croswell, then, had first suggested that Reed put her experiences into writing. In a letter written to the Committee of Publication just two months after the burning of the Charlestown convent, Reed again discussed the origins of her narrative after what she termed "the most interesting and distressing period of my life":

> At the time I related the facts contained in this Narrative to the Rev. Mr. C., he advised me as soon as I was able to put in writing all that I had learned and experienced of Roman Catholicism while among them, and while in the Convent. At first I was able to make only memoranda, but at last I have endeavored, in my own simple language, to place them together in something like the form of a narrative, for your perusal.[84]

Once the original manuscript was completed after August 1833, Rebecca Reed said she gave it "to her immediate friends."[85] In fact, it was in Croswell's possession. The Committee of Publication notes that, for nearly a year before the convent was burned in 1834,

> the manuscript of this Narrative . . . had remained undisturbed in the hands of the reverend gentleman of whose church Miss R. had become a member, after renouncing the Roman Catholic faith; and whatever intention there might have originally been of giving it publicity, all such intention had been abandoned.[86]

It is unclear when the Committee of Publication first approached Rebecca Reed about the publication of her narrative, but they claimed it was not until after the convent at Mount Benedict was burned: "Not one of those at whose suggestion it is now published had ever heard of it until after the destruction of the Convent."[87] This Committee encouraged Reed to transform the "memoranda" she wrote under Croswell's direction into "something like the form of a narrative" for the Committee's perusal and later dissemination. The narrative appeared in March 1835, only seven months after the convent was burned. If the revision took place during this period, it was accomplished quickly.

When Rebecca Reed's character came under attack in the *Report of the Committee,* the Reverend Croswell came to her public defense by writing the following affidavit, which he signed October 20, 1834:

> I hereby certify that Miss Rebecca T. Reed has been, for more than two years last past, a communicant at Christ Church; that I have always regarded her as a devout person and exemplary in her Christian walk and conversation; that I repose great confidence in her sincerity and intention to relate, on all occasions, what she believes to be the truth.[88]

Even the Episcopal newspaper, *The New York Churchman,* expressed surprise at such a qualified recommendation:

> *Intention* to tell what she *believes* to be the truth! This, it struck us, was a most curious expression; and, if such a certificate is to be a passport to public confidence, we may believe all the religious gossips and marvel-mongers and lunatics in the land. . . . It did not strike us as strange Mr. Croswell should give such a certificate, for a clergyman would naturally desire to say as much in favour of a communicant as he conscientiously could. But it did strike us as passing strange, that the gentlemen who had shown so much acuteness as the committee of publication, should be satisfied with such a certificate. . . . [89]

For the most part, it was the Catholic presses that attacked Croswell, calling forth this rebuke from other Protestant presses, which denounced

. . . in the strongest manner, the abusive language used by the Catholic presses, with regard to the reverend gentleman, who gave a certificate concerning Miss Reed's disposition to tell the truth. Such lying accusations can only tarnish those from whom they proceed; and will fade away from his undimmed and irreproachable character, like vapor from a diamond.[90]

The introduction to Reed's narrative also includes a list of "subscribers" who claim acquaintance with Reed "previous to her becoming a member of the Ursuline Community at Mount Benedict." Signing a testimonial, these subscribers attest that they considered Rebecca Reed "a person entitled to our confidence, sustaining as she does a character distinguished for love of truth, for unexceptionable morals, and for meek and modest deportment."[91] In comparing this list against a list of members of Christ Church involved in the Sunday School in 1829, there are no exact matches.[92] Furthermore, none of the prominent members of Christ Church from 1829 to 1835 are listed as giving affidavits of Reed's character and morals. It seems that the Reverend Croswell was one of the few members of Christ Church willing to speak up on Rebecca Reed's behalf.

Moreover, Croswell himself appears to have given the manuscript to the Committee of Publication "after the publicity of the personal attacks which had been made upon Miss R,"[93] since it was in his possession. On September 27, 1834, William's father Harry Croswell, of Trinity Church in New Haven, recorded in his diary:

Rec'd a letter from William, requesting me to send him forthwith by mail, three certain letters from a Miss Kennedy a nun in the convent, to a Miss Reed, who had left the establishment, and which he had left at home some time ago. I accordingly enclosed them in a short letter, and put them in the post office before 12:00.[94]

These three letters appear in a document called *Supplement to "Six Months in a Convent"*—apparently given to the publisher by William Croswell. Croswell played an important role in the genesis of the manuscript, kept it in his possession for two years, and gave it to the Committee of Publication for dissemination. *Six Months in a Convent* reportedly sold 5,000 copies on its first day of publication, and ultimately about 200,000 copies.[95] Fenwick's newspaper *The Pilot* claimed that "30 or 40,000 dollars have been made by Mr. Hallett's ingenious fabrication."[96] This profitable fifty-cent publication was likely the product of extensive revising by the Committee of Publication. Moffatt and others asserted that Rebecca Reed was not intellectually capable of writing the narrative herself. As one Catholic source charged, it did not "come unfathered into the world" and owed its grammatical accuracy to the Committee of Publication.[97] It is probable that in addition to cleaning up grammar, the committee drafted entire sections of the book.

It is doubtful that Reed herself enjoyed many of the profits from the sale of the book. In the case of the wildly popular *Awful Disclosures of Maria Monk,* published the following year, Monk's take was reported to be $80 for every new edition of 1,000.[98] And not quite three years after the publication of her book, Reed died of tuberculosis. Though William Croswell attended at her death, she was not given a burial in one of the crypts available for purchase beneath Christ Church. Instead she was buried in the public cemetery in Cambridgeport. Her body was probably not moved when the public cemetery was closed in the 1850s, because there is no record of Reed's interment in Mount Auburn or the Cambridge Cemetery. It is likely that she still lies beneath what is today Sennet Park—a tiny paved urban park with a playground off Broadway near Inman Square in Cambridge. Had Reed received a significant share of the profits from the book, it is unlikely that she would have been given this pauper's funeral.

Benjamin Hallett is the one most often alleged to have profited from the book, but Croswell denied any role or self-interest. *The Boston Transcript* published Croswell's disclaimer that he had been part of the Committee of Publication:

On the contrary, the MS. was in his hands two or three years ago, and it was in consequence of his influence that the book was not *then published* . . . he had no hand in the writing or revision of the book, was not one of the committee of publication, and has no instrumentality whatever in the publication.[99]

But the balance sheets behind the book remained invisible, even to contemporaries. One publication mused openly about the question,

> There is a general determination to know the names of the wire-pullers of this grand puppet show. . . . The names of this Committee—who are they? By whom were they constituted a Committee? Were they self-constituted? Who of their number wrote the preliminary remarks to "Six Months in a Convent"? Who, besides the publishers, received the immense profits resulting from the sale of this book?[100]

Reed's text was largely devoted to details of what to Protestant readers would have seemed exotic ritual practices such as kneeling and kissing someone's feet, or making the sign of the cross with one's tongue on the floor to demonstrate submission or humility. Reed especially focused on the cruelty of inhabitants of the convent toward Sister Mary Magdalene, the O'Keefe sister dying of tuberculosis, and on the power wielded by the convent's mother superior. However, investigation by the blue ribbon committee appointed to investigate the convent's destruction found no truth to these allegations:

> No penances or punishments are ever forcibly enforced or inflicted; they are not only always voluntary, but can never even thus take place, but by permission of the head of the order, which is not granted unless the applicant be in good health.[101]

While parts of Reed's narrative were clearly based on some of her actual experiences in the convent, other sections appear to be exaggerated to make better reading. One example might be the infamous section that depicts Bishop Fenwick offering to barter extreme unction in exchange for Sister Mary Magdalene's imploring the Almighty "to send down from heaven a bushel of *gold,* for the purpose of establishing a college for young men on Bunker Hill."[102] What finally seems most striking about the narrative is our sense that Reed sees what she is only partly able to understand, perhaps from her lack of understanding of Catholicism or from her own undeveloped intellect.

The charges of confinement and kidnapping, however, appear to be blatantly fictional. The committee investigating the burning of the convent had this to say about the freedom of novices, like Rebecca Reed, to leave.

> During this period no restraints by religious vows or otherwise are imposed to prevent her secession from the establishment, and the Committee have plenary evidence from those who have thus seceded, of their freedom in this respect. . . . Some of those, who after entering upon their novitiate seceded from the Convent, still retain the warmest affection for its members, and bear willing testimony to their unvaried kindess and the purity and excellence of their deportment.[103]

Furthermore, even professed nuns like Elizabeth Harrison were found not to be held against their wills,

> Upon receiving the black veil, the religious vow is taken of devotion to the Institution for life; but even then no forcible means could be exercised to detain any one, who might choose to return to the world; and their legal right to do so, is perfectly understood by every member of that community.[104]

According to the committee, after the convent was burned, Reed

> entirely disclaimed most of those [injurious representations and reports] passing under her name, and particularly all affecting the moral purity of the members of the Institution, or the ill treatment of pupils under their care, and confined her accusations to the system of severe penance for which she alleges, the nuns and novices were compelled to suffer for the most trivial offences, or for the purposes of religious discipline—and to cruelties alleged to have been inflicted in the form of penance upon a member of the community in her last illness, by which her life was shortened.[105]

Reed's claims that she heard plans to send her to the British Provinces and that she witnessed cruelty to Mary Magadalene were denied by both the superior and the bishop. The committee added:

> It was well-known, not only among the members of the Institution, but the pupils generally, that this young woman was not esteemed qualified to become a member of the community, but was to be dismissed at the end of her probation; and of this fact the Committee have the assurance of several of the pupils.[106]

ON THE MATTER OF Mary Magdalene, her two remaining birth sisters and the respected Dr. Abraham Thompson testified on behalf of the nuns "that the tenderest care and solicitude were uniformly manifested for her comfort, and that all was done to smooth the pillow of sickness and death, which religious duty or sisterly affection could dictate."[107]

*The Portland (Maine) Daily Advertiser* summed up the Rebecca Reed episode in this way:

> All things duly weighed, we cannot but look on Miss Reed as a romantic, nervous, passionate and obstinate girl, who without having any fixed principles of action, has taken advantage of a popular prejudice to benefit herself . . . while she at the same time gratified her love of romance and the marvellous by her impositions upon the credulity of the public.[108]

Though Moffatt and Reed had both experienced poverty during their childhood, and shared an aspiration to escape it through entering the hierarchy of the convent, Moffatt could never be described as having no "fixed principles of action." While Moffatt put her considerable energies into building the institution on Mount Benedict, Reed seemed to crave the attention lavished on convenient victims, performing floor kissing and other convent rituals for the entertainment of the institution's detractors. The public's willingness to believe Reed indicated that she was able to tell the public what they already believed to be true. The seemingly decorous and elite women in the convent were dangerous, as were the unkempt Irish working people who presented a different sort of threat to the Charlestown community.

\* \* \*

O N JANUARY 25, 1830, Bishop Benedict Fenwick purchased three acres of land on the summit of Bunker Hill in Charlestown for the purpose of establishing a Catholic cemetery. Five days later, on January 30, 1830, Bishop Fenwick recorded in his diary that the "convent stable is set on fire & burnt." Though Fenwick didn't comment more directly in his journal, later sources suggest the fire was deliberate—and was a warning against the growing Catholic presence.[109] In this and other situations, Fenwick seemed slow to recognize that the Catholic presence could spark violence. The perpetrators of this dress rehearsal for the larger conflagration four years later were never caught. The Charlestown selectmen, though, were fully united in their efforts to stop Catholic burials—and their anger over Fenwick's success with establishing the cemetery would have dire consequences for Mount Benedict. Within a few months, despite the ominous warning blaze, the bishop had erected a fence and enclosed the graveyard.

From the beginning, this new acquisition of land in the Protestant stronghold of Charlestown aroused the ire of many residents. There the Roman Catholics were burying Irish corpses, and the citizens of Charlestown objected to this practice for at least two significant reasons. In addition to concerns about the spread of disease, Irish funeral practices, which featured public demonstrations of grief, offended Yankee notions of decorum. As Marie E. Daly of the New England Historic Genealogical Society notes,

An Irish wake and funeral procession allowed the grieving friends and family to express a full range of emotions from laughter to tears, and to mourn their loss distinctively in the plaintive keening of women. Wrenching their hair and clothes while chanting a high-pitched cry, "och-och-on," female relatives would follow the coffin in an ancient peasant ritual.[110]

In 1819, the first official Catholic burial ground in Boston, St. Augustine's, was established, although unofficially Catholics had been buried in this former potters' field since 1805.[111] By 1830, nearly all the available lots in this cemetery had been taken. Fenwick decided that locating the next cemetery in Charlestown, near St. Mary's Church and the new Ursuline convent, was a sensible choice. The citizens of Charlestown were less enthusiastic. As Fenwick recorded in his diary on November 15, 1831,

> The *B'p* is given to understand that the inhabitants of Charlestown held a meeting yesterday for the purpose of putting a stop to the Catholics of Boston interring their dead in the new burying ground on Bunker Hill. . . . The *B'p* thinks he sees in this step of the town the beginning of a hostile disposition on the part of a number of prejudiced Calvinists to oppose the Catholics as much as possible.

By January 2, 1832, despite Fenwick's rather mild assessment of the level of hostility above, the battle lines were drawn, and it is clear from a document called *Petition of the Selectmen of Charlestown to the General Court* that the issues were class and ethnicity, especially as the law became known to locals as the Paddy Funeral Act. The proposal was voted in at a town meeting held in Charlestown, November 28, 1831, with the petition noting, "during the past summer, a Public Burying Ground has been opened within the territory aforesaid, without the consent of the Municipal authorities, where, for a stipulated price, the dead bodies of a particular class of people, brought from the city of Boston, and the surrounding country are daily deposited." The Act, signed by the selectmen, not only refers to the "particular class of people," but to annoyance caused by "the frequency and offensive peculiarities of these interments," and called for regulation by the Charlestown Board of Health.[112] In March 1832, seeing that the petition was not faring well with the legislature, the selectmen withdrew it for the purpose of amending it.[113] In May, Charlestown officials passed regulations, which Fenwick described as "specially aimed against the Catholics," that established approved burial grounds, required the licensing of undertakers, and stipulated that no bodies be brought into Charlestown without written permission of the selectmen.[114]

Fenwick consulted his lawyer, Mr. J. P. Cooke, about how to proceed on the question of burials. Cooke advised him "to solicit the consent of the Selectmen or a majority of them—and if they refuse permission, to proceed with the burial nothwithstanding, so as to bring the case before Court."[115] Fenwick did not have to wait long before putting the new law to the test. When two Irish children died, he immediately filed a request to proceed with the burials:

> Towards night the B'p receives an answer from the Selectmen declining granting his request. He notwithstanding gives orders to Mr. Murray the Sexton to proceed with the funeral, willing to bring the matter to a trial to try the constitutionality of the interdict.[116]

Ten days after the shooting of the convent dog, the Catholic sexton, Mr. Murray, led a funeral procession in the rain through the streets of Charlestown; there was no immediate response from the selectmen.[117] Burials continued throughout the rainy and unseasonably cold May.[118] In mid-June, 1832, the selectmen finally responded, filing a lawsuit against the sexton and the bishop for burying the dead in Charlestown.[119] Almost a year later, on April 24, 1833, the lawsuit was decided by the lower court in the bishop's favor, but the decision was appealed by the Charlestown selectmen.[120] It would now be brought before the Massachusetts Supreme Court. Irish genealogist Daly has asserted that "The loss of this test case in the lower court frustrated the ignorant and contributed to the mob's motives on the dark night of August 11, 1834."[121] Clearly, this setback in the courts angered the selectmen and the citizens of Charlestown. In October 1834, just two months after the convent was burned, the supreme court finally ruled in favor of the bishop. In January 1835, Bishop Fenwick had a small caretaker's house built at the front of the graveyard for protection, and in response to threats to destroy it.[122]

I N 1832, as the battles over Charlestown's new Catholic cemetery were being fought in the courts and by street vandals, cholera descended upon New England. The worldwide epidemic had originated in 1826 in India, and spread rapidly through the Mideast and Europe over the next six years.[123] The global shipping trade and the far-flung distribution of European armies carried what had once been local diseases to the metropolises of Europe. Bengal cholera spread to Paris and London, where thousands of people died in 1832. It then crossed the Atlantic to Canada, appearing first in Montreal, and then in New York City where it affected the poorer classes disproportionately, largely because of their unhealthy living conditions.[124]

Cholera struck suddenly, and exacted its toll within hours of onset. Spread mainly by contaminated water and food, this frightening disease caused massive vomiting and diarrhea, and a resulting collapse of the circulatory system. Dehydration and capillary hemorrhaging started the process of bodily decomposition even before the victim's death, causing the skin to shrivel and darken. These horrifying physical effects, the seemingly capricious spread of the disease, and its resulting rapid mortality made cholera a nightmarish threat.[125]

Today cholera can be prevented by vaccine, and treated with antibiotics, as well as aggressive replacement of fluid and electrolytes, but in the early nineteenth century there was no effective treatment.[126] In 1832, the "cure" involved drinking fifty drops of laudanum, otherwise known as opium, in a wine glass of hot brandy and water. Caretakers were instructed to apply bags of hot sand to every part of the body and limbs of the patient—along with applications of soaked hot cloths—and to apply hot mustard paste over the stomach.[127]

As the spread of contagious disease was poorly understood at the time, it seemed that cholera was a scourge that struck and killed at random. In the early nineteenth century, most doctors believed that a deadly "miasma" which arose from decomposing corpses and filth spread contagious diseases. One committee of physicians from Harvard Medical School recommended that communities clean up sources of miasma, such as standing water and sewage, in order to slow the progress of the disease in Boston.[128] During this epidemic, cholera became inextricably linked to xenophobic fears about the increasing numbers of Irish, and almost a metaphor for the Catholic threat, descending on New England as it did from Quebec and Montreal. The august body of Harvard physicians was assembled to make recommendations for the best mode of protecting city inhabitants against this scourge. The authorities first targeted the Irish who lived on Broad Street, the scene of an earlier anti-Catholic riot. They debated whether or not the city authorities should have "power to remove the families who occupy the stores and cellars on Broad Street which are not provided with the necessary conveniences for such occupation."[129]

The connection between cholera and Irish Catholicism, though racist, was not entirely inaccurate. Disease has always been rooted in poverty, not in ethnicity. Marie E. Daly described the dismal conditions for the Boston Irish during the 1830s:

> The prefamine Irish immigrants crowded into small tenements along the central waterfront, on recent Boston landfills in the South Cove and the Mill Pond, along the raucous sailors' streets of the North End, the Charlestown Navy Yard and industrial Craigie's Point in East Cambridge. At one point, the occupancy rate in the densely populated North End averaged thirty-seven persons per dwelling.[130]

She notes too that in South Cove, a landfilled area of Boston inhabited by the Irish, the fill began to sink, and even the rudimentary open sewers were incapacitated. Furthermore,

> The population in this neighborhood relied on backyard privies, with sometimes over one hundred people sharing a single privy. Many of the Irish lived in dank basements subject to periodical flooding during high tides. One drinking water well near Quincy Market served the entire North End. The rat-infested waterfront reeked of rotting garbage and swarmed with flies. . . . Trash removal, sanitation, clean water and uncontaminated food were all lacking in Boston's poorest wards of the 1830s.[131]

These deplorable conditions contributed to high rates of contagious disease in the Irish wards of the city. The immigrants arrived from Ireland malnourished and susceptible to bacteria and viruses. Infants and young children were especially vulnerable. Lemuel Shattuck, Boston medical statistician, calculated that out of 1,987 burials from 1833 to 1838, 75 percent of the males and 62 percent of the females were under five years of age.[132] While some died of starvation, others succumbed to diarrhea, scarlet fever, encephalitis, and whooping cough. Among adults, pneumonia, tuberculosis, and dysentery were the most prevalent killers.

Dysentery was especially common in South Cove, where the drinking water was contaminated by sewage. While poverty created these terrible conditions, medical ignorance combined with cultural prejudice to lead Bostonians to blame the Irish themselves for their misery.[133]

The prescribed prevention for cholera in some ways reads like a description of the ideal middle-class life in antebellum America:

> Every house and shop should be made clean, especially provision stalls, should be made clean and sweet. Outhouses should be freed from all offensive matter. Cellars should be thoroughly cleaned of putrid vegetables, ventilated, and thoroughly dried.—Beds and bed clothing should be daily exposed to currents of fresh air.[134]

In addition to domestic cleanliness, hot baths and frequent sea bathing were recommended to enhance personal hygiene. The crowded Irish families were indirectly implicated in this recommendation:

> As few individuals as possible should live in the same room, and where a number are found together, means for dividing and giving them more healthy lodgments should be provided at public expense.[135]

The middle-class ideal of moderation was also prescribed for food, and especially consumption of alcohol: "Cholera attacks the tippler and makes him his first victim. A little excess, even in wine, exposes to the disease." The physicians recommended that the population "Eat a raw onion at breakfast, avoid alcohol, maintain a 'light' diet and conduct a clean, sober and pious lifestyle."[136] Fasting was generally recommended as a preventative measure.

Ultimately, the prevention of cholera was linked to Protestant middle-class values about how to lead one's life:

> Finally, we recommend a *good conscience* and a *fearless performance of duty,* as the best of all preservatives against this disorder. . . . We therefore strongly urge on our fellow citizens, a perfect confidence in the wisdom and goodness of God, and a full assurance that those who perform His will by the devotion of their labors

to the sick and suffering, are taking the surest means to escape the attack of this disease."[137]

Of course, the conditions under which the Irish lived contributed to the spread of cholera: crowding, famine, and close contact with infected persons.[138] But the way in which the recommendations were written suggested to middle-class Protestants that the group which had invaded their community had brought with them this scourge and added to the intensity of their hatred of Catholicism. News reports confirm this. Fenwick's diary of June 24, 1832 reported that "It is stated in the papers that two of the Priests (names not given) in Montreal have died of the Cholera." By mid-August, the disease had arrived in Boston.[139] In September, the bishop's niece died, presumably of the disease.[140]

During the summer and fall of 1832, the disease raged in Boston, bringing certain death to its victims. Many blamed the Irish for bringing cholera to North America. Some believed that this group brought the disease upon themselves with their dissolute lifestyles. Furthermore, they feared that the location of a Catholic graveyard, the burial place for many Irish cholera victims, would produce a deadly miasma in their very midst.[141] The web of tensions that was woven by strained economic relations between the social classes, Rebecca Reed's escape from the Ursuline convent, and the volatile combination of the cholera epidemic and the battle over the Catholic burial ground contributed further to the growing animosity against the Charlestown convent.

During March 1832, a few months after Rebecca Reed "escaped" from the Ursulines, another nun, the lay sister Mary Martha, succumbed to tuberculosis. She was probably the Reverend Woodley's sister, who had taken the veil before so many admiring Protestant eyes. She was laid to rest March 6, 1832, becoming the seventh body to be interred in the convent tomb.[142] But Elizabeth Bennett was admitted as a novice August 30, 1832, so the number in the community remained stable.[143] Bishop Fenwick spent his fiftieth birthday, September 3, 1832, being agreeably entertained at Mount Benedict by a special program performed by the children.

By November, plans were underway for the next spring's planting, as the large field in front of the convent was cleared to prepare for pasture grass, clover, and oats.[144] These were the same crops that many of the brick makers who now worked in the yards surrounding the convent had once grown in their native New Hampshire. In April 1833, the bishop planted "some really Irish potatoes, to see whether they will turn out better than those of this country."[145] A few weeks later, the Ursulines marked the fifth anniversary of their move into their elegant brick building.[146] The community celebrated Thanksgiving 1832 by extending an invitation to the Sisters of Charity to join them for a feast. After Mass, the Boston nuns were given a tour of the house and spacious grounds.

> [T]hey are shewn the garden, places of promenade, the Cottage & the farm and in the afternoon the different apartments of the house with some of the drawings & other work of one of the children who likewise performs several pieces on the harp & Piano for their amusement. The day is spent, in fine, very agreably, the good nuns vieing with each other in their attentions & kindness to the Sisters during the whole time.[147]

Christmas 1832 was a season of peace and joy at the convent. The bishop celebrated by buying himself a new hat and showing it to the nuns, "his old one having been much laughed at."[148] But by New Year's Eve, there was a foreshadowing of the year's increasing troubles, in the form of "Calvinists & others who are going about the town in quest of Catholic children for the purpose of distributing Tracts and anti-Catholic Bibles among them, & holding out rewards for their acceptance."[149] Still, in his end-of-the-year review for 1832, Fenwick proudly listed the population of Catholics in his diary as 16,310. There were thirty boarders enrolled at the Mount Benedict Academy, which by September 1833 would again swell to more than fifty and stabilize at around sixty.[150] On January 17, 1833, another of the O'Keefe sisters took the veil as a professed nun and on May 21, her accomplished cousin, Miss Quirck, arrived from Limerick to join the community as a novice.[151] She became Sister St. Henry on July 31, 1833. Earlier, on June 10, two other novices made their profession ("Sister Mary Joseph & Sister Bernard, the former a Choir & the latter a lay Sister"), and the community seemed to be thriving.[152] Doubtless, these new accessions reminded Mary Anne Moffatt of the loss of her friend, Margaret Ryan. The foundress, Sister Mary Austin, was honored on St. Patrick's Day,

March 17, 1833, as the nuns performed one of her hymns in the cathedral.[153]

In late March, there were ominous hints of problems arising at the academy:

> March 21st (St. Benedict's Day) The *B'p* spends the day at the Ursuline Convent. This being his Patron's festival the children of the Convent present him a complimentary address . . . after which they sing an Ode composed by one of them for the occasion accompanied by two harps & the Piano. The *B'p* returns them an answer. After which they retire to their apartment. No feast is given them this year in consequence of the exceptionable conduct of several of them.

Fenwick's diary does not detail what this "exceptionable" conduct was—but the loss of the traditional feast did not seem to correct it. So, in contrast to the festivities of previous years, Coronation Day at Mount Benedict in 1833 was not a joyous occasion. The white tents were still erected, and the school decorated with flowers to welcome visiting parents and dignitaries. Many of the usual public recitations and examinations took place. But when the most important moment of the day arrived, the crowning of the two best pupils with roses from the convent gardens, Fenwick described the scene that followed in this way:

> In the afternoon the table of Premiums is arranged in the large hall as heretofore, presenting a large assortment of beautiful Premiums. At the appointed hour the Young Ladies are introduced. After the performance of a few pieces on the Guitar & Piano the Superior acquaints the *B'p* that the time of distribution was now come; but that she had the mortification to inform him that none were worthy of being recompensed—that their conduct through the year had been highly exceptionable, so much so that she could not take upon herself to recommend any distribution this year—that there were indeed five of the whole number who had some claim, but that she was afraid to reward these lest they should be persecuted by the bad, & their abode in the house rendered thereby unhappy. After a short pause, the Superior re-

quested that if any young Lady present should deem herself worthy, she might approach. None of them came forward. Upon this the *B'p* took up the subject and addressed them for nearly a half hour. He spoke to them of the evil consequences of such conduct as had been described to him by the Superior, & the bearing it would have upon their future prospects, if not seasonably mended. He expressed his grief & the exceeding pain it gave him to hear so unexpected a report &c, &c. His discourse was frequently interrupted by cries & sobs on the part of the young ladies. As soon as he had concluded they were ordered to retire, & the Premiums, among them an elegant Gold Metal, were left untouched on the table. In their apartments they gave full vent to their tears, & caused for a considerable time the whole house to ring with their cries and lamentations. It is thought that this privation, & this manner of reproof will have its due effect the ensuing year.[154]

Recalling the Ursuline *Règlements* recommendations for mild punishments, administered with maternal tenderness, Moffatt's public humiliation of the scholars on Coronation Day seems shocking. The historical record, unfortunately, is silent on the nature of the girls' trespasses, which the superior must have considered serious indeed. A year later, many of these same girls lost their reserve during an investigation of the convent conducted by the selectmen. The young ladies, contrary to Mary Barber's decorous description of academy scholars, hung out of the windows and heckled the men. Perhaps something of this same lack of reserve may have contributed to behaviors that Moffatt was determined to punish with stunning severity. However, Coronation Day 1834, before the convent was attacked, seemed once again to recall the joyous festivals of earlier years. In its flower-bedecked loveliness, the walls of Mount Benedict Academy rang with laughter—not weeping—as the girls were rewarded for success in their studies. Again, the brick men watched from the bottom of the hill as girls in pink and white gaily rode in handsome carriages down the convent's winding drive.

## CHAPTER FIVE

# THE VINE UPROOTED

## *1834: A Year of Heartbreaks*

*My Beloved had a vineyard on a very fertile hill. He dug it and cleared it of stones, and planted it with choice vines; he built a watchtower in the midst of it, and hewed out a wine vat in it; he expected it to yield grapes, but it yielded wild grapes. . . . When I expected it to yield grapes, why did it yield wild grapes? And now I will tell you what I will do to my vineyard. I will remove its hedge, and it shall be devoured; I will break down its wall, and it shall be trampled down. I will make it a waste; it shall not be pruned or hoed, and it shall be overgrown with briers and thorns . . .*

—ISAIAH 5: 1–7

REFUSING TO BE DISTRACTED or intimidated by rising anti-Catholicism, Bishop Fenwick was ambitiously planning to add a third church to the Diocese of Boston. At the beginning of 1834, he purchased four lots of land on Pond Street (now called Endicott) in Boston's North End.[1] The day after an annual Massachusetts holiday called the Governor's Fast, during which Fenwick wryly noted Catholics "fasted as Protestants, that is eat a better dinner than usual," digging began on the foundation of the new church.[2] Perhaps soured by his experiences with opening the Catholic cemetery in Charlestown, Fenwick wrote of the large number of men who applied for construction work on the new church, grumpily recording that he was being "pestered by Yankees, of every description, applying also for work."[3] The contract for the stone and brick work was awarded to a mason with the distinctly Irish name of Peter Murphy.[4] A month later, at the end of May, Fenwick was attempting to settle disputes between the church's building committee and Murphy's masons.[5] Six weeks after that, just a month before the convent was attacked, Fenwick cancelled the lucrative contract with local brickyards, and opted to build the church entirely in stone.[6] The loss of this income for the local brick makers, including those in Charlestown, could not help but contribute to bad feelings against Fenwick and his thriving diocese.

In many ways 1834 was a difficult year for the Catholics. As the wrangling began with the masons building the Pond Street church, Bishop Fenwick was invited to attend the dedication in May of another church in New Haven, Connecticut. In a journal entry that began with the words, "A fatal day," Fenwick described arriving early at the New Haven church for Mass. After distributing communion and concluding the first Mass, he prepared for a ten o'clock dedication at which fifteen persons were also to receive the sacrament of Confirmation. A large crowd assembled from the town and surrounding countryside to participate in the service. Fenwick's journal also noted the presence of "a very great number of Protestants who were attracted merely to witness the ceremony." The church was packed, and many spectators climbed to some upper balconies to gain a better view.

The gaily clad procession marched through the front doors of the new building, and wound its way to the altar. Just as the bishop reached the altar steps and began speaking the first words of the dedication ceremony, the floor shook with a deafening crash. To his horror, Fenwick turned to see that the crowded balcony had given way and fallen in a heap, crushing the spectators sitting below. Fenwick's journal continued with this recounting:

> The scene of confusion which ensued is indescribable. One boy 14 years old was killed upon the spot, & seven others were dreadfully wounded. Of these one died in the course of the same day. Both of these were converts. The service of course was discontinued. The cause of the disaster is to be ascribed to the Carpenter who had constructed. It appears the original plan required two gothic columns, which the Carpenter deemed unnecessary & in lieu thereof undertook to support the main beam by *trussing*. This

was a terrible blow to the little Catholic Society at N. Haven. But, *fiat voluntas Dei*. Immense crowds of people flocked to the church during the afternoon to see the desolation.[7]

Coincidentally, the accident occurred on May 8, 1834, the eighth anniversary of the laying of the foundation stone at Mount Benedict.

The next day's entry noted carpenters were "employed to remove the fallen timbers out of the Church during the whole of this day, & women to scour & clean the floors in various places stained with blood. Mr. Hardyear & his grandson, the two individuals who had been killed, were interred in the burying ground adjoining the church. Their funeral was attended by a large concourse of people of all denominations who appeared to sympathize much. . . . During the whole of this day also numbers flocked to the Church to examine the injury done."[8]

In July, a terrible heat wave struck New England that was to have yet more fatal consequences. The poor, especially the Irish Catholics who lived in crowded urban centers, were especially at risk, and Fenwick's journals recorded a number of sudden deaths among them from the heat.[9] Once more, the small Catholic community was visited by a bizarre and horrible tragedy. On July 10, 1834, Fenwick wrote,

> The Weather still excessively hot. In the afternoon a dreadful thunder gust comes up succeeded by rain. The lightening struck the school-room attached to the Catholic Church in Charlestown while the children were reciting their lessons which killed three of the Boys upon the spot and disabled two or three of the Girls.

Following so closely upon the accident in New Haven, the Catholics must have felt that God was visiting their community with severe trials. And the greatest of these, in this summer of hardships, was still ahead.

WHEN THE NUNS' DOG had been shot by ruffian brick makers two summers earlier, their Irish servant had carried the animal in his arms and buried him in a quiet spot on the hillside. Shortly afterward, a new man, Peter Rossiter, was added to the convent's caretaking

*The dog belonging to Peter Rossiter, an Irish servant at Mount Benedict who was accused of setting it upon some Protestant women taking a walk near the convent.*

staff. He had his own companion, a brown herding dog with black spots, to help with the cows that were kept for dairy. The new dog was friendly and smart, learning its tasks quickly, and soon his wagging tail warmed its way into the hearts of all the inhabitants of the convent. Rossiter and the dog spent many days watching the cows amble over convent property, grazing in front and back on the gentle slopes.

On the north side of the convent, at the hill's foot, ran the Middlesex Canal from Lowell to Boston, which was spanned by two small bridges. According to John Buzzell, the leader of the gang who attacked the convent, the towpath "ran on the south side of the canal until it reached the nunnery grounds, from which point the opposite side was used, the horses crossing over by means of bridges. Thus there was no towpath between the canal and the grounds of the nunnery, although the canal company owned a strip of land a rod in width on that side, which they could have used for that purpose had they desired."[10] Buzzell vividly recalled these details about the towpath and the canal because, he said, on his days off from the brickyards, like Rossiter, he liked to sit and watch the canal traffic wending its way north and south.

Buzzell also recounted a disturbing tale that foreshadowed the violence to come during the heat of August. One Saturday in June, 1834, he recalled, a man and his wife came from the country to Charlestown on a visit to a local blacksmith named Lamson. During the day, Mrs. Lamson and her guest, accompanied by another local woman, went to look at the canal, which was a curiosity to the country people. "When the party arrived at the bridges in front of the nunnery," Buzzell said,

> they crossed over to the south side, and continued their walk close to the canal. As they strolled along they were seen by the Lady Superior, who sent her superintendent, an Irishman named Rossiter, with a dog, to bring the women up to the nunnery, claiming they were desecrating the holy ground. In attempting to force the women to go to the nunnery, Rossiter was unnecessarily rough, handling one of them so harshly as to leave black and blue marks on her arms, and other parts of her person.[11]

Rossiter's version differed substantially from Buzzell's:

> Two or three ladies were crossing the convent grounds the evening before in order to get into the turnpike road. The superior told me to bring them back and direct them to go the same way that they came. I went towards them, when two of them got over the fence, but the other, who was not spry, remained behind. I took hold of her arm to talk to her. She seemed alarmed— made a noise, but did not scream out. I let her go and she went away. We keep a dog, but I did not set him at her. The dog did not go after her.[12]

But the Charlestown Yankees believed that the women had been assaulted by Rossiter and his dog and planned revenge. For the price of a dinner, Buzzell, who stood six feet six inches tall, agreed to teach the Irishman a lesson he would not soon forget. Buzzell remembered the deal this way:

> Some men who were at work on the canal witnessed the assault on the women, and while I was at dinner they came and offered me one dollar and agreed to pay the costs if I would lick Rossiter. I accepted the offer. On the following morning I caught him about fifty rods below my boarding house and licked him so

faithfully that the doctor [Abraham Thompson] who attended him testified that it was nine days before they could turn him in bed . . . [13]

Buzzell's story of the beating was corroborated during the trial of the convent rioters. Joshua B. Stearns testified in court that he was

> within thirty feet of [Rossiter] when he was knocked down and beaten. I was in my garden, and he came to ask me for some plants. Buzzell came up with some others, knocked him down, threw himself upon him and beat him after he was down. I immediately left my garden, but before I could reach the parties, Buzzell had got up and walked off. Rossetter [sic] was much injured. There was a large bunch upon his temple, and blood was flowing from his mouth. He was on the outside of the fence in the road, speaking to me. Buzzell knocked him down, and struck him after he was down—blood flowed from his mouth—I did not hear Buzzell say a word before he struck Rossiter. He was coming from Kelley's and going towards the brickyard—it was early in the morning, before I had my breakfast.[14]

According to Rossiter's own testimony, the attack was unprovoked, as he had never met Buzzell before. He had lived at the convent not quite two years, joining two other Irishmen on the staff. Pointing to Buzzell during the trial, Rossiter asserted,

> I was beaten while I lived there, last June, by the man at the bar. I don't know what led to it. I never spoke to the man before. It was between the Convent and the neck, in Charlestown. I was standing talking to Stearns. The prisoner came with several others—he asked me if I had beat a woman—a thing I never had been guilty of. He then knocked me down, and beat me as long as he pleased.[15]

The attending physician, Abraham Thompson, testified that Peter Rossiter was very bruised, and that he visited him twice. The doctor de-

*For the price of a dinner, John R. Buzzell avenged the ladies
allegedly insulted by Peter Rossiter.*

scribed Rossiter as "Seriously injured, and so much that I thought it necessary to prescribe to him, and visit him the second day."[16] He noted that Rossiter was "much bruised about the face and breast, and his breathing was seriously affected."[17] Little did the community know that the violence against Rossiter would prove but a taste of the large-scale attack to come by summer's end.

T HE COLD STONE of the wall against her hands sent little shivers of fear down the nape of her neck. She pressed her body against the rough fieldstone and tried to stretch to the rim with her fingertips. The dank smell of the stone assaulted her nostrils as first one foot then the other found hollows that would be her ladder rungs out of hell. She strained until her shoulders cleared the crest, but she slipped back and the climbing roses tore at her nightgown and skin. Just below the narrow gold band circling her left ring finger, the thorns had inscribed a deep gash that welled dark with blood. Again she hurled herself against the wall and willed herself, in all her terror, to be lifted up.

*Jesu Christi, Jesu Christi,* she prayed.

On her stomach now against the wall's broad brim, she wriggled her legs over the top. The thorns had streaked her white cotton nightdress with blood. She rolled and fell to the other side, striking her head as she dropped. Pressing a hand to her cut forehead just below a stubble of hair, she tried to stop the sun from spinning in the late afternoon sky. As the sky whirled, she lay panting in the tall meadow grass. Then with a jerk of her shaved head, she pulled herself to her feet to careen down the hill through July's parched field flowers. Just once, she turned her dark eyes to glance up at the enclosed three-story brick nunnery towering about her, and stifled a bitter cry.

Mr. and Mrs. Edward Cutter had just sat down to dinner when their beagle began a low growl that modulated to a bark.

"Now girl, what is it?" Cutter asked, straightening up.

The dog was at the door, barking louder. The Cutters pulled it open. On their front steps lay the young woman in the torn bloody gown. She rolled her head back and forth in a gesture of tired refusal.

"Please! Don't make me go back! Will you protect me?"

Cutter lifted the lightly clad form in his strong brickman's arms and gazed into the woman's eyes.

"Child," he whispered. "What have those Catholics done to you?"

THE UNBEARABLE HEAT of that fateful summer took its toll on the inhabitants of the Ursuline convent. Sister Mary John (Elizabeth Harrison), who had seven years before written to Trois Rivières about Prince Hohenlohe and other rituals employed to save the life of the dying assistant superior, was particularly troubled in excessively warm weather. The convent's next assistant superior, Mary John had been periodically subject to what those who knew her termed "a disorder in her head."[18] Toward the end of July, she again suffered one of her periodic fits of derangement. Sweating profusely, she chafed against the enclosure of convent life, and asked repeatedly for the doors to be opened. She wanted new instruments to conduct her music classes, she insisted, and behaved in a way that Mary Anne Moffatt called "extravagant." By the end of July 1834, she was in serious decline. Moffatt described her state this way:

> On the same afternoon I had told her that she looked very ill, and that I feared it was too much for her to be attending to the music, to which observation she replied by a burst of laughter, which by no means calmed my apprehensions.[19]

Though the heat wave had somewhat abated, the cumulative effect was too much for Sister Mary John's frazzled nerves. Just as Bishop Fenwick sat down to his evening supper, the bell was rung and Peter Rossiter, recovering still from his violent beating, stood before him. The lady superior had sent an urgent message for the bishop to come quickly to Charlestown. Fenwick immediately summoned a horse and carriage for the two-and-a-half-mile ride, and arrived at the convent soon after. According to his journal record for July 28,

> . . . he finds all the Nuns assembled in the Community room in the deepest desolation. Upon inquiry he learns that Sister Mary John, one of the religious in a fit of mental derangement, occasioned by the complaint called the *Hysterics,* had left the Convent & had gone over to one of the Protestant Neighbours . . . was taken thence, at her request, by him to Mr. Cotton's [*sic*] at West Cambridge, where she then was. This Mr. Cotton had formerly two daughters in the Convent at school. This circumstance had led to her request to be carried thither.

Though it was nearly nine o'clock in the evening, Bishop Fenwick immediately set out on the five-mile trip to West Cambridge, now Arlington, to try to persuade Sister Mary John to return. In the darkness, he stood at the door of the Cotting residence, home of Maria Cotting, who had won a convent medal, asking to be admitted to see the escaped nun.

She refuses to come down to him in the Parlour adding that she had no desire to see him—that she wished to leave the convent & return to the world. The *B'p* requests the messenger to return back & entreat her to permit him to see her. She persists in her refusal. He prevails upon her to return once more & states that he only desired to converse a little with her & that afterwards he should return home. Again a refusal. Seeing no prospect of effecting anything this night in her great excitement, he returns to the Convent & gives an account of his failure.[20]

It was after midnight, and the nuns were awake and waiting anxiously for news of Sister Mary John. When Fenwick reported that she remained at the Cottings', he described the nuns and himself as "greatly afflicted." Certainly, everyone at Mount Benedict that night was thinking of Rebecca Reed's flight two years before, and the trouble it occasioned.

The inhabitants of Mount Benedict and the bishop did not relish the prospect of damaging gossip and allegations printed in the newspapers.

He foresees all the noise & Clamour which ill disposed Protestants would be likely to excite in consequence of this step, which, though taken in a fit of insanity, they would be unwilling in their perversity to allow. In this state of dreadful anxiety the Nuns are unwilling to retire to rest. It being now nearly one OC'k in the morning the *B'p* repairs to his Cottage & there walks the room till day breaks.[21]

Before sunrise the next morning, the convent sent a servant to Boston to call for Mr. Thomas Harrison, Elizabeth's brother, requesting him to come out to Mount Benedict immediately. He arrived at six o'clock. He listened with surprise to the story of his sister's elopement and agreed to go alone to West Cambridge to try to persuade his sister to return. Fenwick reported that though Harrison remained with his sister until four in the afternoon, he was not successful in persuading her to leave the Cottings, and returned to Mount Benedict without her. Harrison was able to gain one concession—the nun agreed to see the bishop that evening.

The *B'p* accordingly loses no time in procuring a carriage & taking Mr. Harrison with him immediately repairs to Mr. Cotton's. He is shortly after introduced to her when he beholds with surprise the great change in her countenance. She had thrown off her religious habit & had assumed quite a worldly dress, which she had borrowed of Mrs. Cotton. Her eyes bore every appearance of one perfectly deranged although her conversation seemed sufficiently connected. The *B'p* perceives at once the state of her mind, & presses her very hard to consent to return with him. After refusing a long time he finally succeeds in prevailing upon her to return. He immediately gives orders to have her clothes put into a bundle not to lose time in changing her dress lest she should in her insanity change her mind & refuse to come with him. In a short time she is led to the carriage & put into it. During the ride back she gave every indication of a perfect derangement. The Ladies of the Convent receive her with raptures of Joy. Having delayed a little while longer at the Convent to give directions respecting her, he returns with Mr. Harrison to Boston.[22]

Elizabeth Harrison, originally of Philadelphia, entered her novitiate in 1822, and became a full member of the Ursuline Community two years later. Her sister had been brought to the community by Fenwick on his return from a trip to Georgetown, but had only remained in the convent a week. Her brother and brother-in-law lived in Boston. As mother assistant and music teacher, Harrison carried a great deal of responsibility at the institution, and before her elopement, she had been giving fourteen lessons a day—each lasting forty-five minutes. As the summer wore on, a "nervous excitement or fever" came over her, culminating in her collapse on the Cutters' doorstep.

The day after her return, a worried Fenwick again rode out to the convent to check on the addled Sister Mary John.

He is quite overjoyed to learn that her phrenzy was over & her mind had again returned. The whole had appeared to her as a dream, & she could scarcely be made to believe what had passed. "O what have I done?" she would incessantly exclaim. "How shall I repair the injury I have occasioned! O God! where were my senses? Can I ever be too thankful to my Creator for having brought me back, &c, &c."[23]

The bishop and the members of the community attempted to pacify Harrison's concerns, and called for the doctor, who pronounced her to be suffering from "*Hysterics* & directs that she should be closely watched, lest the paroxism or fit should return in which case, he stated, she might do injury to herself."[24]

But Mary John continued to improve, as a servant reported to the bishop the next day. Fenwick remained deeply anxious over the negative publicity for the convent this incident was likely to cause. To take his mind off the problem, in the evening, Fenwick joined a crowd of fifty thousand to watch a hot air balloon ascend from Boston Common. It was a beautiful evening, and the colorful balloon with its "aeronaut" was lifted by a west wind, and remained visible for about thirty minutes before it disappeared to the north. But the magnificent sight could not lift the bishop's spirits, which remained "uncommonly low after the occurrence at the Convent."[25]

Three days later, the bishop returned to Mount Benedict to say Mass, and paid a visit to Sister Mary John.

> He is happy to find that all things are still well with her, though in the deepest affliction at her past step, which she seems to deplore beyond measure. She can scarcely believe what she has been told of her leaving the Convent . . . [26]

The bishop and Mary Anne Moffatt remained deeply concerned about the impact of Mary John's elopement, and for good reason. John Runey, a Charlestown selectman, had heard the story of the nun's escape from Edward Cutter. Soon, various versions were spreading throughout the area, many of which conflated Harrison's story with Rebecca Reed's, as this extant letter from Anna Loring illustrates:

> . . . a young lady had disappeared very mysteriously from the nunnery, she was sent there to compleat her education & was so pleased with the place that she was induced to take the veil. After some time she became dissatisfied & went off, but was persuaded

to return being told she might return to her friends in three weeks, & at the end of the time her friends called for her, she was not to be found . . . [27]

Typically, the story mingles the episode of Rebecca Reed, who entered as a student in 1831 and remained for less than six months. Elizabeth Harrison had in fact been a member of the community for twelve years. But in the mind of the public, the stories of Rebecca Reed and Elizabeth Harrison blended to form a powerful indictment of the convent at Mount Benedict.

Anna Loring's letter, in addition to confusing Reed and Harrison, repeats almost verbatim sections of a damaging article that was published in a local paper, the *Mercantile Journal,* on August 8, 1834. The publication by this newspaper of the rumors that had been floating around town as fact was a major incitement to the destruction that was to follow three days later. The article, headlined "Mysterious," seriously distorted the time frame and the events:

We understand that a great excitement at present exists in Charlestown, in consequence of the mysterious disappearance of a young lady at the Nunnery in that place. The circumstances, as far as we can learn, are as follows:—The young lady was sent to the place in question to complete her education, and became so pleased with the place and its inmates, that she was induced to seclude herself from the world and take the black veil. After some time spent in the Nunnery, she became dissatisfied, and made her escape from the institution—but was afterward persuaded to return, being told that if she would continue but three weeks longer, she would be dismissed with honor. At the end of that time, a few days since, her friends called for her, but she was not to be found, and much alarm is excited in consequence.

With its publication, the identification of Harrison with Reed was complete, setting in motion an unstoppable wave of pent-up animosity.

The destruction of the convent seems to have been plotted almost from the day of Harrison's flight on July 28. During the trials of the rioters, the accomplice who turned State's evidence, Henry Buck, testified that that he heard plans for it " . . . over a fortnight before it was burned." According to Buck, groups were meeting at the schoolhouse near the convent grounds, possibly the same school attended in 1826 by Rebecca Reed and her teenage friends. About a dozen men were present, and according to Buck, "they talked some about sending round to get some help to do it—but the meeting broke up without concluding anything. Four nights later, they had another meeting, with about thirty persons present."[28]

These meetings suggest that there was a broader conspiracy to destroy the convent than the eventual indictments of twelve working men demonstrated. The committee formed to investigate the riot offered the opinion that a conspiracy had been formed against the convent, but that "it embraced very few of respectable character in society: though, some such may perhaps be accounted guilty of an offence, no less heinous, *morally considered,* in having excited the feelings which led to the design, or countenanced and instigated those engaged in its execution."[29] One of these the committee may have been alluding to was Benjamin Hallett, who was appointed to serve, but declined membership in the group. He was a key player in the Committee of Publication that brought Rebecca Reed's book to the public less than a year later. Certainly, the committee suspected that the editors of the *Mercantile Journal's* article "Mysterious" published the inflammatory rumors either irresponsibly, without bothering to ascertain the truth, or deliberately. They were almost certainly thinking of Lyman Beecher, who had been doing his best in Boston to whip up the frenzied feelings of the citizenry. And we have seen that the respectable businessmen of Charlestown may have had a hand in promoting anti-Catholic sentiment among union leaders.

These anti-Catholic feelings were given expression in a series of handbills, or posters, aimed at the selectmen that papered Charlestown on Saturday morning, August 9. One of them warned,

> GENTLEMEN—It is currently reported that a mysterious affair has lately happened in Charlestown; now it is your duty, gentlemen, to have this affair investigated immediately, if not, the *truckmen* of Boston will *demolish* the nunnery on Thursday night. Boston, August 9, 1834

Another was directly addressed "To the Selectmen of Charlestown."

> GENTLEMEN—Unless there is a legal investigation of the nunnery affair by Thursday night, August 14, it will be demolished by the truckmen of Boston. Take notice, and govern yourselves accordingly.

And finally, the most dramatic one, that expressed the men's underlying fantasies about illicit sexual activities at the convent:

> GO AHEAD! To arms!! To arms!! Ye brave and free, the avenging sword us shield! Leave not one stone upon another of that curst nunnery that prostitutes female virtue and liberty under the garb of holy religion. When Bonaparte opened the nunneries in Europe, he found crowds of infant skulls!!

On Saturday evening, August 9, prompted by the article in the *Mercantile Journal* and the appearance of these handbills, Edward Cutter, a respected community leader, a member of the Massachusetts House of Representatives, and the man to whose house Sister Mary John had initially fled, paid a visit to the convent. He was accompanied by his brother, Fitch Cutter, and their stated purpose was to warn Mary Anne Moffatt that there were plans afoot to pull her convent down. They did not receive a warm reception. Moffatt was furious with Cutter, who before had always seemed neighborly, for driving Sister Mary John to West Cambridge without speaking to her first. According to Moffatt, she had mentioned to Edward Cutter her feelings on the matter and he had reportedly replied to her that "he would never wish *his* daughter to be brought back to a *prison*."[30] She also believed that Cutter had been partly responsible for the report published the previous day in the *Mercantile Journal*. As she later told her lawyer, J. T. Austin, "He . . . spread a report to reach the newspapers—then came to ask if it was true."[31]

While the Cutters were inside the convent, a group, which Bishop Fenwick described as "a number of evil disposed persons of the dregs of Society," gathered at the convent gates and shouted the refrain that would be repeated two nights later, "*Down with the Convent! Down with the Nuns!*"[32]

During the trial, Fitch Cutter testified to the tenor of that meeting, stating that they had asked Moffatt for an interview with Sister Mary John, who, as a result of the *Mercantile Journal* report, had become popularly known as "the Mysterious Lady." According to Fitch Cutter, Moffatt replied that "if that was my object for calling, she would not gratify my feelings—she said I might bring on my mob—that she had understood that I had applied to the Selectmen for a mob, and that Mr. Runey and myself were to head the mob." Fitch Cutter asked where she had heard such information and insisted his motives for the visit were friendly. But Moffatt was, according to Fitch Cutter, "steaming away." With a toss of her head, the superior directed the following remark to Fitch's brother Edward:

> You may fetch on your mob, the Bishop has twenty thousand of the *vilest* Irish, who might pull down your houses over your heads—and you may read your riot act till your throats are sore, and you cannot quell them—you and Mr. Runey, Fitz Cutter, and Mr. Kelley will have your houses torn down over your heads.[33]

She finally agreed to let them see Sister Mary John, but continued in her defiant manner once the shaken nun was brought into the room.

"There," said Moffatt to the men, "look at her—touch her—see if you can find any marks of violence—question her as you please—ask her if she has been punished." Mary John turned back the sleeves of her dress to exhibit her arms, but no bruises were visible.[34] The superior gave an account of the meeting to the bishop, who wrote:

> The Cutters hearing this from herself are satisfied & withdraw— they lose no time in undeceiving the mob on this subject who shortly after retire. By way of reparation of the evil which they had committed in thus riotously assembling about the house at the dead hour of the night, they agree to draw up a statement of what they saw & ascertained & insert it the following day in the public papers, in order to contradict the false rumour which had been spread.

The entry notes that after the initial crowd dispersed, the superior and the other nuns spent a sleepless night in watching.[35]

According to Moffatt, the visit from the Cutters took place after seven o'clock in the evening, "an hour at which visitors were not admitted, but at their solicitation, as they were labouring men and could not come at any other time, I consented to see them." Moffatt had already seen the article called "Mysterious" in the paper, and airily remarked that "if that was the subject of their visit, I thought it quite a useless one, as they had been our constant neighbours, and consequently, they were sufficiently well acquainted with our institution to know the absurdity of the piece which had been published."[36] In Moffatt's portrayal of the meeting, the Cutters were as much concerned about the safety of their own property as they were about Mount Benedict. Moffatt related that the men "expressed some apprehensions as to the consequences, and said they hope, if anything occurred, their property would not be molested." The Cutters in turn blamed the worst of the rumor-mongering on John Runey, who they said, "for eight or ten days, had given himself no rest, but had been industriously circulating the intelligence of Miss Harrison's temporary absence from the convent . . . thus inflaming the minds of the lower classes of society; had they done all this, they would consider themselves unfriendly, and entitled to have their houses pulled down."[37]

Alvah Kelley, owner of a local brickyard, "who kept a bad set of men," was also implicated by the Cutters for spreading stories about the convent, and Fitch Cutter claimed to have never entered Kelley's house. But Moffatt also noted that "this same Fitch Cutter had told Peter Rossiter that our institution was not a good one, and that it would be destroyed. It would not be my wish that the property of the Cutters, or any one else, should be molested: but I told them I could not answer that it would not be the case, nor can I do so at present." On Monday morning, the Superior sent Rossiter to invite the Cutters to accompany the selectmen on a planned tour of the convent grounds, so that they too could investigate the allegations, "supposing it might be a satisfaction to them to find that it bore very little resemblance to a *prison,* as they had named it."[38]

When the bishop arrived at the convent early Sunday morning to say Mass, he learned about the riotous gathering and the interview with the Cutters on the previous evening. After their sleepless night, the sisters were described as afflicted but none more so than the unstable Elizabeth Harrison:

> Mary John exhibits great remorse herself at having been the cause of so much confusion & disorder. She begs to be put in the last place, & solicits the *B'p* and her Sisters to forgive her what she had done in her phrenzy. The *B'p* says Mass after hearing the confessions of the Nuns & returns to Boston without preaching as usual, his heart being too full to say a word.[39]

On Sunday afternoon, the superior was also visited by one of the selectmen, Mr. Samuel Poor, who expressed anxiety that the convent was

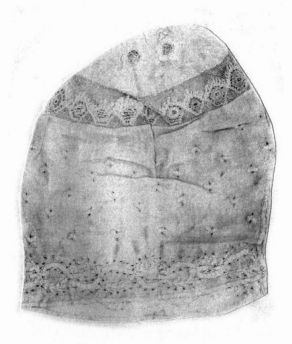

*In appreciation for the warning by Selectman Samuel Poor that the convent was in danger, Moffatt embroidered this baby cap for his new son.*

in danger and encouraged her to cooperate with the selectmen on Monday and to allow them to meet with Elizabeth Harrison. To repay Mr. Poor's kind concern, Moffatt herself, in the months following the convent's destruction, would embroider a linen cap for his infant son which remained in the Poor family for generations.[40] While the bishop and Samuel Poor were visiting the convent on Sunday, the Reverend Lyman Beecher was in Boston on tour, preaching that day at three different churches. Beecher had been involved in the debates with Bishop Fenwick and Father O'Flaherty in Boston during 1831. He had since moved out to Cincinnati, and begun his ministry in the expanding westward frontier. In August 1834 he returned to Boston, seeking support of his Western enterprises.

On the day before the riot, Lyman Beecher gave three anti-Catholic sermons, on Bowdoin Street in the morning, in the Old South in the afternoon, and in Park Street in the evening, each speech lasting roughly an hour.[41] In these speeches, Dr. Beecher focused on drumming up support for his school, the Lane Seminary, giving several reasons why this was crucial. The first reason was to train educated preachers for the West. The second, he asserted, was that financial support must come from New England to spread the concept of New England learning. Interestingly, in this section of the speech, he called for religious freedom, and for an end to persecution, at least of Protestant sects. In grand rhetorical style, he saved his strongest reason for last: "that the Roman Catholics of Europe seem to be seeking an asylum from the contentions and revolutions of the old world and a site for the palace of the Pope and the Romish Church in the Great Valley of the Mississippi."[42] Beecher later issued this speech as a monograph called *A Plea for the West.* The most vivid impression that audiences took away from these sermons were the anti-Catholic themes. One who was in the audience was Anna Loring, who gave the following account of Beecher's inflammatory sermon:

> Dr. Beecher has at last arrived, and preached last Sunday morning at Mr Winslows—his sermon was upon the condition & prospects of the West, & the influence the Lane Seminary would have upon that section of our country—I think he has laid him-

self open to be ridicule by those opposed by the idear [sic] what that institution could do with he [sic] at the head of it—He gave a very interesting account of the soil, climate &c, and the state of the population many facts most appaling of the Roman Catholicks of its influence & its rapid spreading—that they were establishing schools & nunnerys, for the purpose of educating our children . . . [43]

In his sermons against Catholicism, Beecher declared that "the principles of this corrupt church are adverse to our free institutions, from the contempt and hostility which they feel towards all Protestants. . . . Roman Catholic Europe is pouring her population into the Valley in great abundance; and . . . that if the subjects of the Pope increased beyond the increase of our own people, in the proportion which they had in the last ten years they would in thirty years more, out number our native inhabitants. . . . Despotic princes in Europe would empty their coffers of treasure liberally, could they by means of the Romish church, subvert our free institutions and bring into disgrace all ideas of an effective government."[44] He especially warned against "gratuitous schools" established by the Catholics for the education of Protestant children— "while the children of the subjects of the Pope were left to roam in ignorance, many of them incapable of either reading or writing. Hence the necessity that Protestants should be on the alert in the work of early education."[45]

After the convent burning, the Protestant newspaper *The Christian Examiner* published this veiled indictment of Lyman Beecher, referring to him as a "pest":

We doubt not that religious fanaticism, in its lowest and most brutalizing form, had some influence in producing the wickedness which has been perpetrated in Charlestown. It was excited in part by gross calumnies, which had been proved to be unfounded before the deed was committed, and in part perhaps by the writing and preaching of some one or more of those pests of our community, who seem to have little other notion of religion, than it is a subject about which men's passions may be inflamed, and they may be made to hate each other.[46]

By Monday, the public interest in the allegedly missing nun had reached a fever pitch, and a team of selectmen made an appointment for three in the afternoon. The delegation included Abijah Goodridge, Thomas Hooper, Abijah Monroe, Stephen Wiley, Samuel Poor, and John Runey. The superior and Elizabeth Harrison, Sister Mary John, met with the men, who were given a tour of "every room and closet, from the cellar to the cupola, inclusive, and were answered every inquiry which they saw fit to make."[47]

According to Moffatt, the men spent about three hours and "examined from the highest apartment to the cellar—looking into bureaus, and even paint boxes," searching for imprisoned nuns or their bodies. Moffatt could not resist adding with a touch of contempt, "The Mysterious Lady, (Miss Harrison) conducted them over the establishment." During the tour, Mr. Runey earnestly pressed Miss Harrison to pass a few days at his house or with her brother in Boston, but she told him firmly that she wished to remain at the convent.[48] When the superior overheard this, she remonstrated with the selectman, and again brought up what she regarded as Edward Cutter's mistake in carrying Harrison to the Cottings in the first place:

> I told Mr. Runey, if his daughter had come to me in such a state, that I would have acted in a friendly manner, and apprised him of the circumstance, before taking any decisive step. He objected to bringing her back to us.[49]

The superior's comment to Mr. Runey was oddly prescient. In the days following the convent burning, Runey's daughter, who had been in school with Rebecca Reed in Cambridge, suffered a descent into madness, which resulted in her needing to be institutionalized. But that afternoon, the selectmen found "that every thing was right" and they made plans to publish their findings in the papers the next day.[50]

Just as the investigating committee was leaving around six o'clock that evening, they had the unpleasant experience of being subject to a volley of insults from the students at the convent. Though convent education had aimed at shaping decorous and pliable girls, on that nerve-frayed day, all social rules were bent. According to one student, Lucy Thaxter, on Monday afternoon, during the selectmen's investigation of the convent, one group of girls was accosted on their walks through the gardens by the shouts of several men already gathered at the gate below. The men called to the girls "and asked 'if we did not wish to go away?' and that, 'now was our time, if we would come down to the fence they would assist us over.' Some of the girls replied that we did not wish to go away and they need not trouble themselves."[51] Four of the selectmen later wrote that the pupils addressed them in "a very rude and improper manner, inquiring, 'Have you found her? Did you find her in the tomb? Was she buried alive?'"[52]

Louisa Whitney, another student, recorded overhearing a heated conversation between the superior and one of the selectmen:

> "There, sir," she cried, "if you want to play the spy in *my* house, you shall do it alone. I won't allow any one of the sisters to enter that cellar on your account. Go down, sir, with your lantern, and look about at your leisure,—there is no man here to prevent you." The poor citizen from Charlestown hesitated, stepped forward, the gulf below yawned dark as Erebus, he stepped back again; and at last, fairly daunted by the Superior's eye, he suddenly put down the lantern, and hurried out of the building as fast as he could. The Superior's laugh of derision followed him, and it was echoed by the girls, who had crowded into the hall to witness the proceedings. Probably the poor man drew a breath of relief as he prepared to walk down the avenue, after leaving the Convent; he was seen to stop and mop his face, as he emerged from the door, with a yellow bandanna handkerchief—another object of derision for the girls. But his troubles were not yet over; he was assailed with a volley of sarcastic remarks by the pupils, who had rushed out upon the balcony to watch his departure.[53]

The unruly behavior of the boarders toward the men carrying the responsibility to investigate improprieties at the convent was jarring to say the least. Though the selectmen had found no nuns in the dungeon, they must have left with the uneasy feeling that something was truly amiss.

While the selectmen were conducting their investigation, rumors were flying through the surrounding brickyards that this was the night that the convent would be destroyed. John R. Buzzell, the ringleader of the convent rioters, recalled that on Monday morning, " . . . one of my strikers went to Boston, and on his return in the afternoon came to me and said: 'They are coming out of Boston to take down the nunnery tonight.'" That evening, he stated, he was a little late in finishing work. On his way home, Buzzell stopped at Ford's store. There, according to a trial witness named Jesse Templeton, he and John Buzzell ordered a gin and molasses.[54] While they were drinking, Buzzell told Templeton that "he was ready to be the first man to break into the convent—I am old R. and will be on hand."[55] By the time Buzzell had reached the boarding house where he lived with several other brick makers, the others had finished dinner. Buzzell sat down alone to eat, and had hardly begun when a stranger came in. The stranger said he was looking for "Old R."

> I answered that I was the man, and he asked me to step to the door, as he wanted to see me. I told him to wait until I had finished my supper . . . he went out, but came in twice or three times before I got through. Finally I went out, and found about thirty men gathered about the door. They said they wanted to go to the nunnery . . . they insisted on going, saying: 'You are the man who licked Rossiter, and just the man to lead us.'[56]

John R. Buzzell, the imposing brick maker who in that moment became their leader, was described by contemporaries as having the appearance of a "giant." He was born in Northwood, New Hampshire around 1805. In 1825, he married Tamson Drew in nearby Strafford, and by 1834, the twenty-nine-year-old Buzzell and his wife had five children. Both his parents were still living, and he had at least one brother, James. One Catholic source portrayed him unflatteringly during these years as a "great wretch" and a "regular tenant of the New Hampshire state prison."[57] Sometime after his marriage, Buzzell left Northwood to learn the trade of brickmaking, which ultimately brought him to Charlestown, where he lived with other men employed in the same line of work.[58]

The nineteenth-century *Boston Globe* invested Buzzell with some of the legendary appeal of such American folklore giants as Paul Bunyan.

In his youth he was noted for his tremendous strength and extraordinary agility, which were tested in many a hard struggle with the bullies of the Massachusetts coast. In form he was a perfect picture of physical manhood, measuring six feet six inches in height, while his broad shoulders and stalwart limbs gave him the appearance of a giant. It is told of him that at the time of the burning of the nunnery he could stand with a cross bar at the height of his chin, and leap over it at a single spring, without touching his hands. . . . The stories of his youthful prowess in wrestling and hand-to-hand fights contain many thrilling episodes, and, if half of them are true, it is little wonder that he was looked upon as a hero in those days when duelling among the bloods and fighting with the bare hands among the workingmen were the accepted methods of settling all personal difficulties.[59]

This giant of a man had been employed for some years in Benjamin Parker's brickyard, a quarter of a mile from the nunnery. It can easily be imagined that the violence of which Buzzell was capable had been expressed in the early 1830s, in the torching of the stable and the shooting of the convent dog. During his years in Charlestown, he boasted that he "had acquired considerable reputation as a fighter and a wrestler." Certainly, Buzzell had exercised his prowess against Peter Rossiter, the convent's servant.

With the group encouraging him, Buzzell "marched off at the head of the crowd, which increased rapidly as we proceeded toward the nunnery." Louisa Whitney reported that when the mob crossed the Charlestown bridge it gave a roar—which she heard from more than a mile away.[60] Several witnesses placed John Buzzell at the gate around sunset. One described him as "a stout tall man in shirt sleeves, light pantaloons, tarpaulin hat, clothes spattered with clay like a brickmaker's . . . he was called 'old R.' and bragged he whipped an Irishman."[61] Another portrayed Buzzell as having "broad shoulders and a sharp nose" and as having bragged, "they know me up there; I whipped their Irishman, and they'll know more of me yet." (It is not clear why Buzzell was called "old R."; perhaps it was a reference to his middle initial.)

During the day on Monday, some of the parents of the convent pupils had heard rumors that they might be in danger, and came to investigate. Levi Thaxter, the father of Lucy Thaxter, who published her account of the riot in 1843, and Judge Fay, father of Maria Fay, who had greeted the Sisters of Charity with pretty speeches on the day the convent dog was shot, drove by the convent in the early evening and noticed only two men near the gate. According to the parents, the pair loitered, looking suspicious. Judge Fay got out of the carriage and went up to them. The loiterers began to speak angry words about the convent. According to Fay, "One said a great deal about blood shed by the Roman Catholics and about Convents . . . [and] . . . ordered me to take my horse out of the gateway as it would be in the way by and by." Fay continued that he was afterward convinced the man he spoke to was John Buzzell. He recalled that Buzzell had once again boasted, "I am the man that whipped the Irishman down on the canal." Fay said he then demanded of Buzzell, "Mr. Tall Man, what is your name?" But Buzzell only replied with profanity to the question.[62]

It is difficult to believe that the fathers of the girls would have been satisfied that there was no problem at the nunnery, but in fact, they drove away convinced their daughters were safe. Perhaps their reaction was the same as Bishop Fenwick's, who had also heard on Monday rumors of the convent's destruction. Though the rumors were floating through the community, virtually no one believed that such violence was possible in a sophisticated nineteenth-century American city—and furthermore that the violence would be enacted against a defenseless community of women. On the day the convent was destroyed, the bishop recorded in his journal that he had received advance notice that the convent would be attacked that night. However, like Thaxter and Fay, Fenwick confidently noted that "he can scarcely credit the rumor not believing that any body of men could be so lost to themselves as to presume to proceed to any such acts of violence."[63] Even when it was reported to Fenwick around eight o'clock that evening that "a hord of vagabonds of the worst description were on the march thither," he still relied upon the public authorities and trusted "no violence would be offered."[64]

When Thaxter and Fay rode off in their carriage, groups of men emerged from the dark bushes surrounding the convent gates, and the two lone men at the foot of the hill swelled to a crowd of thirty. Buzzell strode before the mob, with a large club in his hand. He began to encourage them to give three cheers—and to goad them on, saying some thought they were not men enough to do it. By nine o'clock, the crowd had grown considerably, as more people arrived on foot or in wagons. Finally, the mob began its march up the winding drive to the front door of the convent. About forty or fifty bold fellows stood before the front door, using violent and threatening language, repeating "Down with the Pope! Down with the Convent!"

Mary Anne Moffatt appeared at an upper window. Louisa Whitney later wrote,

I can imagine how she appeared as she stood . . . high above them, her tall erect figure dimly outlined in the starlight, her black robes fluttering back and blending with the dark background. . . . The mob saluted her with a storm of objurgation, which she bore without flinching, interrupting them at last in her clear, loud voice, with some word that intimated her desire to speak.[65]

"What do you want?" she demanded.

In return, the crowd shouted that they wanted to see Elizabeth Harrison. Moffatt retorted, "The Selectmen have already been here to see her—go speak with them." If they would come at a suitable hour the next day, she continued, she would welcome them to meet with Harrison—but this was an outrageous violation of the peace. They were, she said, disturbing the repose of the daughters of many of their most prominent citizens.[66] This argument, typical of Moffatt and her pride in her elite institution, seemed to have some effect on the crowd. One man then asked if they were protected, meaning were there any armed men in the house. To this Moffatt replied in a strong clear voice, "Yes, by legions," adding demurely during the trial, "for I supposed the Celestial Court was looking on."[67]

As they stood before the convent's heavy wooden door, Buzzell recalled, Moffatt had come out only "to harangue us." In his portrayal of her as "the sauciest woman I ever heard talk," he reported that Moffatt concluded her remarks to the crowd by saying, "If you meddle with us, the Bishop has 30,000 men, who will burn your houses over your heads."[68] At this, the men's language grew more "threatening . . . gross and indecent." Moffatt, out of patience, chided the rioters—and demanded to know if any selectmen were present. When she learned John Runey was in the crowd, she called out to him. The selectman announced he was there for her protection. Moffatt scoffed that without other selectmen present she would certainly not trust her establishment to him. If he was there to protect her, she asked, why didn't he start by dispersing the mob?

Runey then tried to reason with the men, saying indeed the selectmen had met with Harrison, and that the stories reported concerning her were untrue.

"Young men," said Runey, "the Selectmen have been at the Convent, and they are satisfied; and something is coming out in the papers in the morning that will satisfy the public."

For this, he was at first met with a storm of mockery. But then some of the men assured the selectman that if the statement coming out was satisfactory, it could be well; but if not, then on Thursday night the convent must come down.[69] Satisfied at their response and feeling as though he had fulfilled his duty, John Runey returned home and went to bed.

As the crowd lingered at the convent door, two to four gunshots rang out as a warning. According to the Catholics, the discharge came from under the willow tree, and served as a signal for the accomplices to collect. Moffatt denied that the shots came from the convent, saying, "there were never any firearms either in the convent or the farm house."[70] At the sound of the discharge, the crowd apparently dispersed and went back down the hill to the street below. According to Buzzell, there they "held a consultation at which a motion to tear the buildings down being unanimously passed." They continued to give evasive and impertinent answers to passersby about what they were doing there. Buzzell would later claim that it was the convent's men "including Rossiter" who "fired pistols in the air to intimidate us." But Buzzell noted that the guns had the opposite effect, "and made us all the more determined to clean the establishment out."

Calling the men together, Buzzell said, "There's a factory down here where they make tarred twine. Let's get some tar barrels and build a fire, and that will bring out the fire boys, who will help us tear down the buildings." Taking two men with him, Buzzell pulled three tar barrels from the factory and set them up on the neighboring property of Alvah

Kelley, just along the fence that formed the boundary line between Kelley's property and the convent's.

"When they got well to blazing," contined Buzzell, "I ran down the street shouting 'Fire!' at the top of my voice. Then Walker's meeting-house bell struck the alarm, and this was followed by a general alarm in Boston, Medford and other neighboring towns, the fire being on a high hill and visible from a great distance. The boys had torn down the fence and piled it upon the tar barrels, so that from a distance it looked like a great conflagration."

Buzzell's narrative continued,

> Enough engines responded to have flooded the whole hill, but only one, the North End, No. 2, of Boston, went to the nunnery, the others stopping at the foot of the hill. Not one of them played a stream during the entire conflagration, while many of the firemen were aiders and abettors of the mob, which by this time numbered over four thousand people.[71]

As the blaze lit up the hill, bells pealed out the signal for fire, and more people, as well as local fire departments, raced to the scene. As Buzzell noted, the watching crowd now numbered in the thousands. Interrupted from his night's rest by the clanging of the bell, Runey hurriedly assembled the other selectmen, including Mr. Hooper. Hooper testified that he again tried to reason with the crowd, but they shouted, "That cross must come down!"

The Charlestown and Boston engines arrived at the scene. While the Charlestown engines stopped at the bonfire, the Boston engine proceeded into the avenue leading up to the convent, lined with the cherry trees the bishop had planted. Engine 13's arrival was greeted with a shout from the rioters on top of the hill, as well as those hiding in the shrubbery. The men emerged from the bushes and began to pull the engine's ropes, drawing her up the hill to the front of the convent's circular walk. Using the engine as a safety base, the men began to pull up the fences, and hurl stones and clubs against the windows and doors. Once this violence was begun, the engine's commander ordered it to be carried down into the road, and be positioned opposite the gate, where it remained during the whole night of violence.

As the darkness deepened, the mob again charged up the hill shouting obscenities. Lucy Thaxter recalled stepping over to a dormitory window, from which she had a distant view of the convent gate.

> There I could see a dense, black mass, apparently moving up the avenue toward the house, and the sound of their prolonged huzzas, came upon my ears, like the yells of fiends. Never shall I forget that sound . . ."[72]

Louisa Whitney wrote that as she gazed out the window at the gathering crowd below, a shooting star, from the annual Perseid meteor shower that occurs this night, blazed across the sky in a downward arc, a kind of heavenly sign of impending doom.

Sister Mary Benedict (Mary Barber) later testified that she was awakened "between nine and ten o'clock by the Superior, who desired me to dress quickly, and collect the children together and the young ladies. I tried to tranquilize them. The mob [was] collecting in front of the Convent. They used vulgar language toward the Superior, called for the 'figure-head,' and said it was made of brass. . . ." This epithet likely had its origins in a contemporaneous controversy surrounding the USS *Constitution*, in which a newly installed figurehead of Andrew Jackson on the ship's bow had been decapitated in the Charlestown Navy Yard just before the Fourth of July.[73] The man who had ordered the controversial ornamentation of *Old Ironsides* was Commodore Jesse Elliott, whose daughter attended the Mount Benedict Academy. Commodore Elliott was a staunch defender of the convent and a friend of the superior's, sending a gift for her to Bishop Fenwick after she left for Quebec. Commodore Elliott had been lampooned in the press for his proposal to honor the president this way, and had to rely on Irish labor to transport the heavy carving when Yankee workers refused to touch it. Newspapers had howled over the sacrilege of using a national treasure like *Old Ironsides* as a partisan symbol, calling the figurehead of Jackson "a graven image" and a "wooden idol." The Puritan language, the vandalism, and threatened violence associated with this incident suggest that the rioters associated taking down the convent's high and mighty superior to the symbolic beheading of Jackson, whom a local newspaper had satirized as Andrew I.[74] The Workingmen's party had played an active role in the

*Old Ironsides* controversy. A man named John Coon later testified that it was Buzzell himself who verbally abused the superior.[75]

Mary Barber shepherded a small group of students to the home of Edward Cutter. Around this same time, two men named O'Callaghan and Walsh who resided in Charlestown informed Bishop Fenwick in Boston that the riot was fully in progress.[76] By then, the mob had begun breaking down the convent's front door. The sound of splintering wood and breaking glass sent the young girls inside the dormitory into panicked hysterics, as Louisa Whitney vividly narrated.

> "Wake up, wake up, the mob has really come!" The younger girls ran up to [Sister Mary Austin] and clung to her screaming "O, the mob, the mob,—we shall all be killed! O what *shall* we do, and what *will* become of us?" The older ones wept and wailed and wrung their hands, and those who were intimate friends threw their arms about each other, and vowed to keep together whatever happened.[77]

Inside the convent were some fifty girls and ten women, including Sister St. Henry (Miss Quirck), the novice from Limerick who was suffering in the final stages of tuberculosis. The Mysterious Lady, Elizabeth Harrison, was reduced to a state of near delirium by the excitement. When Mary Anne Moffatt heard the men begin breaking the windows, she knew they were coming into the building. Her first thought was to evacuate the young girls, so she directed them out the back door to the summer-house at the bottom of the garden. There, the frightened children cowered next to the mausoleum that held the bodies of the seven dead nuns. Louisa Whitney later recalled that although the children were as terrified of the tomb as they were of the rioters, one sensory impression stood out in her memory:

> The court was planted with white rose bushes, yet in bearing, and shall I ever forget how the full-blown roses were set among the dusky branches, like so many ivory cups, nor how they seemed to hold a sweeter perfume than ever rose-cups had before.[78]

Once the children were temporarily safe, Moffatt told them to wait for her and returned to the building to make sure everyone was evacuated. Moffatt's lawyer, J. T. Austin, described Moffatt during the trial as traversing the entire building, "from basement to cupola, looking for the children," but all were for the moment out of danger. Moffatt then returned to her office, in order to save some of the property of the institution. In a curious letter written to Austin two days before the beginning of the trial, she wrote:

> After the rioters had entered the convent, when I went to my room, the principal object that I had in view, was to secure my mother's miniature; but were I to say that I had gone for this miniature, my sensibility would be aroused to that degree, that I should be overpowered, and unable to say anything more. (This, dear Sir, is a *private* communication, for yourself, and I should not wish any mention to be made of it.) I should therefore be much pleased, if the question should not be placed—*For what purpose I went to my room?* I had gold watches, chains, money, and other valuables, in the same drawer with this miniature, which I should have taken up with it; but I must admit now candidly, that only the miniature, would, at that moment, have been an object of concern to me; and it is for that reason that I should prefer not having the question placed—or, could I safely say, as I did at Concord, that I went to secure some valuables, (which is true;) but I have thought of it since, and feared that my reply then, was not explicit enough.[79]

What Moffatt actually removed from her office remains a mystery, though she almost certainly pocketed the small portrait of her mother, who was then living in Canada. She later testified that her drawer contained one thousand dollars in cash which was stolen by the rioters. The rioters would deny taking it. On emerging from her office, Moffatt saw the hallway was filled with armed men. She turned down another passageway, and there was another band coming toward her. Louise Whitney wrote afterward that the men were tracking the superior with the purpose of killing her.[80] But as Austin told it during the trial, "She then retreats to the garden, where she finds the cowering children, driven like doves from their dove-cote."[81]

After the first assault on the door, the rioters paused to see if there would be an answering volley. When it was clear to the rioters that the women were entirely defenseless, the men began their penetration into the cloister. Mr. Runey was on hand with some of the selectmen, and entered the building with the rioters. The selectmen later testified that they had entered to assist the nuns and students. But now the mob had full possession of the house, and cried loudly for torches and lights. Mr. Runey, taking pride in his quick thinking, deterred them briefly in this search by reminding the rioters that if they had lights, they might well be identified. To the committee appointed to investigate the riot, selectman Hooper testified that this advice was not heeded, and three or four torches "which were, or precisely resembled engine torches, were then brought up from the road."[82] The rioters began their search of every room of the building, rifling every drawer, desk, and trunk. They broke up furniture and tossed it out the windows. Much of their fury was vented upon "costly piano fortes and harps, and other valuable instruments," as well as on the children's abandoned treasures, and the vessels and symbols of Christian worship.

According to John Buzzell, "the first thing that was done, after getting in, was to throw the pianos, of which nine were found, out of the windows." So many men pressed into the convent's foyer that Buzzell, "with great difficulty . . . got upstairs to the chapel, which was located on the second floor. When I finally succeeded in forcing my way into the chapel I found a fire about the size of a bushel-barrel blazing merrily in the middle of the floor. It was made of paper, old books, and such other inflammable stuff as they could lay their hands on, and soon spread in all directions."[83]

Meanwhile, Moffatt was making her escape from the dangerous passageways in an attempt to rejoin the shivering band of children and nuns cowering next to the mausoleum. When the curtains in the convent window above them went up in a blaze, the nuns waiting in the garden knew they needed to get the children off the property. Suddenly, they heard men's voices calling and steps approaching. Certain that they had been discovered by the mob, a few of the girls began to cry. Then Mr. Cutter and a friend appeared. After securing Mary Barber and a small group of girls at his house, Cutter had come to assist the rest of the girls, about forty, who remained in the garden with eight nuns.[84]

During the trial, Cutter testified that when they arrived at the rear of the building, they saw the nuns in a circle in the garden. Cutter asked them if they would accept his protection. One of the nuns spoke up, asking, "Is that you, Mr. Cutter?" They indicated that they would be glad to have it. They then asked if their lives were in danger. Yes, he told them, he thought they were. Cutter inquired where the superior was, and the nuns replied they didn't know. He asked them to follow him to safety, but they told him he should look after the children already sheltered at his house.

"If we find our lives in danger," they assured him, "we will come down."

Shortly after Cutter left, Mary Anne Moffatt returned, and the group, as she had directed them, was waiting for her. Determined to evacuate the children, the superior began prying at portions of a picket fence at the rear of the garden, and the nightgown-clad girls and the nuns climbed through the small opening and hurried down to the road below. Cutter discovered them there, near the front of his house, dazed and wandering aimlessly:

> . . . two seemed to stray away, and walked off in another direction. They appeared to be lost, like a couple of silly sheep separated from the flock . . . I put my hand upon her shoulder, and discovered, by her voice, that it was the Superior.[85]

Moffatt later testified that

> On the night of the fire, Mr. Cutter and another person took me forcibly by the arm, and endeavored to carry me into his house; but I resisted, and would not go in. He said my life was in danger from the mob.

Cutter denied that he had handled the superior roughly, saying he had only wanted to shepherd her to safety. But she refused to accompany him, saying, "Mr. Cutter, I do not want any of your assistance, and will not enter your house." Standing in the road, Moffatt berated Cutter, saying that he delayed in making his statement to the paper "on purpose to have the convent attacked by the mob, and that our own houses would be torn down."

Refusing Cutter's offer of hospitality, the superior decided to take the children to the home of Mr. Adams, on nearby Winter Hill. She led the disheveled group down the road, away from Mount Benedict. Louisa Whitney described the hastily dressed children's motley array:

[O]ne had on only a petticoat outside her nightgown, another a nightcap under her bonnet. . . . A third displayed one leg bare, with a garterless stocking on the other; a fourth had a shawl pinned over a flannel skirt; a stringless shoe and a slipper down at heel.[86]

Not long afterward, from the safety of Mr. Adams's house on Winter Hill, the girls were able to watch from the windows as flames enveloped their convent.

Just after midnight, having ransacked every room, the men prepared to set the convent on fire. Warren Draper, who had allegedly supplied the information for the article "Mysterious" to the *Mercantile Journal*, reported seeing the men break the lower windows with clubs. He watched as chairs, mirrors, and books came flying out. Then some of the men appeared at the window with a large book, and said, "Here goes the Bible. Set fire to it with a torch."[87] Broken furniture, books, curtains, and anything else that would burn were placed in the center of the room. The first fire was lit, and then the Bible was cast, with shouts of exultation, into the blaze. The beautiful embroidered vestments that Bishop Fenwick had brought back from his trip to Canada were tossed in with the holy book, followed by sacred ornaments. The cheering continued until finally the cross was yanked from the altar and cast into the flames. Local resident John C. Tenney recalled seeing the blaze from Boston:

That night I stayed in Boston, and was aroused by the policeman springing his rattle and calling out that there was a fire. A little after that he sprang it again, and cried out that there was a fire over in Charlestown. I slipped into my clothes and went out. The sky was all red across the river, and I saw that the fire was in the convent on the top of Nunnery Hill. I could see every window clear, with the red flames behind it.[88]

Outside the burning convent, Henry Creesy and a few others had found the tabernacle from the chapel's altar, hidden in a rosebush by two nuns when they heard the rioters at the door. Inside was the silver chalice, or ciborium, containing the consecrated hosts. Laughing and tossing the silver vessel aside, Creesy shoved a few of the wafers into his breast pocket, and looked up to see flames coming from the convent window. His gleeful declaration that God was now in his pocket was the prelude to the madness that would shortly lead him to take his own life in the Newburyport tavern.

As the flames engulfed the convent, the rioters moved on to other areas of the property. John R. Buzzell gave this vivid description of what happened next:

> When the main building was enveloped in flames we went for the cook-house and ice-house, which were separate buildings, and set them on fire. . . . At a little distance from the main building stood what was called the Bishop's lodge, where he had a library, and where he used to keep his robes, etc. After the ice-house was fired I started for this lodge, and was the first to get in. I picked up a heavy desk and was giving it a swing to heave it out of the window, when the mob arrived, and not knowing I was within, smashed the glass. The broken pieces were thrown violently into my face, cutting many bad gashes, from which the blood flowed freely. However, I wiped my face, and getting out the Bishop's robe, put it on in a spirit of deviltry. The others stripped it off my back, and winding the remnants around poles, used them as torches, lighting them at the main building and firing the lodge with them.[89]

The rioters who had joined Buzzell inside the lodge began tossing books and pictures out the window to a waiting group outside, which threw them into the flames. It was here that sixteen-year-old Marvin Marcy acted the part of the mock auctioneer and cried, "Going once" and "Sold" as he threw books into the fire.

Next the men targeted the renovated farmhouse, first pounding the doors with stones and sticks to see if any defenders might be inside. They entered and set fire to this building. The red skies seen by John C. Tenney from Boston began to lighten to mark the coming of day. But the rioters were unwilling to leave a single building standing, so though day had broken, they proceeded to burn the barn. Finally, with the pink skies of morning spreading a dim light, they entered the convent tomb. At the small altar, they pocketed the sacred vessels, wrested the plates from the coffins, and exposed to view the mouldering remains of their tenants.

John Buzzell, in his account more than fifty years after the event, mixes fiction and fact in his recollection of the visit to the convent tomb, where they specifically went, he recalled,

> to see if the body of the music teacher Mary St. John was there. The door of the tomb was broken open, and within was the body of a young girl who had evidently been dead but a day or two at most, and whom I religiously believe to this day to have been Mary St. John, although I had no positive proof of her identity.[90]

We have seen that Sister Mary John, Elizabeth Harrison, had herself conducted the selectmen through the building that very afternoon, so clearly she was not immured in the convent tomb. One eyewitness reported that Buzzell was petitioned by the mob to conclude the evening by leading the crowd in a vulgar song.[91] The destruction had taken place before town officials and a crowd of thousands who stood on the convent grounds watching the events unfold. Half a century later, Buzzell would recall,

> There was a very pretty moon that night. It was not at its full, but, I should think, in its second quarter, and as the bonfire died down, that crowd of excited faces, with the building looming up against the sky, took on a weird aspect in the moonlight, which is as vivid to me to-day as it was over fifty years ago.[92]

EARLY THE FOLLOWING DAY, Bishop Fenwick sent carriages to transport the nuns to the Sisters of Charity's convent in Boston. Louisa Whitney and some of the other students were placed into a stagecoach by the father of one of the girls, and driven along Main Street in Charlestown the morning after the fire. Whitney reports that some of the rioters had no difficulty in identifying the passengers [in] the interior, full of pink calico, and crowned with childrens' heads, half of them bonnetless. We looked as ill-conditioned as a body of little paupers broken loose from the almshouse, and those of the mob who first caught sight of us broke into loud cheering and rude laughter. Fortunately it happened that the crowd was in a mood of high good-humor, and its heart may have warmed to our disreputable appearance, so like its own. At any rate, the idea of acting as our escort to the city seemed to seize upon it as a good joke. So we slowly rode the gantlet between a double file of amiable ruffians, who saluted us with jests, yells, shrill whistles, and cat-calling, roars of laughter, rough jokes and questions. "Saved yer diamonds?" shouted one young man. "I've got something of yours, I guess!" bawled out another, holding up his clenched fist which probably contained some valuable he had stolen. "We've spoiled your prison for you," cried a third. "You won't never have to go back no more."[93]

Whitney's account of this motley procession following the riot underscores her perception that the rioters were men of the lower class, who themselves recognized the class distinctions. But the jovial mood of the rioters as depicted here quickly gave way to strained tensions in Boston following the event.

Anna Loring wrote to a friend that

last night the nunnery at Charlestown was burnt to the ground . . . —a party of men begun first pulling down the shead the Abbess expostulated with them saying that there were but women & children in the house, but no they went destroyed & setting on fire to the building & furniture pianos' harps & every thing was destroyed even the articles the nuns had taken into the garden was brought back burnt, horrid most horrid . . . [94]

As Loring's letter goes on to recount, Boston was in turmoil as news spread of the convent's destruction. It was reported that the Irish laborers on the Worcester, Lowell, and Providence railroads were on their way to the city, in great numbers, for the purpose of aiding their Irish brethren in avenging the insult that was offered to them by the destruction of the Catholic seminary at Charlestown. Bishop Fenwick dispatched five or six priests in different directions during the afternoon to intercept the laborers and instruct them not to raise a finger in retaliation.

On Tuesday afternoon, the authorities called an emergency meeting at Boston's Faneuil Hall to try to calm the excitement. One of the speakers called upon was the Honorable Harrison Gray Otis, who gave a speech condemning the violence of the previous night. A contemporary publication gave the following description:

> . . . the Hon. H. J. Otis rose to address the meeting amidst the most deafening applause, which was more than once repeated in the course of his most animated and eloquent remarks. It was pleasant once again to meet the splendid orator on the theatre of his youthful glory, and totally unprepared as he was, we must say we have seldom, if ever, heard him to greater advantage. There was the same music in his voice, the same elegance in his gestures, the same beauty and felicity of expression, for which he has so long and so justly been conspicuous. The frost of age is on his brow, but the glow of youthful ardor was still predominant at his heart, and the thunders of applause which made old Faneuil Hall ring again, were sufficient evidence that he still occupies the same high place in the affections of his fellow citizens.[95]

At this public meeting, six resolutions were adopted, condemning the riot as cowardly and unlawful, and nominating a committee from the citizens at large to investigate the proceedings. Twenty-eight were selected, including Anna Loring's husband, Charles, who would serve as chairman, and Benjamin Hallett, the probable publisher of Rebecca Reed's narrative. These twenty-eight were advised to consider the expediency of providing funds to repair the damage done to the convent. In order to stem further violence, Mayor Theodore Lyman, Jr. was "authorized to offer a very liberal reward to any individual, who in case of further excesses, would arrest and bring to punishment a leader in such outrages."[96] Subsequently, on August 15, 1834, the Governor of Massachusetts, John Davis, would issue a proclamation condemning

*Destruction of the Ursuline Convent by Fire.*

*The flaming convent high on Mount Benedict could be seen from Boston as it lit up the night skies.*

the violence and offering a reward of $500 for the arrest of the perpetrators.[97]

To assist with these incentives against further disturbances, a militia called the Independent Light Infantry Company was called to alert to protect Boston from retaliatory action on the part of the Catholics and more violence on the part of the Protestants. On the evening of August 12, 1834, around six o'clock, several hundred Catholics assembled in the cathedral on Franklin Street. Bishop Fenwick addressed them for thirty minutes, on the subject of avoiding retaliation. The sermon was hailed by both Catholics and Protestants as effective in diffusing the threat of a retaliatory riot:

You have heard that it hath been said, an eye for an eye, and a tooth for a tooth. But I say to you . . . if one strike thee on thy right cheek, turn to him also the other . . . I say to you, love your enemies, do good to them that hate; and pray for them that persecute and calumniate you. . . . Turn not a finger in your own defense, and there are those around you who will see that justice is done you . . . tell this to anyone you know coming from other cities.[98]

But while Fenwick was trying to soothe the Catholics, Protestant mobs were arming for still more destruction. Fenwick recorded in his journal that on the night after the fire, a large crowd gathered at the Franklin Street cathedral around nine in the evening, with the stated object of destroying it. With the militia on patrol,

Nothing is attempted. The *B'p* & Clergy remain up all night as well as the good religious & Sisters in Hamilton Street, who are similarly threatened.[99]

Frustrated with not being able to destroy the Catholic cathedral, the mob marched across the Charlestown bridge to Mount Benedict. The burned ruins stood silently in the August moonlight, but the magnificent gardens still bloomed relatively untouched. This time, the crowd of men vented their fury on fruit trees and vines. A man with a scythe cut down the roses growing against a stone wall and rued that the valuable silver ciborium had been lost through the carelessness of Henry Creesy. A New York Catholic newspaper, *The Truth Teller,* later called Creesy a "blasphemous wretch, who laid his hands on the divine Host, and boasted that he had the Papist's God." The next night, as we have seen, Creesy "went away and cut his throat so dreadfully that the head scarcely remained connected with the body."[100] Like most of the rioters, Creesy was far less economically privileged than were the victims of his fury. One local newspaper reported in his obituary,

At the time of his death, Henry Creesy's personal effects consisted of a fragment of an old letter, a memorandum book, and a pair of cotton socks. He was buried in Newburyport, Massachusetts at the public's expense.[101]

Despite further threats throughout the following week, no further violence was enacted in Charlestown or Boston.

U LTIMATELY, THIRTY-EIGHT men served on the blue-ribbon investigative committee which met starting August 13, from nine in the morning until sunset, daily except Sundays, until August 27—two full weeks. They dispatched subcommittees to ferret out intelligence in various neighborhoods, and summoned voluntary witnesses to meet with the committee. Assurances had to be given to some of the witnesses that "no use would be made of the information they might give, unless it should be thought necessary to summon them as witnesses before a magistrate or judicial tribunal. This latter assurance was given to most of the persons who appeared in the Committee Room, in order to remove the apprehensions entertained by them or some of them, for their personal safety."[102] More than one hundred and forty persons appeared before the committee, some of them several times. Because of the enormity of the task, more members joined the committee than had been originally appointed. Some of the gentlemen, including Benjamin Hallett, Reed's publisher, declined to serve. Apparently none of the committee was Roman Catholic, since the committee's report said all of the members were "unanimously opposed to its [Catholicism's] characteristic tenets."[103] The committee's investigation ultimately led to the arrests of thirteen men, eight of them to be arraigned on charges of a capital nature. Opponents of Catholicism charged that the report, which they alleged had cost $7,000 to produce, had been prepared from written statements by the superior.[104]

T WO WEEKS AFTER THE RIOT, Harvard freshman Theodore Russell paid a visit to the ruins of the Ursuline convent, which had been left much as they were on the eve of their destruction. His eyewitness account of the state of the ruins, including the convent tomb, is as follows:

> I visited the ruins of the Ursuline Convent on Friday. The buildings and grounds remain precisely as the mob left them. Even the

Tomb is left as yet in the same condition in which it was found the next morning except filling up the entrance. The coffins are split open and the bodies out. I was informed by a gentleman we found there, that some of the mob he saw (I think) *actually took out the teeth* from the mouth of a female corse (probably a nun) and *coolly put them into their pockets.* This is a thing at which humanity shudders. . . . When I looked upon these ruins but a few days ago one of the pleasantest and most beautiful places in the vicinity of Boston; when I wandered through the gardens and walks green and blooming with a varied luxuriant growth of flowers and summer vegetation and saw the havock and devastation, trees of most choice fruit broken down and destroyed, when last of all I saw that the . . . hand of the destroyer had broken through the sacred enclosure of the tomb and cruelly and wantonly disturbed the rest of the slumbering dead in presence of the living friends the sight was truly heart rending.[105]

O N SEPTEMBER 3, the bishop's birthday, he visited the site of the Ursuline convent for the first time since its demolition, probably because it would have been too dangerous to go earlier. That evening, he expressed his sorrow at the scene in his diary, confessing, "His heart bleeds to see the devastation which had been committed. Nothing but the walls of the old building remain, the fire having consumed every other thing." The murderously hot summer of 1834 departed, giving way to a brief autumn and an unusually early start to winter. On October 26, as the bishop traveled to Roxbury, Massachusetts to celebrate Mass for the Ursulines in their new rented home, the first snow began to fall and continued for several hours. Later that day, some of the members of his congregation offered to go out to Mount Benedict to dig up the "real Irish potatoes" the bishop had planted with such optimism the previous spring.[106] By the next day, the weather had moderated a little, and Fenwick along with Father Healy rode out to the ruins of Mount Benedict. There, he recorded, he had "the pleasure to behold 50 or 60 good Irishmen, who had volunteered their services, digging and carting the Potatoes to the new establishment of the Ursulines at Roxbury." On his return from the old convent, he traveled by way of Bunker Hill, stopping to survey the Catholic cemetery, which was now open to the Catholics for burial, the lawsuit having been decided by the supreme court in his favor. With his cartful of Irish potatoes, the bishop stopped to give thanks for small blessings. He was happy to see the cemetery was in good order, and recorded his gratitude to the Almighty, noting in his journal that night, "Thank God! the Catholics can now bury there without molestation."[107]

## CHAPTER SIX

# THE LOST GARDEN

## Indictments and Trial

*We are not the people whom we thought ourselves to be.*

—*The Christian Examiner,* September 1834

*The events you are investigating are to be recorded in the history of your country; the connection you have had with them is to be recorded also, and both will go down to posterity as long as history shall exist.*

—JAMES T. AUSTIN, Argument to the Jury, December 1834

T HE CLOSE-KNIT NEIGHBORHOOD of Charlestown, Massachusetts has long been famous for its code of silence, which protects its own from the enforcement side of the law. The placards posted on the Charlestown Bridge as the investigations were beginning were an early indication of this practice. Shortly after the convent was burned, a crudely lettered sign warned:

All persons giving information in any shape, or testifying in court against any one concerned in the late affair at Charlestown, may expect assassination, according to the oath which bound the party to each other.[1]

Before the trials even began, Bishop Fenwick recognized the slim chance that a Yankee jury would convict the convent rioters. Despite the attorney general's attempt to impress the jury with the historical significance of its deliberations, the protective code prevailed, and the rioters were, almost to a man, set free. From the beginning, the legal question of whether or not the men charged were guilty of destroying the convent was relegated to a distant position behind less relevant questions. Esoteric inquiries into the peculiarities of Catholic doctrine and tangential explorations of various events that occurred on the night of the crime were the focus of the defense's examination of witnesses. The strategy of putting Catholicism on trial, instead of the rioters, proved to be an effective one.

John R. Buzzell was taken into custody even before the investigating committee completed its work. According to his own account, within three days after the convent was burned, on August 14, 1834, "I was arrested by Deputy Sheriff Coleman and taken before a justice for a preliminary examination. Two days were consumed in this examination, and at its conclusion I was sent to Cambridge jail without bail, to await the action of the Grand Jury. About one hundred others were arrested at the same time I was, but only twelve beside myself were ever indicted."[2] Buzzell's role as ringleader was so widely known that even the protective code could not shield him.

With Buzzell in jail, the investigations into the incident began with a specially appointed committee interviewing over a hundred witnesses. In the end, the committee suggested that a larger conspiracy was behind the riot, but failed to prove that it was hatched by prominent and respectable men who enticed the lower classes to do their dirty work. This suspicion, however, has persisted ever since. The committee pointed its fingers at "conspirators who were led to design the destruction of the convent, and to avail themselves of the aid of those miscreants . . . activated by 'the love of violence, or the hope of plunder.'"[3] Aware of the class implications of the event, the committee expressed apprehensions that the well-placed men who had planned the riot would escape and justice would fall "upon the humbler instruments of their villainy."[4] The men of property who sat on the committee also focused on the implications for people like themselves, who were also the main clientele for the convent school. Announcing that the state of affairs surrounding the convent's destruction had "come upon us like the shock of an earthquake," the committee bemoaned the implication that "if for the purpose, of destroying a person, a family, or an Institution, it be only necessary to excite a public prejudice, by the dissemination of falsehoods and criminal accusations, and under its sanction to array a mob; and there be neither an efficient magistracy nor a sense of public duty or justice sufficient for its prevention, who among us is safe?"[5]

The roiling tensions of the event can be seen most clearly in the perception that the notion of democracy had been undermined in the age of President Jackson to mean social equality as well as lawlessness. The *Christian Examiner* called for a recognition of "the necessary order of society," referring both to social station as well as greater lawful regulation of the lives of citizens. In the wake of the destruction of Mount Benedict, the *Examiner* opined that

> There are those who would confound that equality of civil rights, which our institutions are intended to secure, with an equality in all things, which God has made impossible. When they recognize any one superior in the gifts of nature, or in the advantages to be secured by good conduct and industry; or more fortunate in the lottery of life, which with us is equally open to all, they have a feeling as if their rights were invaded. Hence there is a struggle against the necessary order of society, that order which may be disturbed by violence, but as soon as that violence is removed must immediately restore itself.[6]

For the wealthy men of Boston, whose daughters attended the convent school, protection of property was paramount. Theodore Hammet explains that this is why people like the Beechers, who were liberal abolitionists, could be anti-Catholic at the same time. In the nineteenth century, perceptions of slavery were strongly rooted in perceptions about ownership and property. The wealthy supporters of the convent were often supporters of slavery—making their stands based upon the protection of property as much as upon moral issues.[7]

The committee was unable to find any report in circulation critical of the community at Mount Benedict that could not be traced to Rebecca Reed and her friends—and discovered no proof of the charges of abuse. It also called for a return to the ideals of the Founding Fathers, especially the notion of religious freedom:

If there be one feeling which more than any other should pervade this country, composing, as it were, the atmosphere of social life, it is that of enlightened toleration, comprehending all within the sphere of its benevolence, and extending over all the shield of mutual protection.[8]

To foster this idea of enlightened toleration, the committee recommended a restructuring of the laws, and especially focused on the responsibility of the magistrates. It called for indemnification—at the hands of the town of Charlestown who so failed to observe the concept of a community formed for mutual protection. Its report ended with a ringing indictment of the convent burning,

And if this cruel and unprovoked injury, perpetrated in the heart of the Commonwealth, be permitted to pass unrepaired, our boasted toleration and love of order, our vaunted obedience to law, and our ostentatious proffers of an asylum to the persecuted of all sects and nations, may well be accounted vain glorious pretensions, or yet more wretched hypocrisy.

In an age where the rule of law seemed increasingly undermined by unruly Jacksonian democracy, another contemporary magazine called for a strengthening of the law to preserve freedoms for all:

[L]iberty, by which, in the widest sense of the term, is meant nothing more than the full enjoyment of all our rights, cannot exist unless there be power enough in the state effectually to defend those rights. Power in the government is necessary to the enjoyment of liberty by the individual. There are false notions maintained by some among us, respecting . . . the tendency to license, disorder and that worst form of tyranny, that is controlled by no laws and no restraints of opinion.[9]

The destruction of the convent meant that social disorder ruled, and only reparations would ensure a return to the necessary order of society.

\* \* \*

O N SEPTEMBER 6, 1834, Mary Anne Moffatt, along with Mary Barber, received notice that they were to appear before the grand jury in Concord, Massachusetts to give testimony in relation to the convent burning. At six o'clock on the morning of September 9, accompanied by Mr. Kielchen, the Russian consul stationed in Boston, they set out to appear in court.[10] On Monday, September 14, 1834, indictments were made against twelve men at Concord, Massachusetts by Attorney General J.T. Austin. The main indictment was handed down against John R. Buzzell, brick maker, of Charlestown. Also charged were William Mason, a gardener; Sargent Blaisdell and Alvah Kelley, brick makers; and Ephraim Holwell, a rope maker. From Boston, Rebecca Reed's brother-in-law, Prescott P. Pond, a cordwainer, or shoemaker; Nathan Budd, Jr., a baker; Aaron Hadley, a carpenter; Benjamin Wilbur, a mariner; and Thomas Dillon, a painter, were also indicted. The young mariner, Marvin Marcy, Jr., of Cambridge, had tried unsuccessfully to board a ship heading out of New Bedford, Massachusetts on a long sea voyage, but had been intercepted. In addition, Isaac Parker, a cordwainer from Cambridge, "and sundry other evil disposed persons to the number of twenty whose names are to said Jurors as yet unknown" were charged.[11] Several counts were handed down, including breaking and entering with dangerous weapons, stealing, and setting fire to the convent. The men were accused of stealing a thousand dollars in cash, fifty dollars in coins, and fifty dollars worth of goods from Mary Anne Moffatt. In addition to Moffatt, the other aggrieved nuns named in the indictment were Elizabeth Harrison (Sister Mary John), Mary Anne Barber (Mary Benedict), Sarah Chase (Mary Ursula), Frances O'Keefe (Mary Austin), Ellen O'Keefe (Mary Joseph), Mary Rebecca Theresa DeCosta (Mary Claire), and Grace O'Boyle (Bernard).

The indictments concluded with a call for the arrest of the twelve men, who were to be held in a Cambridge prison. Arson and burglary were punishable by death from hanging. Seven of the men, Buzzell, Pond, Mason, Marcy, Blaisdell, Parker, and Kelley, pleaded not guilty, and Isaac Parker was discharged. Buzzell summed up the response to his arrest by the public, "As fears were entertained that I might be rescued, I was taken to old Concord, where I remained in jail until court convened—in November, I think."[12] Because an attack on the jail had been planned, it was deemed too risky for Buzzell to be held in Cambridge, so close to Charlestown.

Naval Commodore J. D. Elliott, who had angered so many with his role in the *Old Ironsides* incident, as well as other convent supporters, vowed to defend the jail. Because Elliott voiced indignation at the prospect of an attack, his own home was threatened. Later, he was one of the first to place his daughter with the Ursulines for further study when the school reopened in Roxbury a few months later, at Brinley Place.[13] For these reasons, the attorney general expressed his fear that unless the convent rioters were removed to a more distant county for the trial, justice would not be served. He was unsuccessful in having the location moved and in mid-October, the trial date was set for December 2, 1834 in Cambridge. Fenwick was already pessimistic about the outcome, writing to his brother that "Their friends (and they have a good many among the rubbish of both towns) are very apprehensive they will go to the Gallows—but I do not think that will be the case; for, in all probability a Yankee Jury will prefer perjuring itself to sending them to the Gallows."[14]

During the two months they spent in a confined space in Boston with the Sisters of Charity, the health of all the nuns deteriorated. Elizabeth Harrison (Sister Mary John), the escaped nun, who was supposed to testify at the upcoming trial, earnestly solicited to leave. Moffatt herself seems to have made the decision to let her depart for Quebec, along with six other nuns. This placed the Canadian convent in an uncomfortable situation, since the Boston nuns arrived virtually unannounced. The superior, meanwhile, had taken it upon herself to rent Brinley Place in Roxbury as the site of her new school. Because the new house at Brinley Place was being renovated, and it was necessary to take in some boarders to pay rent and make the improvements, Moffatt chose to lighten her burden by sending the six nuns, including Elizabeth Harrison, to Quebec. In all likelihood, these decisions, taken independently, marked the beginning of the breakdown in relations between Fenwick and Moffatt. Fenwick was placed in the uncomfortable situation of having to apologize for the unannounced arrival of the nuns, and to ask that Harrison be sent back to testify. Fenwick, after the fact, penned a note of apology to Bishop Signay in Quebec, saying, "I should have written to your Lordship before to reclaim your charity in behalf of our poor afflicted persecuted Nuns of Mt. Benedict six of whom have sought shelter within your convent, but the situation in which I was placed & the precipitancy with which they left . . . urged by their fears, rendered it impossible."[15] This letter suggests Fenwick was somewhat out of the loop on this decision—he had only just returned from a trip out of town when the nuns made their departure.[16]

Moffatt thought that Elizabeth Harrison, even after her time in Quebec, would prove too unstable to testify, and urged the attorney general to prevent it. Writing to him confidentially, she said, "I include two letters which she had written, one from Montreal, and the other from Quebec—By the latter, you will perceive in what state her mind is."[17] When it became clear that the fragile Harrison would be required to appear, Fenwick wrote to ask for her return. In the letter to the bishop of Quebec, Fenwick summed up his dark mood as "Persecuted, insulted, with a heart half broken & laboring under all the difficulties of an infidel sect who are every day seeking to insult and entrap us."[18] But other Catholic communities attempted to help, with the City of New Orleans collecting $3,000 for the benefit of the Ursulines.[19] On a warm fall day, " . . . the weather precisely like a day in April . . . Mr. Kielchen, the Russian Consul, starts this day for Quebec at the request of the Superior of the Ursulines here for the purpose of accompanying St'r Mary John back to Boston, her testimony being required on the trial of the rioters which is to take place on the 2d of Dec'r next."[20]

As soon as the indictments were handed down, it became clear to the cloistered Ursulines that their appearance in a sensational and very public trial would be necessary. Extant correspondence between Mary Anne Moffatt and Attorney General Austin provides a fascinating glimpse of some of the preparations behind the scene for the court appearance of the nuns. A small work box belonging to Mary Barber, Sister Mary Benedict, that was requested as evidence by the attorney general, was sent a few days late with the superior's apologies. When it was necessary for the nuns to appear at Concord, the attorney general arranged with a woman named Mrs. Davis to provide rooms for the nuns to wait. With gratitude for this kindness, Moffatt wrote, "The circumstance of our appearing at court, would have been much more unpleasant, had it not been for your extreme politeness."[21]

In another letter, dated only "Friday morning," Moffatt wrote to the attorney general that

All the articles, accompanying the small red work box, were *in* the box, when it was returned to us, but *mixed together.* Recollecting perfectly well, where each article was left, I have written the place on the outside, and wrapped up the different things *separately,* that you may be able to judge what time they had for plunder. If these were taken, though concealed in closets and drawers that were locked, can it be supposed that most valuable articles, such as splendid work boxes and fancy ornaments, which were *on the same bureaus and in the same closets and drawers,* were not likewise taken? As yet, nothing of any value has been returned.—The three pieces of ivory were not returned with the box, but all the other articles were.[22]

Moffatt carefully used these plundered objects to help draw a map of the rampage through her convent, and suggested arguments for the attorney general to use in court.

In mid-November, as the trial was about to begin, Moffatt wrote a long letter to Austin discussing many aspects of her testimony. She began by admitting that the ivory pieces and other small articles that were later returned to the Sisters of Charity came from an unknown source—that the sisters did not inquire who brought them.[23] Her main concern is anxiety over her upcoming court appearance:

The more I reflect, dear Sir, on our appearing at Court, the more desirous I am of being exempted from it. Our evidence cannot be of much importance, as we could identify no one; and everyone tells us, likewise, that the criminals will not be punished. I do not think, moreover, that I could have courage to get through. I thought, when we went to Concord, that the obligation was a most painful one; and I have been astonished that I was able to support it, even as well as I did. Had I had an idea how things were, I do not think I could have gone. At Cambridge, it will be public, and therefore, much more painful,—I beg you will excuse us, and by so doing, you will confer on us a *very great favor.* Be kind to take it into consideration, and our man will call for your answer on Monday.[24]

Moffatt ended this letter of November 15, 1834 with a repeated request to be exempt from testifying.

On the same day as Moffatt petitioned to be excused from appearing in court, Bishop Fenwick received an unpleasant surprise: a visit from the tax collector. For Fenwick, already burdened with loss, this was an unpardonable offense. In his diary of November 15, 1834, the bishop recorded that:

> Solomon Hovey, Collector of the taxes in Charlestown, calls on the *B'p* stating that the taxes on the Ursuline Convent for the present year amount to $79.20 & demands payment of them. The *B'p* expresses his surprise at so unreasonable a demand. The Convent burnt on the 11th of Aug't and still the taxes on it demanded for a whole year, as if it was yet standing! He inquires the names of the Assessors? He is informed they are the following: viz. Timothy Fletcher, Benjamin Badger Jun'r and Joseph Miller. He is informed further more that the property destroyed was valued by the above assessors at $12,000, that is today, at the rate of $6.60 pr. thousand. The *B'p* intends consulting a lawyer before he pays the above.

Two days before the trial was to begin on December 2, Moffatt again wrote to Austin. She informed him that the earliest Elizabeth Harrison would arrive was Monday night, at the end of the first day of the trial, ruling out her appearance on Tuesday. Moffatt again made clear her own anxiety about the court appearance: "I fear that I should have some difficulty in relating circumstances unless I were *questioned*. I therefore request the favor of your placing questions and as many as you think proper." In the same letter, Moffatt brought up the mysterious circumstances under which she returned to her room on the night of the fire, denying that she herself removed the valuables from her room, including the thousand dollars in cash. Whether Moffatt took only the miniature or the money as well has never come to light. It seems unlikely that a shrewd business woman like Moffatt would leave such a large amount of cash available for plunder and the rioters consistently denied that they found the money. Six months later, when Moffatt returned to Quebec,

*Moffatt presented her lawyer, J. T. Austin, with an engraving of the convent
to show her gratitude for his help.*

she seems to have had in her possession a great deal of money to buy
lavish gifts for her nieces.[25] It is possible that Moffatt's spending money
consisted of profits from the sale of her successful book rebutting Rebecca Reed's. But Moffatt's sentimental response that she went back
only to save her mother's picture, while her mother was very much
alive, raises doubts that she was entirely truthful.

On December 17, convinced of the futility of the trial, Moffatt again
wrote to Austin, asking to be excused from testifying further. She enclosed an engraving of the convent as a sign of her esteem.

> I take this opportunity to assure you again of the favor you would
> confer on us, by exempting us from appearing any more at court,
> or by discontinuing the trials altogether.—The parents of the pupils
> whom we have are much alarmed for the safety of their children.

By the rumors that are spread abroad, and the bold threats that are made, it appears that the people, concerned in the riot, as well as their friends, believe that we appear joyfully against them, and are thirsting for their blood—This is far from being the case—Nothing but respect for the laws, has induced us to go to court, and we should be sorry that any of the prisoners should suffer.[26]

But as the wronged party, the appearance of the nuns was deemed essential.

As part of their preparation for the trial, the Catholics were asked to estimate the value of the property that had been lost. Bishop Fenwick estimated the loss of property at the convent to be $40,000 and the property of the students to amount to $50,000. The list of articles belonging to Mrs. Russell, whose two daughters were enrolled in the academy, might be typical for each of the approximately fifty girls who were in the convent on the night of the fire. Each girl could have lost about a thousand dollars worth of property in the fire. The unvalued items on the list consist of two down beds and two mattresses, four silver spoons, two silver forks, and articles of clothing and embroidery. Chamber furniture is valued at $50, two silver cups at $10, four books of music at $30, and one English harp at $800.[27]

As part of this accounting, the superior published her list of the names of pupils and their lost property, noting that "As many of the scholars owned much valuable property, such as Piano Fortes, Harps, Guitars, Silver Cups &c., upon which their initials were engraved, and which were stolen at the time of the conflagration, the publication of this list may lead to the detection of the thieves."

One student, Miss Mary Anne N. Fraser, who would later enroll in the Quebec academy, had especially substantial losses. Some evidence suggests Miss Fraser may have actually been the niece of Mary Anne Moffatt, for whom the lavish gifts were purchased. Miss Fraser apparently brought with her to the school

one Harp, Piano Forte and Guitar, 13 Music Books; a Portfolio containing about 200 pieces of loose Music; a Silver Tumbler, inlaid with gold; Dessert and Tea Spoons; two Settees, of mahogany, covered with rug work; rosewood Desk and paint box, completely furnished, inlaid with brass, (imported); fancy work of every description; more than 300 pieces of Drawing and Painting, a gold Watch, Cross, and two Chains, with other articles of jewelry. Books to the amount of more than a hundred volumes, and all her wearing apparel, except what she had on at the time of her escape. . . . The other Young Ladies, as far as can be ascertained, lost their Silver Thimbles and Spoons, Music Books, Drawing and Painting materials, valuable Birth-day Presents, Gold Watches, Rings, Chains and various other Jewelry, Work Boxes, Books, and *all* their wearing apparel. . . . All the Plate of the community, except what belonged to their place of worship, was marked Ursuline Community, in full . . . the community had two libraries, one for the community, and one for the girls. . . .[28]

Losses by Mary Anne Fraser and her sister Jane apparently eclipsed those of the others, and the Frasers are the only girls whose parents' names do not appear in the indemnity petitions. Though Mary Anne Fraser was only nine years old, no parent or guardian was listed, which raises suspicion that she may actually be Moffatt's niece. And Jane, or Genevieve, was also the name of Moffatt's mother. Though the Frasers' losses were high, even the poorest girl on the list would have been wealthy compared with most of the men who attacked the convent.

The Mount Benedict Community and its patrons, however, did not suffer the only losses. There was an additional Protestant casualty, which followed upon the suicide of Henry Creesy. During the period before the trial, the daughter of John Runey, the selectman who had been blamed by many for inaction on the night of the riot, herself went insane. Runey had written a letter to the *Bunker Hill Aurora* claiming that Elizabeth Harrison told him "that the step she had taken, was the consequence of dissatisfaction with her condition as an inmate of the convent; and that she had good and sufficient reasons for being dissatisfied, some of which she should never disclose." But sometime in the early fall, Runey's daughter was herself stricken. In a letter to the *Bunker Hill Aurora* on November 6, 1834, Moffatt noted the irony of Mr. Runey's not understanding the nature of Elizabeth Harrison's illness, asking "Will Mr. Runey's daughter, if she ever recovers, be responsible for what she has said or done since the destruction of the convent?"[29]

According to Catholic sources, "Miss Runey, the daughter of one of the Selectmen of Charlestown . . . had exalted when she saw the burning."[30] However, one of the convent pupils disputes this interpretation, and suggests that for a daughter to witness a father perpetuating such an outrage could lead only to madness. Lucy Thaxter recalled that on the night of the fire,

> Mr. Runey's wife and daughter received us very kindly—and went to look for the other pupils and teachers. . . . We had gone but a little way, when we saw flames bursting from the windows of the room which we had occupied as a school room. Involuntarily we took each other's hands, and gasping for breath, stood for an instant motionless, gazing into each others faces in silent horror. Could such things be? Were they men, with the hearts of fathers and husbands beating in their bosoms? Alas for human nature! Those hearts were turned to stone by the violence of restrained and gratified passion.[31]

The real reason for Mr. Runey's daughter's madness, and her fate after this illness, remains a mystery.

ON AN EARLY DECEMBER DAY in Boston that began with drizzle a black-robed priest mounted the scaffolding where hung a strong rope knotted in a noose. By his side, a swarthy man in a white blouse and pantaloons stood in prayerful resignation, then mounted a stool. The hooded executioner placed the noose around the neck of the prisoner. After the priest and the prisoner uttered a final prayer, the executioner pushed the stool out from under the prisoner's feet. A sound of cracking bone was followed by the silent swinging of the corpse. All together, seven captured Spanish and Portuguese pirates—all Roman Catholics—would be tried and hanged for crimes on the high seas while the trials of the convent rioters were in session.[32] Two days earlier, the sun had been eclipsed at three o'clock in the afternoon, and had looked ominous to many.[33] But the trials that began on December 2, 1834, in Cambridge were not to result in any Protestants swinging from the end of a rope.

The court proceedings were presided over by a distinguished panel of judges, including the Honorable Samuel Putnam and Marcus Morton, and Chief Justice Lemuel Shaw, who a few years later became the father-in-law of the writer Herman Melville. According to contemporary accounts, his appointment four years before the trial had been marked by acclamations. He was described in glowing terms:

> Endowed with eminent abilities, his mind is imbued with a vast store of judicial learning, and embellished with an extraordinary stock of general acquirements. On the bench he is distinguished by his legal attainments, by patience, penetration, impartiality, integrity, and all other elements essential to high and responsible station . . . no magistrate in this commonwealth ever enjoyed more universally the confidence and admiration of his fellow-citizens.[34]

This trial would be one of the most sensational of his career.

Of its start, John Buzzell recalled that his "trial lasted ten days, and during the whole time the court room was crowded to its utmost capacity by men and women, while hundreds were turned away every day. The interest was the greater because I was tried in principal, while all the others were either accessories or indicted for minor offenses."[35] The brick maker was the first to be put to the bar, charged on three counts with the commission of arson during the night time; with entering with intent to steal and having at the time in his possession a dangerous weapon; and with breaking and entering with intent to burn. Each of the offenses was punishable by death.[36]

According to a published account of the trial, Buzzell's lawyers were George F. Farley and S. H. Mann, known for their success in defending desperate causes. The prosecuting attorneys were James T. Austin, the attorney general, and Asahel Huntington, the district attorney. The trial opened with Austin admitting to a weakness in the government's case—the absence of important witnesses. He attributed this dearth to the notifications in circulation threatening death to any who appeared for the prosecution. Apparently, these threats were effective, given the potential pool of over four thousand witnesses who had seen the events unfold.

The twenty-four-count indictment was read, and included all the prisoners—although each prisoner was to be tried separately to give them each a better chance of defending themselves. The indictment stated that the prisoners,

> not having the fear of God before their eyes, but being moved and seduced by the instigation of the devil, on the 11th of August last, with force and arms, did feloniously and burglariously enter with clubs and bludgeons the dwelling house of Mary Anne Ursula Moffatt, otherwise called Mary Edmond Saint George, and steal certain sums of money, break the furniture to pieces, and set fire and burn the dwelling house of said Moffatt, against the peace of the Commonwealth, and contrary to the force of the statute in such case made and provided.[37]

To these charges, Buzzell and the other rioters pleaded not guilty.

The jury was empaneled. As each juror was confronted with Buzzell, Judge Shaw asked him if he had formed any opinion as to the guilt or innocence of the prisoner, or that of any other of the prisoners—or if he had conscientious objections to convicting in a capital case. A jury was selected: William Farris of Natick was named foreman; the others were Abner Albee (Hopkinton), Nathan Brooks (Acton), Joseph Bigelow (Natick), Artemus Cutter (Malden), John Cutting (Weston), Perry Daniells (Hopkinton), Osgood Dane (Lowell), Thomas J. Eliot (Charlestown), Reuben Haynes (Sudbury), John Jones (Weston), and William Rice (Sudbury).

Mr. Huntington, the district attorney, next described the charges. Arson was defined as the malicious and willful burning of the house or outhouse of another. This was punishable by death. Burglary was breaking into the house in the night time, described as an offense which causes terror to the inhabitants and invades and disturbs the basic right of habitation. Until 1805, Huntington noted, burglary was also punishable by death.

After recounting the burning of the convent, Huntington asserted that the government would be able to prove that John R. Buzzell was on the scene at eight o'clock that night, acting as a leader and fomenting the riot, wielding a club and using abusive language—refusing to tell his name to friends of the convent who questioned him, but boasting of beating an Irishman. The government had proof, continued the prosecutor, that Buzzell had been on the convent grounds, and that he had entered the building. J. T. Austin then rose to remark that the court was not in session to try the merits of this or that denomination of Christians, or to decide whether the Catholic institution was a good or bad one. If an unpopular sect is to have its property destroyed by a mob, Austin contended, no one can be safe. The attorney general firmly maintained that it was the duty of every good citizen to condemn such acts.

Mary Anne Moffatt was the first witness to appear in the packed courtroom. She arrived in the black gown that was the full costume of her order. A cross hung from her waist, and a white linen tucker fell over her breast in the front. A white scarf was pulled tightly across her forehead and passed from the temples under her chin, and her black crepe veil fell over her shoulders to below the waist from the crown of her head. When Moffatt entered the courtroom, her veil was drawn forward entirely, concealing her face. Contemporary newspapers gave this account:

> The lady appeared in court in the costume of her order, and closely veiled. One of the counsel for the prisoner (Mr. Farley) expressed a desire that she should unveil. With this requisition the witness hesitated to comply, but on being informed by the court that it was absolutely necessary for her to do so, in order that her voice might be distinctly heard, she reluctantly removed the veil from her features.[38]

The dramatic unveiling began Moffatt's first full day of testimony, which was not complete when the court adjourned at four o'clock. At nine the next morning she would again unveil herself before the court and give testimony against John R. Buzzell.[39] But her main role would be to defend the practices of her community and of Catholicism.

"My name is Mary Anne Ursula Moffatt," she began softly. "I was born in Montreal, and entered the convent at Quebec at age seventeen." In a subdued voice, she noted that after two decades in the Quebec monastery, she came to Boston to begin her life there. The first ques-

*Cartoon depicting the mother superior unveiled, as she appeared at the
trial of John R. Buzzell, ringleader of the rioters.*

tions were posed—about the way nuns chose their religious names—
which she answered in the same quiet voice. The court requested that
she speak more loudly, but Moffatt replied she could not; that she and
the other sisters were still suffering from the ill effects to their health
from the night of the fire. Despite her quiet voice, her words indicated
the key role she played in convent life, as she asserted, "I have entire ju-
risdiction in regard to all the temporal concerns of the institution—I
hire domestics—provisions are purchased by my direction." Moffatt
then noted she had held this station for ten years, and that, as directress,
she personally received the money for the board and tuition.

Austin then asked Moffatt when she first heard that the convent was in danger, and she replied, "I was told on Thursday before the 11th of August, that the Convent would be pulled down." She continued her account this way:

> On Saturday, a paper containing an article, headed "The Mysterious Lady," was sent to the Convent. On Sunday, Mr. Poor, one of the Selectmen, called at the Convent, and told me that the house would be destroyed, if the Mysterious Lady should not be seen. I understood him to refer to Miss Harrison. Next, was a visit from the Selectmen of Charlestown, on Monday, to investigate every part of the institution—they remained about three hours—and examined from the highest apartment to the cellar—looking into bureaus, and even paint boxes—there were five Selectmen—the Mysterious Lady, (Miss Harrison) conducted them over the establishment. It was in the afternoon, between 3 and 4—it might have been 5.[40]

Austin then asked the superior about the night of the fire, carefully avoiding, as she had requested, inquiring about her reasons for returning to the room where she slept. Moffatt testified,

> I did not remove any of my valuables. I removed nothing; there was money there—more than $1000 in my room—in bills—and some silver—all United States money. It belonged to the institution—it came from the pupils. I account to the institution for the money I receive of pupils. I had not yet accounted for this. These men were in the room where the money was. The money was locked in a desk—all in one place—I cannot come nearer to the sum, than more than $1000.

After searching the third-floor dormitories of the main building and both wings to ensure that all pupils had been evacuated, Moffatt stated she then returned to her room. "It was when I came down again," she said, "that I saw the men in my room."[41] As she had requested, the miniature of her mother was never mentioned.

Austin continued to solicit Moffatt's testimony about the value of the property lost on the night of the fire. Moffatt told the court,

There was about $50,000 in property of the pupils—there were three Spanish children, who had great quantities of jewelry. The children were required to have a silver tumbler, tea-spoon, desert-spoon and table-spoon. There were harps and pianos—a harp is worth from 300 to 400 dollars—about 4 in the institution—9 or 10 piano fortes—3 of them perfectly new, and worth from 350 to 370 dollars each—an harmonicon that cost $110.

It was at this point that the attorney general most likely held up the silver ciborium from which Henry Creesy had taken the consecrated hosts on the night of the fire, before carelessly tossing it into the rose bush. Moffatt identified the sacred cup, saying, "We had a chapel—there were silver ornaments." She also identified a pedestal upon which the cross had stood.[42] Moffatt noted that the silver piece had been presented to the institution by the eminent Reverend Cheverus, Archbishop of Bordeaux.[43]

The defense attorney for Buzzell, Mr. Mann, then rose to ask further questions about her role, specifically asking Moffatt what she was called by the other nuns. To this she answered, "I have no other title than Lady Superior—they sometimes call me 'president.' The nuns called me *Ma Mère,* the French for My Mother—they never called me their Divine Mother." In response to his further inquiries, she added, "I do not, in the office I hold, represent the Virgin Mary." Following this impertinent question, Mann then asked, in open court, the even more outrageous question of whether two nuns ever slept in the same bed.[44]

Mann then began his line of questions about Roman Catholic practice, especially confession. When he asked Moffatt if the nuns confessed to her, she replied, "no—they confess to the bishop, or some other priest, once a week." She answered other questions about images in her office ("no—she didn't have an image of the Virgin Mary") and stated that nuns were not restricted in what they could talk about during recreation—but that silence must be observed in the convent after seven in the evening. Mann then continued with further questions about confession, such as about how loud the person must speak. After discussing the role of the priest in confession, Moffatt ceded that "Once a week, we meet to tell our small faults to each other—and I advise the nuns what to do," but denied that the nuns kneel to her or to the bishop. Finally, Moffatt showed her exasperation with the defense attorney's line of questioning, objecting "that she thought the subject of auricular confession had nothing to do with the present case."[45] The focus of these questions, about the female-centered cult of the Virgin Mary, and the perceived antidemocratic practice of confession, only stoked the anti-Catholic feelings in the coutroom.

Moffatt was next asked about the escaped nun, Rebecca Reed. To this she replied,

> She was taken into our community out of charity, so as to be able to get her living by keeping school. She was privy to things which took place in the convent. We restricted her access to the school room. She was much older than the young ladies in it, and very ignorant. She wanted to join us—we promised that if she had strength of mind, constancy and chastity enough, we might take her in, or send her to some other community. She ran off after four months because I would not let her take the white veil.

The questions about Reed's escape led logically to the elopement of Elizabeth Harrison, Sister Mary John. Moffatt testified that Harrison's derangement began two or three days before she left the convent, and she detailed some of the ways this madness was manifested.

"On Saturday," recalled Moffatt, "Mr. Cutter said the mob would destroy the convent if they did not see the nun." She admitted that she told him that the bishop had influence over "ten thousand brave Irishmen" who would destroy the neighbors. Then, on the night of the fire, Moffatt testified, "Mr. Cutter and another person took me forcibly by the arm, and endeavored to carry me into his house; but I resisted, and would not go in. He said my life was in danger from the mob." In his closing statement, J. T. Austin praised Moffatt's performance in court, asking the jury: "Does she show any heat, zeal, or malignity of heart? Nothing, but the sublime spirit of her religion could have presented her in court, so mild, so calm, with such resignation, as she displayed on the stand."[46] Yet it seems the jury was unimpressed.

When Mary Anne Moffatt stepped down, the mistress of the senior class, Mary Barber, Sister Mary Benedict, was called to the stand. Her appearance sent a murmur through the crowded courtroom. Her unusual parentage and upbringing in the cloister after her mother and father became celibate monastics gave her an ethereal manner that added to the porcelain loveliness of her face, which was set off to advantage by her black habit. One local newspaper gave this account of her testimony:

> This beautiful young lady gave her evidence with great dignity and propriety. Her appearance and dignified deportment attracted the attention of the whole court, and her loveliness made many a poor fellow's heart ache.[47]

Another newspaper added,

> This lady is very beautiful. She gave her testimony with great clearness and self-possession, and her manner and language were those of a highly educated and accomplished female.[48]

To the spellbound court, Barber recounted the following,

> On the night of the 11th of August I was awakened between nine and ten o'clock by the Superior, who desired me to dress quickly, and collect the children together and the young ladies. I tried to tranquilize them.

Barber recalled that she stood at the window and saw the mob collecting in front of the convent. They used vulgar language toward the superior, Barber said, mocking her as a "figure-head." When they began breaking the windows, the beautiful nun continued, "I conducted the young ladies to the summer-house at the bottom of the garden. I was unable to save anything."

The crowd in the courtroom waited anxiously for the next testimony, that of Elizabeth Harrison, the "Mysterious Lady," who had returned from Quebec the night before. Timidly, Sister St. John took the stand. Obviously pained, Harrison testified that she had been mentally deranged. "I should have thought it impossible, if any one had told me I should do what I did." She said she could barely remember what happened during her delirium. With this admission, Mr. Farley was proceeding to put other questions, when she suddenly covered her face with a handkerchief and burst into tears. The defense lawyer, under these circumstances, and considering what had been said respecting and considering the witness's state of health, expressed his willingness to refrain from further interrogations. Miss Harrison was then allowed to retire from the court, which she did under the escort of that staunch friend of the convent and devout Catholic, the Russian consul.[49] On December 5, 1834, Bishop Fenwick granted her permission to return to the Quebec monastery.[50]

Fenwick, who had expected to testify on the first day of the trial, was finally called during the second day. As he sat on the witness stand, the clerk held out the Book of the Evangelists and asked Fenwick to be sworn in. When the clerk offered the text, Fenwick asked if it was the usual mode of administering the oath. Protestant witnesses were offered a complete Bible. Surprised, Judge Putnam inquired, "Are you a Catholic?"

"Yes," Fenwick answered. "But the Catholic religion does not prefer one mode [of swearing in] to another."

Chief Justice Shaw then intervened, saying, "It is usual to administer the oath in the form, in which it is considered by the party taking it, to be the most obligatory. Catholics are usually sworn on the Evangelists since it was believed they considered that form more obligatory than any other."[51]

"I have understood that the idea has been common that Catholics do not feel themselves bound unless sworn on the book," Fenwick replied in measured tones. "It is not so. Every well instructed Catholic feels himself bound by an oath, however administered. It has been regarded as a stigma on Catholics that they are required to take an oath differently from other persons. I have no objection to taking the oath in any way the Court may prescribe."[52]

Following this exchange, Fenwick's testimony centered on the circumstances surrounding the elopement of Elizabeth Harrison. When he found her at West Cambridge, Fenwick said, "She was much excited, and looked very haggard." He described her conversation as "unconnected—she would laugh and would then cry immediately."[53] Fenwick noted that he offered to bring her to her family a few days after she returned to the convent, "but she entreated me to let her stay."

Following the questions about Harrison, the bishop was asked about his house on the convent grounds. The purpose of keeping a house there, he said, was "for me to retire to for purposes of study and not to incommode the community in their duties." He added that on the night of the fire, part of his library was burnt, consisting of Latin, Greek, French, and English books. A continued fascination with confession was pursued during the questioning of the bishop, along with questions about celibacy of the clergy. Fenwick noted that he received confessions as any priest does. To another question, he responded, "Priests and bishops do not marry—we live like the Apostles of whom we are the successors."

As the opening of his testimony began with a discussion of Catholic perceptions of Bibles, Fenwick was then asked if the Catholic Church prohibited the use of the Bible. Fenwick replied that Catholics are discouraged from reading any but Catholic Bibles—and that the Church prefers that the reading be guided by a priest. The listening Protestant audience took away the distinct impression that Catholics presumed to censor the direct word of God. Following the testimony of two domestics at the convent, Ann Dunley and Margaret Hulbert, the Catholic testimony concluded.

The next witness called was Warren Draper, Esq., the person said to have furnished the *Mercantile Journal* with the information for the article titled "Mysterious." He was a fireman—and on the grounds on the night of the burning. Draper testified he saw the men break the lower windows with clubs—and watched as chairs, mirrors, and books flew out the window. Some of the rioters, he stated, came to the window with a large book, and shouted, "Here goes the Bible. Set fire to it with a torch."[54]

One of the Charlestown selectmen, Thomas Hooper, appeared next. He tried, he said, to disperse the crowd, telling them that the stories about Elizabeth Harrison's imprisonment were false. But one of the men yelled "That cross must come down!" and began breaking up the furniture. "Now for the torches!" called another. Hooper described his visit to the convent the day before: "We examined the cellar, for there had been reports of some places there where children had been buried. Mr. Kelley, (who is now a prisoner), wanted me to examine the cellar."

Next came Levi Thaxter, father of one of the pupils, Lucy Thaxter.

In driving by the convent, he said, he saw two men near the gate. They stepped up close to it, which looked suspicious. He and his companion Judge Fay got out and went up to them. Loud talking soon commenced. One said a great deal about blood shed by the Roman Catholics and about convents. Buzzell "was not there at first, but spoke thus immediately on his coming. He came striking his hands, and ordered me to take my horse out the gate-way, and said that it would be in the way by an' by. Some one came and put his head into my chaise, and told me in a low voice, that I had better take away my children before Thursday night. I think the prisoner is the tall man . . . he was in a working dress, his pantaloons spattered with mud. Fay asked him his name; the answer he gave was obscene."[55]

At this, Judge Shaw intervened, saying it was of importance that the precise words should be known. Since several ladies, however, were in court, the witness was directed to write upon a piece of paper what he had heard, instead of stating it from the stand. This was done, and the paper passed to Judge Fay, who also wrote the reply made by the "tall man." It was then handed to the jury.[56]

Judge Fay continued his testimony along the same lines as Thaxter's: He saw a man who answered perfectly the description of the prisoner: "he had a thin nose—he was an athletic man . . . he looked like a man just off his work—he had on a low crowned hat."[57] Fay testified that Buzzell said, "'I am the man that whipped the Irishman down on the canal. Didn't I trim him well?' When I heard his voice at the examination, it struck me as being the man I had seen."

Peter Rossiter, the convent's hired man, then walked slowly to the stand. Yes, he said, he belonged to the convent. Buzzell accused him of having beaten a woman, a thing he denied. Buzzell had knocked him down, and beaten him on the Medford Road. When asked why he never pressed charges, Rossiter replied, to the great merriment of the packed courthouse, "I did not *prostitute* him, for fear that he might waylay me, and take revenge." Still confused about the laughter from the spectators, Rossiter stepped down.[58]

Dr. Abraham Thompson was called next and reported that he had dressed Rossiter's wounds, noting that both his face and breast were wounded. Dr. Thompson also testified that the niece of the original foundresses, Sister St. Henry, who had died of tuberculosis about six weeks after the convent was burned, had her life no doubt much short-ened by the events of the night. According to her physician, she was car-ried out of the convent in a great terror, and the shock produced a spasm, resulting in premature death. Thompson would maintain that her death was murder attributed to the perpetrators of the riot.

Two men, Colonel Elbridge Gerry and Edward Phelps, next testified that they saw thirty-five to forty persons milling around the gate. One man wanted them to make a ring and agree upon a plan to attack the building. Another said they had "better wait till another time, and get better organized, as they were but poorly organized then." But then an-other man swore the convent should come down that night. A *tall man,* they testified, then proposed to get some tar barrels. In half an hour he came back with four others, who were carrying several tar barrels. The tall man carried one barrel. The convent's board fence was torn down and the boards laid upon the tar barrels to make a bonfire—this was to raise a signal alarm. Phelps, who had been with Col. Gerry on the night of the fire, confirmed that it was Buzzell who brought the barrels. "I no-ticed him from his being so tall and very noisy, I marked him out as a leader." When asked if he himself assisted in the riot, Phelps became in-dignant, which raised another laugh of derision from the courtroom spectators: "If I did, I should not own it. I think a criminal has no right to criminate himself, I should think it rather an improper question to ask a fellow."59

Henry Buck, aged nineteen, had been an accomplice but turned State's evidence, and was considered the most valuable witness for the prosecution. Buck said he came from Claremont, New Hampshire and lived at Winter Hill with Mr. Adams, the man who sheltered the nuns on the night of the fire. Buck testified that he heard plans for the burn-ing of the convent at least two weeks before. Some people, Buck said, met down near the convent, at the schoolhouse. There were about a dozen present at the meeting. They talked about sending round to get some help to destroy the convent—but the meeting broke up without deciding anything. Four nights later, they had another meeting, with some thirty persons present.

According to Buck, Alvah Kelley told them they had better wait three weeks. On the Saturday before the fire, a barn was burned in Charlestown and a large group of people from that fire were the same that collected at the gate of the convent. Buck also testified that Buzzell was at the gate, with a large club in his hand, and that he appeared to be at the head of the crowd. Every three or four minutes, Buzzell would tell the crowd to give three cheers—and goaded them by saying that they were not men enough to do it. Henry Buck himself was one of the forty or fifty men who entered the convent.

"I assisted in breaking the door in," he testified. "I helped to throw the furniture out, and tear down the inside work of the building." The fires were set in the lower and second stories—the first fire he saw was in the chapel.

"I saw a number put things in their pockets," continued Buck, "I saw one fellow take a watch, put it into his pocket, and carry it off." He said he did not see any silver things taken, or money. Buck recounted that if the rioters found a door shut, they jammed it open with clubs. He also testified that when a fireman tried to stop another building from being set on fire, Buzzell cried out, "Let it alone; don't meddle with it."[60]

When he was cross-examined, Buck also made damaging testimony against Edward Cutter, supporting Mary Anne Moffatt's unfavorable views of him. Buck heard Cutter say that he wished the convent was down—that it hadn't ought to be there—and hoped it would be torn down. Buck was the one who found the small work box belonging to Mary Barber. It was covered with red morocco and had needles and thread in it.[61] Buck also testified that he had escaped from jail after testifying before the grand jury—but was retaken.

An Irish immigrant named James Logan testified that he heard that the torch for the fire came from "No. 13," the engine from the Boston Fire Company. Logan testified that during the riot he was able to save "$400 or $500 worth of property, consisting of four sets of priests' vestments valued at $100 per set, two silver candlesticks, and some other articles and delivered the whole of the property to Bishop Fenwick." When questions were put to him about confession, like Moffatt, this witness became rather choleric, and answered very sharply to some questions put to him by the counsel for the defense.[62]

"Who is your confessor?" asked the defense lawyer.

"I will make you my confessor," snarled Logan.[63]

The moment for which the crowded court had long waited came when Rebecca Reed was called to the stand. The newspapers informed readers what they already suspected about the twenty-one-year-old future authoress: "She looked very interesting and handsome." Most of Reed's testimony centered on countering the mother superior's testimony that it was not the practice of the nuns to prostrate themselves before the bishop. In fact, the trial was a kind of rehearsal for many of the charges that would be laid out in her coming book.

Though most of the crowded courtroom watched these proceedings with rapt attention, some of the jurors found the testimony less than diverting. One newspaper reporting on the trial noted, "We noticed a juror asleep on his post yesterday, and perceived him dozing again to-day. His name will be forthcoming, should this conduct be repeated."[64]

The speeches in court were lengthy and detailed. In his concluding statements, the prisoner's lawyer, Mr. Mann, argued for four hours, unfolding the grounds on which he expected to obtain acquittals. Mann's

*The packed courtroom waited with great anticipation for the testimony of Rebecca Reed, the novice who fled the Ursuline convent in 1832.*

argument was that the rioters should never have been indicted as a group—the statutes were only meant to apply to individuals. The whole transaction should be covered under provisions of the riot act—not arson. The case offered great liability to error—it being so difficult to identify with certainty at night—and this was a capital case. He went on to verbally attack the convent at Mount Benedict. Why bring the lady superior to court, Mann asked, except to make an impression? Her testimony, he said, was of no use in the case. "Although she is highly accomplished, beautiful and well-educated, her testimony is liable to impeachment, by that of the domestic by whom she was followed."[65] Then he continued with a startling assertion:

> We shall show you that the Superior sent her a message that she (the Superior) should commit suicide unless she returned—and then Miss Harrison said, "I shall have the blood of the Superior and my vows on my conscience," and to save herself and the Superior, she returned, on condition that she should remain three weeks, and then should be sent home to her friends in Connecticut. She was treated kindly and changed her mind.[66]

Following this assertion, defense attorney Mann went on to note sarcastically, "All the female witnesses pretended to have colds, caught on the night of the fire." The lawyer then argued that the prisoner at the bar could not be convicted without Catholic testimony—and he would show what Catholic testimony was worth. He first would demonstrate that Peter Rossiter, the convent's hired man, perjured himself. Mr. Mann would show Rossiter did set the dog on the woman and did know why Buzzell struck him. Buzzell first charged him with this unmanly conduct, and then "showed him how things of this kind were settled in this country." When Mr. Mann made this comment, a low murmur of applause could be heard throughout the court.[67]

"As to Peter Rossiter," Mann continued, "I think his testimony should give a tone to the Catholic testimony; he is a fair representative of the 20,000 Irishmen. We submit that you cannot believe a word he has said; he shows the tone of the foreign *imported* testimony; and I class Buck with the imported."[68] Throughout his closing statement, Mann attacked the state's witnesses, Buck and Logan, on the basis of character. John Buzzell's life is now at stake, he argued, "[and] depends on the *imported* testimony of Buck and Logan; and he appeals to you with confidence to say that such evidence as this is not to rob his children of their father and protector."[69]

With this open attack on the value of Catholic testimony, Chief Justice Shaw interceded, saying:

> The Court thinks it proper to remark that the religious faith of the witnesses is not a subject for argument or proof. I may add that not only in conformity with the principles of the law generally, but by our constitution and laws, witnesses of all faiths are placed on the same footing, and each is to stand on his own individual character.[70]

Following Mr. Mann came Buzzell's other lawyer, Mr. Farley, who set his sights on Moffatt. In his summation, Farley laid bare popular feeling about the leader of the convent community, who was described elsewhere as a "termagant scold."[71]

> There is still another witness. To call her the Lady Superior is ridiculous. There are no ranks among us, but those obtained by integrity of virtue. Dress yourself as you please, deform the beauty of the human person by an uncouth garb, and put a cross around your neck, this will not add to your credibility. I cannot believe Mary Anne Moffatt, but I do believe Edward Cutter. Did she tell Cutter that the bishop had 20,000 of the vilest Irish at his control, that they would pull down the houses of him and others, that he might read the Riot Act to them till his throat was sore? Cutter says she did. She denies it. If Cutter tells the truth, did she not mean to mislead?[72]

With this, Farley again warned the jury of the necessity of patient investigation in this case. Peculiarities of character, he said, had been drawn out and exhibited during the previous examination of witnesses, and the jury might occasionally be amused by circumstances which came under their observation. But they should remember that they were not called to decide upon a question of property—but upon a question of human life. Quoting *Hamlet,* Farley asked, should Buzzell be sent from this world "with all his imperfections on his head"? Farley disputed the assertion that Buzzell's voice could be recognized—because the prisoner himself had a bad cold on the night of the fire. He brought up the conflicting testimony of whether or not Buzzell had whiskers. He called into doubt the testimony of Buzzell's whereabouts—and of whether he bragged of beating Rossiter.[73] After his concluding attack on the case of Miss Harrison's insanity, he attempted to undermine the testimony of the state's witness Henry Buck and his accusations against Buzzell, Cutter, and Kelly. Appealing to the notion of reasonable doubt and the value of the Protestant family, Mr. Farley reminded the men of the jury that John Buzzell had a wife and children, and aged parents, and that his life, therefore, should be spared.[74]

Following this four-hour oration, the prosecuting attorney rose and offered the following speech:

> The crowd who have assembled in this Court-house, day after day, look upon it as the trial of John R. Buzzell alone. It is not so. You, Gentlemen,—I say it with all respect,—you are also on your trial before your country, before posterity, and before your God. The events you are investigating are to be recorded in the history of your country; the connection you have had with them is to be recorded also, and both will go down to posterity as long as history shall exist.[75]

Austin began first with the outrage committed on the old Revolutionary fortification of Ploughed Hill—that Mount Benedict had been established

> [O]n one of those hill-tops, which, less than sixty years ago, was consecrated, by the best blood in our country, an altar to liberty and the rights of man. . . . [T]his defendant, and his associates, have left a blackened and mournful memorial of the manner in which that freedom has been exercised by the race that have succeeded them.[76]

Turning and gesturing toward Moffatt, Austin continued,

> Look at the state of this lady. All her property is gone. Everything
> she was worth in the world—her institution—her school, has been
> consigned to the flames. You have seen her here. Do you think she
> came to this court with malignity of heart? She had not mixed
> with the world for many years before she came from her convent
> upon the present occasion, with as much reluctance and alarm as
> would be felt by a modest female in appearing before you habited
> in the costume of her bed-chamber. But an all-controlling power
> was operating on her mind. Nothing but the sublime and holy in-
> fluence of religion could have rendered that woman so calm, so
> mild and so resigned as you behold her. Her testimony was cor-
> roborated by that of the other nuns, and the counsel for the de-
> fence had no objection to make to them but their dress.[77]

With this most moving appeal to the helpless state of the victims, Austin
concluded his remarks, calling for justice to be done.

Chief Judge Shaw now charged the jury in an able and impartial
manner. He explained the statutes under which the prisoner had been
indicted:

> It was laid down by the Court, that, according to the Statute of
> 1830, upon the crime of Arson, if no person was *lawfully* in the
> Convent, when it was set on fire, it did not amount to a capital
> offense, and was not punishable by death. The Attorney General,
> in reference to that principle, called the attention of the Court,
> that Messrs Balfour and Logan, who were in the building when
> fire was applied, were lawfully there; but the Court were of the
> opinion that they were not there lawfully, in the sense of the
> statute, though in other senses, their presence there was both law-
> ful and laudable, viz: to afford protection and assistance, if there
> had been any persons in the Convent requiring it.[78]

Therefore, concluded Judge Shaw in his instructions, this was not technically arson—because no one was lawfully in the building. The judge
next instructed the jury upon the charge of burglary:

It was laid down to be a capital offence to break into a dwelling-house, while there were persons in it, with a felonious intent, and armed with a dangerous weapon. Nor is it necessary to *prove* the intent, if the party be armed with a weapon competent to do the mischief, and does it. The court considered the testimony of the Superior, that she was in the Convent, when the rioters made their forcible entry, corroborated by the other witnesses, and they therefore fell within the scope and effect of the principle. The Court did not sustain the proposition advanced by the Attorney General, that the Nuns, being in the summer house, a part of the curtelage of the dwelling-house, they were in the eye of the law, also in the dwelling house.[79]

The jury were instructed that they could acquit or convict the prisoner upon all, or either of the counts in the indictment, on those that were capital, or on those which were only punishable with confinement to hard labor in the state prison.

The chief justice then entered generally upon the evidence of the cause, with the remark that the commission of the crime had been conceded. The whole case, he maintained, was resolved into a question of identity; and the evidence upon this point he stated to the jury with great impartiality. Reports of the trial note that Shaw abstained scrupulously from all remarks or suggestions calculated in the remotest degree to interfere with the peculiar province of the jury to decide upon the evidence. The chief justice stated that Buzzell was the man identified by the first series of witnesses in front of the convent; yet, after the bonfire, there was no evidence given against him except for that of Buck and Logan, who saw him inside the building with a club in his hand, doing mischief. As Logan's character for truth had been questioned, Shaw instructed the jury to regard principally the *intrinsic* probability of Logan's statement, and its corroboration by the other witnesses, and also the circumstance that he was not contradicted in one fact. A witness may be incompetent from infamy or interest, said Shaw, but a surmise by counsel against a witness ought not to have any bearing on the minds of the jury.

His Honor charged the jury to disregard absolutely and entirely the remark, if they heard it, that stolen property had once been found in Logan's possession, as Logan was not allowed to explain that circumstance, although he brought witnesses into court upon very short notice to testify upon that point. The imputation that he was an accomplice, and a participator in the plunder, continued Shaw, was also unsupported. Shaw noted that Logan went to the convent with a good motive, to look after the safety of the women and children, and took possession of a number of valuable articles to rescue them from destruction.

That this was his design, continued Shaw, was known from the proof that he sent a message to the priest informing him that he had the property in his possession. His being a Catholic, and a regular member of Mr. Byrne's congregation, precluded the presumption that he was in the convent for plunder; and if all the material particulars of his testimony were to be believed, and if he was not mistaken, then the defendant would be guilty. With respect to Buck, Judge Shaw agreed with the attorney general that the tendency of admitting the evidence of accomplices was beneficial to the community, by destroying the confidence in each other which criminals might otherwise feel. The fact that Buck did not intend to implicate Buzzell in every transaction he witnessed—as a corrupt witness might be expected to do—lent further credibility to his testimony. The judge also noted that Buzzell made no attempt to prove an alibi; nor did it appear that he was at his home that night.

With the closing of his instructions to the jury, Judge Shaw sent the men to deliberate in chambers. The large crowd filed out of the courtroom into the darkness of a late December afternoon, and the nuns and Fenwick stepped into a waiting carriage for a gloomy and silent ride home. In the days before the trial began, both Moffatt and Fenwick had expressed pessimism about its outcome. Following the defense's successful diversion of lines of questioning to extraneous issues, they must have known that all hope was lost. But the next day—just before Christmas—they dutifully returned to court, along with throngs of spectators anticipating a verdict. After twenty hours' sequestering, at ten o'clock in the morning, the jury returned to the courtroom. The verdict, delivered coolly by the foreman, was "Not Guilty." At his announcement, the audience erupted into thunderous applause, and the house resounded for several minutes with their claps and stampings.

During the commotion officers sprang in the courtroom and arrested one John Flanders, and another person named Joseph M. Ford, who stood at the time near the bench. Both men were brought to the bar and put upon their oaths to answer for the offense. Flanders stated he was not aware of having committed any impropriety, and did not know the regulations of the court in this respect. Ford, when called to answer, stated he was never in court before when a verdict was declared—and seeing others cheering, thought it proper. The court, under these considerations, and it being the first offense of the kind, ordered them to be discharged. Chief Justice Shaw then remarked that any expression of applause or disapprobation made by any person present, on the declaration of a verdict hereafter, would cause such measures to be taken against the offenders as the law provided. John Buzzell was summarily discharged from custody and retired from the courthouse to the green in front of the building, where he received the congratulations of thousands of his overjoyed fellow-citizens.[80] Years later, Buzzell remarked, "The testimony against me was point blank and sufficient to have convicted twenty men, but somehow I proved an alibi, and the jury brought in a verdict of not guilty."[81]

According to an account in a Catholic source,

When the jury retired to deliberate, and agree on a verdict; at night there were *seven* for conviction and *five* for acquitting; in the morning *ten* desired to *acquit* and *two* to *convict,* and astonishing to relate, those two changed their minds while on the way from their place of deliberation to the court. This is, indeed, a most extraordinary piece of business—one which we know not how to account for, except by a firm conviction that improper influence was used over the jurors; and an unalterable belief that their verdict was given under fear or interest, and not as a result of a careful, unprejudiced, and honest deliberation. . . . There was another indictment pending against Buzzell, and yet, contrary to the well-established rules of law, he was discharged from custody.[82]

Buzzell recalled that "When the verdict was announced such a shout went up as I never heard even in a New Hampshire town meeting. So beside themselves were the spectators that several were fined by the court before order could be restored. Standing at the door were three mounted horsemen who, the instant the verdict was rendered, started on the gallop, one for West Cambridge, one for Boston, and the third for Charlestown, each swinging his hat and shouting, 'Not guilty,' 'Not guilty.'" As Buzzell remembered, the streets were lined with people, and the news of the couriers was received with wild huzzas and cheers. He added that "I afterwards learned that plans had been carefully laid for my rescue from jail had I been convicted, but I knew nothing of it until after my acquittal, and the twenty . . . hours while that jury were thus out were the most solemn of my life."[83]

So overwhelming was the support for Buzzell that one day after his acquittal, he issued the following statement in local newspapers on December 23, 1834:

> John R Buzzell begs leave, through your paper, to tender his sincere thanks to the citizens of Charlestown, Boston, and Cambridge, for the expressions of kindness and philanthropy manifested towards him on his acquittal of the charge of aiding in the destruction of the convent; also, would gratefully remember the gentlemanly deportment of Mr. Watson, while imprisoned in the Charlestown Jail.[84]

T HE ATTORNEY GENERAL renewed his motion to have the remaining cases continued till the next term, and urged as a reason the recent expression of the public feeling on the subject. This was overruled by the court. So Marvin Marcy, Jr., Isaac Parker, Prescott Pond, Alvah Kelley, and the others were placed at the bar for trial, and informed that they had a right to challenge, each, twenty jurors peremptorily.[85] Buzzell was subsequently detained by his counsel until the others had been tried, as it was thought he might be needed as a witness, but he was never called upon.

The trials of this group of convent rioters began immediately. In East Cambridge, on December 31, 1834, the jury again came in at ten o'clock, and returned a verdict as follows: Marvin Marcy, *guilty;* Isaac Parker, *not guilty;* and in the case of Pond and Kelley, they could not agree upon a verdict. The attorney general then informed the court that another indictment had been found against Parker, but he should pursue the prosecution no farther. Parker was fully discharged. The court then decided that Pond and Kelley might be admitted to bail in the sum of $5,000 each, with sufficient sureties. Marvin Marcy was sentenced to state prison for life. The boy who had burned the books at the bishop's lodge was thus made the scapegoat for a community's shame, but even he was pardoned, after serving a few months, by the governor.

Marcy's lawyer, Mr. Prescott, immediately filed a motion for a new trial, arguing that during the proceedings, the jury had separated. Prescott contended that at different times, under the care of an officer, members of the jury had visited a barber's shop, where they had read the *Morning Post,* in which evidence of the case was incorrectly reported. To support this contention, an affidavit from the barber was produced. Prescott also called for testimony, under oath, from Thomas Gill, Jr., who was employed as a reporter at the paper. He testified that the reports furnished by him to the *Post* had contained "misapprehensions of the case," and he said that in some cases, the reports had been misprinted. Prescott also produced the affidavits of several persons to show that part of the jury had, under the care of an officer, visited the glass works, where there was conversation respecting the trial, which might have been heard by them. Finally, Prescott unsuccessfully argued that since Marcy was indicted together with Pond and Kelley, he was therefore entitled to a new trial with them.

Following these arguments, the attorney general moved that the court should not have proceeded to pass sentence, as there were other indictments against each of the prisoners which had not been disposed of, but that all the prisoners should be remanded. With this, the court adjourned until 9 o'clock the next morning, to decide whether Pond and Kelley should be admitted to bail, another indictment having been found against them.[86]

Seventeen-year-old Marvin Marcy, Jr., who after the night that he "auctioned" the books at the bishop's lodge had attempted to change his name and ship out of New Bedford, became the only rioter to be convicted in the burning of the Ursuline convent in Charlestown. His heartbroken father had died while Marcy was in prison awaiting trial, and now he was sentenced to three days' solitary confinement and to hard labor in the state prison during his natural life. On the afternoon of his conviction, about three o'clock, the boy was discovered insensible on the floor of his cell. The prison physician, Dr. Anson Hooker, was immediately called in, and Marcy could not be roused for some time. Reports of the incident noted that the cause of his illness was not known, but Marcy had been frequently heard to say that

he never would be carried to the States' Prison.—Dr. H. states there is no appearance of poison; some suppose he has eaten ground glass. In the midst of the medical examination, the sheriff called to convey him to Charlestown. He of course was not removed.[87]

Like Henry Creesy, John Runey's daughter, and his own father, the teenage Marcy became a victim of psychological distress after his conviction. On February 23, 1835, Dr. Hooker wrote that

Young Marcy, confined in East Cambridge Jail, was attacked on Thursday between one and two o'clock with delirium, and has continued in that state till this morning, occasionally struggling violently, and at other times remaining very quiet for some minutes. . . . I do not perceive his attack to be induced by pounded glass, or any other poison, but to have been brought on by the great anxiety he has felt about the decision of the court—so great as to prevent his sleeping but very little in the past week, by the sentence of the court, and by the agony of his mother, sister, and friends, the recent death of his father, and his great horror of the State Prison. Signed A. Hooker, Physician, Cambridge Jail. NB— He will recover in a few days.[88]

On February 26, 1835, Mary Anne Moffatt, having read the report of "poor Marcy's decline in the newspaper," wrote directly to Marcy's physician, Dr. Hooker.

I am *deeply pained* that any one should suffer on our account; and it was my intention, from the commencement, to do all in my power, to obtain pardon for any of the criminals who might be sentenced to punishment; for I am well convinced they knew not what they did. Moreover, Marcy was not one of those who *con-*

*certed the plot:* he was young, and joined in the riot for *sport,* as many other boys would do. I *beg* of you to *console* him and his afflicted mother, and to say that I will *supplicate* the governor for his release. My sisters, as well as myself, would feel miserably, if his sentence were put into execution. Have the kindness to let me know by the bearer, if he is better to-day.[89]

The next day, true to her word, Moffatt wrote to Governor Davis:

We have felt miserably, since hearing of Marcy's sentence, and of the effect which it has had upon him. I therefore solicit *most earnestly,* in the name of my Community, that he may be pardoned; and, in granting this request, you will, Hon. Sir, confer on us a favor that can never be forgotten. I believe he was a thoughtless boy, and knew not the extent of the mischief he was doing. If he is released, he may have received a salutary lesson, and *we* shall be relieved of many a *heartfelt pang.* I take the liberty of *entreating* that he may not be sent to the State's prison, but enlarged *as soon as possible.* For this kindness, we should be *very* grateful.[90]

To the citizens of Boston and Charlestown, Marcy's sole conviction was a clear injustice. A petition for his pardon was signed by upwards of five thousand persons, including Bishop Fenwick and Moffatt.

In February, while Marcy remained in distress, the trial of Pond and others was continued from the sitting of the supreme court in Cambridge to Concord in April. Meanwhile, the Catholic Church's petition for indemnification moved forward. An appropriation of $10,000 was at first approved by the state legislature, but then voted down. In response to the denial of indemnification, an angry citizen wrote the following:

We cannot refrain from comparing this indignant condemnation to the sorrow of a certain company, in which the misfortune of a companion was mentioned. Every one declared that he was exceedingly sorry—filled with regret, &c. About two or three thousand dollars would afford relief. One of the least wealthy said, "Gentlemen, we are all very sorry, but the value of that sorrow has not been estimated. I shall begin. Let us relieve our companion. I am sorry five dollars. I should like to know the worth of your sorrow." One, and another, and another stole away, and it was found that their regret was like the vindication of the honour of the commonwealth of Massachusetts—VALUELESS![91]

Like Buzzell, the other rioters, including Hadley, Budd, Pond, and Kelley, were acquitted, and many of their accomplices discharged without trial. Though it was proven in the trial that Budd, in a conversation with a woman named Maria Hull asserted, "We are going to burn all the Catholic Churches" and admitted that he went to the fire and described his part in the affair, no one was convicted. Reminiscent of the celebrations upon the release of John R. Buzzell, when the acquittals of the other convent rioters were announced, young men in Boston fired fifty guns as a *feu de joie*.[92]

The following October, the only convicted rioter, Marvin Marcy, was pardoned and released. Acting Governor Samuel T. Armstrong remitted the sentence—but attached strict conditions. Marcy was not fully restored to citizen rights, but had to serve a term of probation:

> Under full consideration in the premises, we do hereby remit to the said Marvin Marcy the residue of the punishment which he was sentenced to endure, on condition that within one day of his liberation from the State Prison he becomes bound to some good citizen of this Commonwealth, until he should have reached the full age of twenty-one years, to learn some useful trade; and within the period of said apprenticeship shall not come within the distance of fifteen miles of the city of Boston,—of which all our judges, justices, magistrates, and officers of every denomination, and especially the Warden of the State Prison, are to take notice.[93]

On October 9, 1835, Bishop Fenwick recorded the following entry in his diary:

> Weather dry & clear. Marcy, the young vagabond who was condemned to the State's Prison for having been concerned in the burning of the Convent last year was pardoned this day by the

Lieutenant Governor & let out of jail. The Citizens of Charlestown fired *feu de joie* on the occasion.

Though the historical record is mostly silent on Marcy's life after this
dramatic event, a source dated 1870 averred, "Marcy is now a useful citizen of New Hampshire."[94]

## CHAPTER SEVEN

# THE ASHES SCATTER

O N THE DAY AFTER the fire, Bishop Fenwick sent carriages for the nuns, who were scattered around various houses in Charlestown. They were brought back to Boston to lodge with the Sisters of Charity, where they received "every attention that can possibly be imparted to them & every comfort which a small contracted house can afford."[1] Within ten days, the bishop was actively looking to purchase a new home for the Ursulines. His diaries from August 21 to September 10, 1834, show almost a daily effort to find a new location. On August 28, Mary Anne Moffatt's forty-first birthday, Fenwick wrote, "No house yet. The *B'p* visits the Nuns, this being the birth day of the Superior. Poor congratulation!" The eight Ursulines would remain in the small house of the Sisters of Charity for two months.

While the bishop was in Washington and Baltimore between September 10 and October 11, 1834, Moffatt appears to have made two decisions—one that the bishop may never have known about and one that he would find out about when he returned. The first involved a mysterious burial noted in the records of St. Augustine's cemetery in South Boston. According to the description of the devastated convent written by the Harvard freshman Theodore Russell on August 31, the tomb on the convent grounds remained just as it had been left on the night of August 11, with the bodies still in disarray. Bishop Fenwick visited the site only once on September 3, 1834 before his departure to the southern states, and his diary records no action on his part during the visit— just a lament over the devastation.

But on October 7, 1834 a strange listing appears in the *Index for South Boston Cemetery, 1850.* It says, *"Ryan, Mary. d. October 7, 1834 from the Ursuline convent, age 38."* The *Index,* in fact, lists two burial records for Mary Ryan, the convent's original superior, who died June 4, 1825. In the first listing, no age is given, though other records indicate she was born in 1785. After her death, Mary Ryan was buried in the South Boston cemetery, and her body moved to Charlestown when the new mausoleum was built on the Mount Benedict grounds. Had she lived to see the destruction of the convent, she would have been forty-nine years old. Her sister Catherine would have been forty.[2] Moffatt's beloved friend, Mary and Catherine's younger sister Margaret, who had also been buried first in St. Augustine's and then moved to Charlestown, was twenty-seven years old when she died in 1827. In 1834, she would have been only thirty-four.

It appears that, with the bishop away, Mary Anne Moffatt arranged to have one of the bodies removed from the desecrated tomb at Charlestown. But whose? Decently burying the original superior, Mary Ryan, in St. Augustine's would have shown respect for the office. However, it is also possible that Moffatt arranged to have her dear Margaret's body removed from the Mount Benedict mausoleum and quietly interred at St. Augustine's. Significantly, this burial took place four days before Bishop Fenwick returned. It is also unclear where the other six bodies were ultimately reburied—there are no records for this in the Catholic cemetery in Charlestown, or in St. Augustine's. Less than two weeks later, on October 18, the niece of the original foundresses, Mary Quirck, Sister St. Henry, succumbed to the tuberculosis that had plagued the other members of her family, and she was buried with great ceremony beneath the altar in the chapel of St. Augustine's. Five thousand persons joined in her funeral procession, and the bishop officiated. It seems that no one but Moffatt knew of the quiet burial the previous week of one of Sister St. Henry's three aunts.[3]

The very evening the bishop returned from his month-long visit to the South, he hastened to the house of the Sisters of Charity. To his surprise, he wrote, he found only Mary Anne Moffatt remaining in Boston, "the religious having removed to Roxbury in the house of George Dearborn which the Superior had taken for 18 months. After just saluting the Sisters the *B'p* at the instance of the Lady Superior accompanies her to her new abode with the Russian Consul, Mr. Kielchen. It being late he returns immediately."[4] Two days later, he returned to Dearborn's house, known as Brinley Place, to see the nuns in their new Roxbury establishment. Sister St. Henry, the nun dying of tuberculosis, was "very low, though cheerful." After examining the premises, Fenwick recorded that he was "not quite satisfied with them. The house, though large, is not very convenient. Yet, it may answer for a time."[5] With seeming irritation he would later note that instead of purchasing a property as he had wished them to do, they had rented, and "are compelled to occupy a house not their own and for which they have to pay a very high rent although much too small for their present number."[6]

Brinley Place is described in Francis S. Drake's *The Town of Roxbury: Its Memorable Persons and Places* (1878) as once "one of the grandest houses in Roxbury." The house was built about 1723 by Colonel Francis Brinley and sat on an estate of eighty acres.[7] To the rear was a large garden, filled with rare trees and beautiful shrubbery.[8] During the Revolutionary War, it had served as an encampment for George Washington's army. Drake includes a description by Mrs. Emily Pierpont

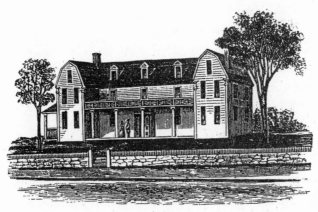

BRINLEY PLACE.

*Brinley Place in Roxbury, where the Ursulines tried to reestablish their school, was threatened with destruction by a mob.*

Lesdernier from her book *Fannie St. John* that details the estate when it was in its glory:

> [I]t was situated in the midst of a large domain of park and wooded hills, and presented a picture of grandeur and stateliness not common in the New World. There were colonnades and a vestibule whose massive mahogany doors, studded with silver, opened into a wide hall, whose tessellated floors sparkled under the light of a lofty dome of richly painted glass. Underneath the dome two cherubs carved in wood extended their wings, and so formed the centre from which an immense chandelier of cut glass depended. Upon the floor beneath the dome there stood a marble column [and there were] grand staircases at either side of the hall entrance. All the panelling and woodwork consisted of elaborate carving done abroad, and made to fit every part of the mansion where such ornamentation was required. Exquisite combinations of painted birds and fruit and flowers abounded everywhere, in rich contrast with the delicate blue tint that prevailed upon the lofty walls. . . .[9]

The cherub is a popular symbol with the Ursulines of Quebec, frequently found in the artwork of the nuns there, and perhaps it was the cherubs on the chandelier, in addition to the other opulent features of the house, that appealed to Moffatt. The nuns, however, had lost everything in the Charlestown fire, and had next to nothing with which to furnish it. At their request, Bishop Fenwick advanced them $500 for the purpose of purchasing necessities.[10] In addition to the $3,000 sent to the nuns by the city of New Orleans, the diocese of that city donated $792.[11]

The house was in need of renovation, and some of the pupils had already begun boarding there.[12] The safety of the students became a great concern once the trials were underway in December, and this is one of the reasons the superior requested to be excused from testifying. In a letter to her lawyer, Moffatt wrote:

> We feel an obligation to take every precaution for the safety of the children, confided to our care. Should any accident happen,

our loss would likewise be very great, for we are much in debt, all the furniture and instruments having been got on credit. It is true, everything has been insured, but that can have no effect, in case of destruction by a mob. As the place is quite unprotected, I feel continual alarm.[13]

The move from Charlestown to Roxbury did not shield the nuns from harassment. The threats against them continued, and required them to rely on the protection of about a dozen men, many of them Protestants, who became known as the Roxbury Committee of Vigilance. It was formed on December 15, 1834 when the sheriff of Middlesex County, B. F. Varnum, wrote to Norfolk County Sheriff John Baker II: "Dear Sir— . . . I have received information, that threats have been made to pull down or destroy the building, used a[s] a Nunery, at Roxbury."[14] With this knowledge, the Roxbury selectmen appointed a nightly patrol of six to watch the building, and formed a secret committee of three to collect information about threatened attacks. Part of their plan involved regular meetings with the superior, who knew about the threat against her convent at least a week before the bishop.[15]

Just before Christmas 1834, "a young gentleman of respectability in Roxbury" named Mr. Brewer called on the bishop with ominous news: "that a new riot was hatching having for object the destruction of the present Convent there." Mr. Brewer, however, assured the bishop that "a sufficient guard of young men would be on the spot for any emergency." On hearing this, Fenwick hastily called a meeting at the Cathedral of the Holy Cross in Boston, "thinking that the Mob in all probability would make an attempt to fire the Church the same night." At seven o'clock that evening, a large group assembled and formed ranks to protect all the Catholic properties in the area.[16]

The next day, while the trial of John R. Buzzell was winding down, rumors abounded that the convent in Roxbury would be attacked by a mob and lie in ruins by Christmas Eve. Once again, threatening placards had been posted around town, and the Catholics grimly prepared for their defense.

Mr. Brewer calls on the *B'p* to let him know that he has procured a sufficiency of arms & ammunition & men to use them. Com-

modore Elliott calls also to inform him that an order has been received by the Secretary of the Navy charging him not to interfere
in case of a riot, but to leave matters solely to the Civil authorities. We live in awful times.[17]

While Commodore Elliott was barred from raising a guard for Moffatt,
the Roxbury Committee of Vigilance prepared for her defense. It consisted of John J. Clarke, Ebenezer Seaver, and other prominent and influential citizens. Captain Spooner's company guarded the premises.
The company's orders, which were made public, were "to fire ball-car-
tridges only." This information seems to have given pause to the would-
be rioters.[18]

Mary Anne Moffatt was largely in charge of handling matters with
the committee. Documentation of this group suggests she took a very
active role in the protection of her convent, acting as a kind of general,
and providing for the needs of her army under the cherubic chandelier
in the great hall of Brinley Place. The names of the nightly watch were
handed to the superior and they reported to her. She, in turn, offered
the use of the mansion's hall, with a fire and refreshments, for the guard.
The superior reported to the committee that she "could not express the
gratitude she felt for the energetic steps which had been taken by the
Citizens of Roxbury for her protection—a kindness greater than she
had ever experienced before."[19] The committee secretly voted that the
watchword *Protection* be reported only to the superior. When this pass-
word was given, Moffatt knew that a member of the Committee of Vigilance was at her door, and could be safely admitted.[20]

The tension continued for several weeks through the Christmas season. On Christmas Day, the snow fell heavily as the bishop left Boston
at six in the morning to celebrate Mass for the Ursulines at Brinley
Place. After a silent night, he was able to record,

Nothing has as yet been attempted against Brinley Place or either
of the Churches. A man was, however, (the servant of Commodore Elliott, a Catholic) severely beaten yesterday in Pond
Street by a gang of Ruffians for no cause but that of being an
Irishman & a Catholic.[21]

But despite the relatively quiet Christmas, on December 29, 1834, Bishop Fenwick wrote to his brother:

> The new asylum of the Ursulines was to have been broken in upon again and the house set fire to. But the timely guard set to protect it defeated the scheme. All is again quiet. Certainly, some lives will be lost in case of another attack; for our good Irishmen are now wound up to a point where if you go one step further the chord will snap.[22]

Many of the Boston newspapers reacted with indignation at this new threat against the Ursulines. The *Boston Centinel* reported that Buzzell's acquittal had "emboldened the incendiaries to devise a similar demonstration upon the quiet retreat of the Ursuline Community at Roxbury." A Catholic newspaper congratulated the town of Roxbury, and commended the Committee of Vigilance.

> [T]he inhabitants of that town assembled at the Town Hall, on Tuesday evening last, which was filled to overflowing. After adopting some spirited resolutions, they chose a committee of vigilance and protection, consisting of twelve gentlemen, who, we are glad to learn, have taken such energetic and decisive measures, that should any person or persons attempt an outrage upon the building, now occupied by the Ursuline Community, they will meet with such a reception as they deserve. This is as it should be, and we congratulate our brethren of Roxbury upon their promptness and decision on this occasion, which show that their hearts are in the right place, and that their hands are ready to act when their rights as citizens are threatened.[23]

But even with the formation of this committee, and the descent of a deep freeze on New England, the new year of 1835 began with continued threats against the Roxbury convent. On January 3, the bishop recorded that

> This day the two Brewers of Roxbury, Father & Son call on the *B'p* to apprize him that information had been received in Rox-

bury that tonight the Convent on Brinley Place is to be attacked by a Mob. The *B'p* is satisfied with the precautionary measures adopted in Roxbury in case of such an event.

In the intense cold of the next morning, the bishop set out to say Mass at Brinley Place, not certain that it would still be there:

Jan'y 4th (Sunday) . . . The *B'p* repairs to Roxbury—is happy to see the house of the Ursulines still standing notwithstanding the alarm of yesterday. Nothing was attempted during the last night. He says Mass, during which Mr. Kielchen, the Russian Consul, enters, for the purpose of hearing it. He had been one of the Committee of Vigilance during the night & had watched with a number of others apprehensive of an attack. He breakfasts with the *B'p* after Mass & returns with him to Boston.

The cold snap lasted almost a week in Boston, freezing the harbor almost to the Narrows, "a circumstance which has not occurred for the last ten years."[24] The following Sunday, the bishop again went to celebrate Mass for the Ursulines at the Roxbury convent, only to learn that

during the whole of the preceding night bands of ruffians in sleighs were passing, repassing & stopping in front of the house where the Ursulines were now lodged, using the most profane language & singing aloud; down with the Convent! & the most lascivious & indecent songs to the great annoyance of the poor religious. This practice, he learns, has been in operation for the last week. The poor Nuns are disconsolate—not having enjoyed any rest the preceding night. None of them are ready for confession or communion this morning from the state of confusion into which they are thrown in consequence of these proceedings.[25]

With disgust, the *New England Magazine* also reported these doings, saying,

On the last Fast-day, a host of these rioters, in gigs, drove by the dwelling, and bellowed forth volleys of abuse, shouting names too vile to be repeated—applicable, doubtless, to their own female associates.[26]

By mid-January 1835, the most serious threats to the convent seemed to have passed, and some of the nuns had returned from Quebec to work at the school. By January 20, 1835, the Catholics were preparing to file a request with the legislature for indemnification of their losses.[27] The Catholic cemetery in Charlestown remained a target for threatened violence and the bishop proceeded with his plans to establish a house for a caretaker there.[28] Violence against Catholics now seemed to be erupting in other areas. Local newspapers reported that in Lowell, Massachusetts, the cemetery was attacked and monuments destroyed. In Wareham, the house in which a number of Catholics were assembled with their priest for the purpose of performing divine service was assailed by men calling themselves "Convent Boys." Their threats compelled the priest to desist and the congregation to disperse.[29]

THE DISAGREEMENT OVER the rental and security of Brinley Place opened a rift between Bishop Fenwick and Mary Anne Moffatt. He may not have approved of her supervising an armed guard of men, the Committee of Vigilance. Or maybe these additional threats from hostile Protestants were more than he could bear. Fenwick earlier had been strangely blind to the faults of Rebecca Reed, and slow to ascribe violent outcomes to anti-Catholic hostility. He now focused the blame for his problems squarely on Moffatt. Because the superior had been such an object of the rioters' animosity, and had, by her independence of will, seemingly brought on herself additional problems in Roxbury, Fenwick's heart hardened against her during those subzero days of January. He began to believe that if he could get rid of Moffatt, his problems would be solved. On January 28, 1835, Fenwick wrote to Bishop Signay of Quebec, and again sent three of the sisters, Sister Mary Ursula, Sister Mary Joseph, and Sister Mary Austin, back to Quebec because the house at Brinley Place was too small for the nuns and about twenty-five boarders—and because of the continuing harassment. In the same letter, Fenwick confessed his pessimism over the success of the reparations being sought in the Legislature for indemnification,

If the Legislature grant us a sufficient sum to rebuild that establishment, all will again be well; but if they refuse, which is very probable considering the Puritan's spirit which prevails with the members generally, it will not be possible for the Ursulines to continue any longer in this Diocese. They will not be able to live as a community ought to live; & therefore I should be very unwilling to compel them to remain where they will be continually exposed to every persecution, & where, in fact, they will be able to do no good. Under such circumstances I shall advise them to seek some other asylum where some respect is paid to the laws, and where they may live in peace.[30]

By the end of January 1835, Bishop Fenwick was already skeptical that the Ursulines should remain in Boston, even if the entire convent could be rebuilt with donations.

But alas, even supposing this, what greater security will the second convent have than the first? Will they not have it as much in their power to demolish the one as they had to demolish the other? It is true, if a law be passed during this session making the town responsible for the act of the townsmen there will be some security so far as regards the loss of property, but I see none for the Nuns themselves. . . . For my own part I have but little expectation that things will wear a more favorable aspect than they do now; but all is in the hand of God . . ."[31]

With the writing of this letter, the bishop was already forming plans to dismiss Mary Anne Moffatt and the Ursuline sisters from the diocese of Boston.

On Sunday, March 1, 1835, the bishop took a late winter sleigh ride to Brinley Place, where he celebrated Mass. Afterwards, he asked to speak privately with Mary Anne Moffatt, recording in his journal:

After Mass he proposes to the Superior & recommends strongly the propriety of her removing with her remaining Sisters to Quebec & of there remaining till better times. He sees the gradual decline in the health of the Sisters (Ursulines) & deems a change of this kind under existing circumstances necessary for their health.

The proposal was not well received by Sister St. George, who had already managed to rebuild her school to twenty-five boarders.[32] In fact, Fenwick wrote, "The Superior is violently opposed to the measure; yet, the *B'p* means to insist upon it deeming the change absolutely necessary."[33] This was the opening sally in a three-month battle between the superior and the authorities of the Roman Catholic Church, the bishops of Boston and Quebec. While St. George had been successful in supervising her knights to provide Brinley Place adequate protection, ultimately she could not muster the forces that would allow her to remain in Boston and rebuild her school.

Two weeks later, the bishop received help in his efforts to remove the band of Ursulines from Roxbury. It came in the form of a letter from Madame St. Henry McLaughlin, superior of the Ursulines in Quebec. In that letter she, too, urged "the removal of the Ursulines in Boston to that city or to the *Convent at Three Rivers* in Canada." Fenwick penned his hearty agreement with these sentiments in his journal: "The *B'p* consents to the measure & is resolved to take the necessary steps without delay to effect the object. He sees & is more convinced daily of the necessity of this measure in the existing state of things."[34] The state of relations between Moffatt and Fenwick at this point can be easily imagined, though Fenwick's journal does not go into much detail. Earlier that year Moffatt had remarked, "I think it would be a difficult matter for any man to control me!"[35] The bishop was beginning to see the truth of this statement. On March 17, when Fenwick received his yearly St. Patrick's Day invitation to spend the day with the Irish Charitable Society, he did not decline, as usual, in favor of spending the day with the Ursulines. Instead, he remained at home, spending a meditative day alone.[36]

The week after the first of many Catholic petitions for indemnification of their losses in the Charlestown fire was rejected by the legislature "by a great majority in the lower house"[37] and as the trials were winding down in favor of the convent rioters, the beleaguered Fenwick had a new public relations disaster to contend with: the publication of the narrative of Rebecca Reed. On March 19, 1835, Fenwick wrote:

Yesterday an infamous Book teeming with calumnies against the Ursuline Convent was issued from the Press in the City got up under the ostensible sanction of the noted Miss Rebecca Reed, who left said Convent in an abrupt manner in Jan. 19, 1832, & of whom mention has been already made. The Presbytarians & Calvinists are evidently at the bottom of this villainy, anxious to destroy the reputation of the Convent after having already destroyed its building. But some of the many lies the book contains are so absurd that little or no credit will be given to any of its forgeries by the respectable portion of this community.

The same day as Bishop Fenwick made this entry, he wrote to Bishop Signay in Quebec with a renewed determination to send the Ursulines back to Canada:

> . . . I have to acknowledge the receipt of your very kind & obliging favr and to express my gratitude for the generous offer you have made in behalf of our poor desolate & afflicted Nuns. This offer [to take them at Quebec and Three Rivers] I accept with transports of joy convinced that in the existing state of things it would be more than madness to detain them any longer. The Legislature has refused to grant our petition for indemnity— poverty already begins to stare us in the face—the health of all is gradually diminishing from the load of care & anxiety which continually press upon them. Add to this the want of a proper house, a house adapted to religious exercises &c. &c. so that I see no other method to put a period to all anxiety on their account than to deliver them over to that protection which alone can secure them the inestimable blessing of peace.

But to his friend Bishop Signay, Bishop Fenwick also confessed his concern that this would not be so easily accomplished, because of Mary Anne Moffatt's "violent opposition" to the remove. To enlist Signay's aid in the matter, he asked Moffatt's supervising bishop to revoke her obedience, or orders to stay in Boston, which she had been granted until 1840:

I see no obstacle in the way but *a want of consent to it* on the part of our good Mother who cannot bear the idea of removing from this quarter. To effect the object therefore it will be necessary for your Lordship to address her a letter and to withdraw the *Obedience* which she has been granted, stating for reasons *that I see no prospect at present of having such an establishment as is fitting for religious of the Ursuline order, and your unwillingness to expose her any longer in an unprotected state.* As soon as I have notice of such a communication from your Lordship I shall immediately direct the others to repair to Canada as soon as possible. I have calculated that immediately after Easter they may be in readiness to depart. I have lately addressed a letter to the excellent Mad. St. Henry on the same subject & to the same effect.[38]

Moffatt, who was only on loan from the Quebec monastery, would find herself no longer welcome in Boston by her sponsoring bishop, Fenwick, and in direct violation of her Canadian superiors and her vows should she persist in the insubordination of remaining in Boston. But even in the face of this powerful pressure to depart, ironically, Moffatt had a new ally in the most unlikely of persons: Rebecca Reed. The publication of Reed's book, which charged the Roman Catholics with plotting forced kidnappings of unwilling nuns to Canada, probably helped to buy Moffatt the additional three months that she managed to remain in Massachusetts. Reed's accusations made it imperative that Moffatt herself agree to willingly leave the diocese.

On March 20, 1835, Fenwick again visited Brinley Place, "principally with a view of urging it upon Mad. St. George the Superior of the Ursulines, to leave this section of the Union where they experience nothing but trials & contradiction and withdraw for a time to Canada. The *B'p* is fully impressed with the necessity of this measure & intends to insist on the adoption of it."[39] Moffatt was clearly feeling the building pressure, for the next day, March 21, the superior wrote two letters, one to the bishop of Quebec and one to James T. Austin, her lawyer and the attorney general, in response to the possibility of her being recalled. To Bishop Signay, she wrote,

Understanding from the Rt. Rev. *B'p*. Fenwick, that you are alarmed about our situation, and wish me, as well as my sisters, to go to Quebec, it appears to me a duty to let you know there is no danger at all; we are never molested; our health is excellent; we have a fine school, the authorities are desirous we should remain, and the glory of God, as well as the good of Religion, seem to require it. Under these circumstances, I am sure your Lordship will not urge, or even wish us to abandon the work of God, particularly as we are told by influential gentlemen, that, if we once leave, we can never again expect to be re-established. The *total extinction* of the Ursuline Order, in the New England States, is a thing of great moment, as well as a great responsibility, seeing what influence it already has had, in removing prejudices against our holy religion. The seeds, now sown, will fructify in the ensuing generation; and I believe none of my Community will shrink from the prospect of labors, when posterity will reap so *plentiful* a *harvest.* Be so good, my Lord, as to take all these points into consideration, and I doubt not that you will concur in the expediency of our not abandoning our post. PS The Rt. Rev. Bp. Fenwick did not inform me, until yesterday, that you wished us to leave, and that you made this decision, fearing our health might suffer, and the Comy had had a little alarm but the physician has decided, if I go north, that I will not live one year, and that only a warm or very temperate climate can agree with me. I hope to be able to send for my four sisters, who are at Quebec, in the month of July—[40]

Moffatt was no doubt overstating the case in several places in an attempt to convince Signay to let her remain in Boston. Certainly, to claim that the community was "never molested" and that their health was "excellent" stretched the truth. The superior's assertion that their presence helped remove prejudice against the Catholic religion, though, probably represented what she believed—that the destruction of the convent had roused sympathy for them among the people of New England. Having alerted Church authorities that she had been discussing her options with friends outside the hierarchy, the "influential gentlemen" to whom she alluded, Moffatt also wrote to her attorney, asking for his advice. Here too she admits she had sought out secular opinions to supplement those being offered by her Roman Catholic supervisors:

For a few weeks past, the Rt. Rev. Bishop has been advising us to leave for a year or eighteen months, and he seems inclined to think this would have the effect of turning the public feeling in our favor. He tells me that after we are gone, the storm will blow over, and that we will be requested to return. But the parents of the pupils and our other friends, advise the contrary. They say our leaving would have a bad effect, and that we could never be reestablished, for which reason it would be better for us to remain, though we might receive no remuneration for our losses at the destruction of the convent. If you will be so kind as to favor me with your advice, you will Hon. Sir, much oblige . . . Signed the Superior—PS Our man will call for the answer tomorrow afternoon.[41]

By seeking outside advice, and alerting several lay persons that she wished to remain, Moffatt in effect was ensuring that she could not be forced to leave against her will. That she had written to friends was a source of irritation for the Catholic authorities, and made the issue of her removal a delicate matter. In late March, Bishop Fenwick was still attempting to persuade Moffatt of the wisdom of this step:

MARCH 25TH (Annunciation) Cold & clear. The *B'p* sets out at six OC'k for Brinley Place to give Mass to the Nuns—good sleighing. After Mass uses every argument in his power to induce the Superior to go to Quebec & leave Boston where there is so great excitement against her & her establishment without effect. He is determined notwithstanding that the other Nuns at least, shall go, so well is he convinced of the propriety of the measure . . .

The next day, with the weather bright and clear, the bishop recorded in his journal the good news shared by the Russian consul, who had recently returned from Canada, that there was now an additional faster means for travelers to reach Quebec from Boston. He painstakingly recorded the route and costs, and was clearly calculating that this new road might more quickly rid him of his problem with the nuns:

The *B'p* understands through Mr. Kielchen that the new route to Quebec through the state of Maine is completed & that stages travel it weekly. The following is the route from Boston with the prices, viz. From Boston to Portsmouth 49 miles—cost of stage 12S, 6D. From Portsmouth to Portland 47 miles—cost is 12S, 6D—From Portland to Augusta 55 miles; cost 1—From Augusta to Milburn 30 miles; cost 7S, 6D. From Milburn to the Forks of the Kenebec 45 miles; cost 10S. From the Forks of the Kennebec to Hiltons 40 miles; cost 12S, 6D—From Hilton to Quebec 33 miles; cost 1, 10S. Whole distance from Boston to Quebec by this route 355 miles; whole cost 5 (pounds), 5. It takes four Doll's to make a pound. The distance is now performed by the regular stage in six days . . . [42]

For Fenwick, the notion that six days could rid him of his problem had strong appeal. Assistance for the plan arrived two days later, in the form of the revocation of St. George's obedience by the bishop of Quebec. In an accompanying letter, Signay confided to Fenwick that he had acted quickly for two reasons. The first was that Moffatt had embarrassed the bishop, and the second was that her departure would procure for the Quebec Ursulines " . . . a subject of first rank and rare capacity." Despite Moffatt's stubbornness, she had done a fine job directing the Ursuline establishment.[43] To Moffatt, in a letter sent with her revocation, Signay wrote,

In circumstances other than those in which the Bishop of Boston finds himself, I would have been acting with cruelty to take away such a precious subject as yourself from the community—but because the bishop has no hope of reestablishing the institution—it becomes pardonable to recall you.[44]

Moffatt herself was not persuaded by this gallantry, and for her, the recall could never be pardonable.

During the first week of April, Fenwick was called away from Boston for three days on diocesan business.[45] Upon his return, he learned that Moffatt had taken the extraordinary step of preparing for publication her own book in response to Reed's, an *Answer to Six Months in a Convent*.[46] Though he did not openly express surprise in his journal, it is clear that the writing and editing of the book were unknown to him until the week the book was actually to appear in print. Fenwick's own views on the publication are not known, though in the weeks following his notation, the relationship between himself and the superior grew even more strained. Elsewhere, Moffatt's step received mixed reviews. One contemporary magazine, while lamenting the superior's step in publicly answering Reed, cited a positive review:

> We shall wait for the answer of the superior; though we regret she condescended to answer. One of the Boston papers has the following paragraph, announcing publication of the book—
>
> "This answer is written in a style, which shews its author a woman of an excellent education, fully adequate to the important task of presiding over a seminary of young ladies, and eminently worthy of the praises which are bestowed upon her by the intelligent parents who have placed their daughters under her care. We have been told, by ladies who have conversed with her—in confirmation of her own denial of the vulgar phrases attributed to her by Miss Reed—that her conversation is elegant and her manners refined."[47]

In Quebec, the murmuring was less muted, as the *French Quebec Gazette* wrote:

> . . . we hope that the Lady Superior will not persevere in the intention which she has of answering any persons who are guided by such a spirit. Nothing is to be gained by it. Their ignorance or their malice is sure to misconstrue every word . . .[48]

The book, however, which answers Reed's text in a point-by-point format, enjoyed immediate success. One source reports that on the day of its publication, 5,000 copies of the lady superior's *Answer* were sold in Boston.[49] Shortly afterward, the *New York Times* reported 23,000 copies sold, and an order of 5,000 more to be printed.[50] The printer for the City of Boston published the book, so it is unclear who benefited financially. If the superior had arranged a similar profit margin for herself as that arranged by the uneducated Maria Monk, the Canadian escaped nun, eighty dollars for every thousand copies sold, this would have resulted in more than two thousand dollars in royalties, a significant sum that could have supported her. No record of the earnings from the sale of this book has come to light, and it is likely that the worldly Moffatt arranged an even more lucrative margin for herself. Technically, any money made from this venture would have belonged to the Ursuline community, but no mention is made in the existing documents.

In Boston, Protestant-Catholic tensions were again mounting, and only added to the bishop's resolve to rid himself of the Ursuline problem. The day after Fenwick made the notation about Moffatt's upcoming literary debut, he recorded in his journal:

> The *B'p* is given to understand that tomorrow being the Fast-day recommended by the Governor of the State, which is kind of holiday among the Protestants in this quarter, a Party of disorderly People propose to go over to Mount Benedict to commit further depredations upon the Ursuline property there; and among other insults to carry over the effigy of the *B'p* & Lady Superior & to fire at them on the spot. The *B'p* to prevent as much as possible further damage to the fruit trees & fences, gives directions to two Constables to station themselves on the Premises, although he is aware that but little dependence is to be placed either on their good will or exertion.[51]

Despite these fears, the Governor's Fast Day passed uneventfully.[52] Still, the fact that Moffatt herself was a hated target only added to Fenwick's desire to see her depart. The showdown between them came four days later, on Sunday, April 13, 1835. After riding out to Roxbury to look at land for a new church, the bishop

> afterwards repairs to Brinley Place & hands the Superior Mad. St. George an order from her Bishop, the *B'p* of Quebec, to return to his Diocese—he having become highly dissatisfied with the precarious state of things in relation to the Ursuline community since the destruction of the Convent on Mount Benedict.

Apparently, the meeting was very unpleasant, for the bishop added to his journal the following aside:

It may be proper here to observe that Mad'me St. George was appointed Superior over the Ursulines here prior to the arrival of the present Bishop of Boston & that she was allowed to come to this Diocese to fill that office by the consent of her Superior in Quebec & the industrious *B'p* of that City, which permit he now recalls. The *B'p* of Boston, aware of the situation of things in consequence of the great excitement which prevails, acquiesces with pleasure in the recall.[53]

No doubt some angry words had passed between them, for the next day, Fenwick took an extraordinary step. He removed St. George as superior of the Ursuline Community, dissolving "all connection between Mad. St. George, late Superior of the Ursulines here, and this Community." In her place, Fenwick appointed his namesake Mary Barber, Sister Mary Benedict, as superior.[54] Fenwick's action was so distressing to the remaining five Ursulines that they pleaded with him to undo it. Consoling himself that he would only have to endure the situation for a few weeks longer, "the *B'p* consents to continue Mad. St. George as Superior until the affairs of said Community are wound up."[55]

Fenwick's actions spelled St. George's final defeat. Having suffered the indignity of being removed and then restored as superior, Moffatt apparently accepted that it was time for her to leave. On the same day as she was restored to her office, she wrote to her lawyer informing him that under the bishop of Quebec's directive, the time had come for her to return to Quebec.

My friends there being also very anxious that I should do so, and deeming my stay here unsafe, I have yielded to their entreaties, and shall depart in about two weeks.[56]

Five days later, on Easter Monday, Fenwick set off for Brinley Place to say Mass, and wrote only that he returned to Boston afterwards "a little indisposed."[57] The following week, he signed permission for Elizabeth Harrison, Sister Mary John, and Grace O'Boyle, Sister Mary Bernard, to return to the Quebec monastery.[58] But after his next visit to Brinley Place to say Mass, the bishop began to doubt whether, in fact, he would be successful in ridding himself of St. George. Upon his return home, the bishop wrote the following to his colleague in Quebec:

> It may be proper to inform you that on the arrival of your *obedience* to Mad. St. George, expressing your desire that she should return to Canada as soon as convenient, she with Sister Mary Benedict had been summoned to appear at court again on the 1st of June. In consequence of this summons I have been obliged, though with exceeding reluctance, to allow her & the other sisters to delay their journey till after that period.

Fenwick considered the pending court appearance a serious setback for his plans, and felt compelled to add, for extra insurance:

> I need not apprize your Lordship that Mad. St. George is very unwilling to leave the United States, and that she will use every exertion in her power to induce your Lordship to consent to her remaining as I have already communicated this to Mad. St. Henry with a request that she should so inform yr Lordship. *But it will not do by any means that any of them should remain under existing circumstances,* and so long as the present excitement lasts they are in danger; & I cannot be responsible for the consequences. Thus, My Lord, availing myself of your kind invitation, my determination is that they (les Religieuses) shall all go as soon as the trials are over, and I shall be greatly obliged to your Lordship if you will have the kindness in all your communication with Mad. St. George to impress strongly upon her the importance of her speedy departure, & that she should not on any account delay after the above mentioned term. She may possibly write to yr Lordship on the subject & state things as they appear to her; but I can assure your Lordship very differently from what they are in reality. I trust therefore yr Lordship will not be influenced by her representation of things. I am equally on the spot, and I know that religion will not benefit by their staying any longer in this ungrateful country, nor would I have them return to it after they shall have left it till all excitement shall have ceased & a better order of things established.

Having raised Signay's doubts about Moffatt's truthfulness, Fenwick still was concerned about her stubbornness, and added this postscript:

> Pardon me, Monseigneur, for the trouble I give you; but I cannot do otherwise in the deplorable state of things in which I now find myself. . . . I intreat Monseigneur you will aid me with your advice to Mad. St. George to urge their departure from this Diocese for Quebec.[59]

The next day, Sisters Mary John and Mary Bernard left Boston for Quebec on the stagecoach through Burlington, Vermont, and Fenwick recorded his fervent wish that the "other Ursulines . . . will leave as soon as the trials are over, that is in June."[60] The two nuns arrived in Quebec four days later, on May 10.[61] At this point, only three remained in Roxbury, the lay Sister Mary Claire, Sister Mary Benedict, and Mother St. George, who watched over the school's twenty-five pupils.

With the safe arrival of the first of the Boston sisters, plans were underway to retrieve the rest, whose testimony, as it turned out, would not be needed in the upcoming trial. The Annals of the Ursulines of Quebec record that the Reverend Father Maguire, confessor to the nuns in Quebec, was planning to visit New York soon, and would return via Boston to accompany the remaining nuns to Quebec.[62] But a letter in the Archives of the Archdiocese of Quebec casts a different light on Maguire's journey, suggesting that Maguire was sent to perform the delicate task of persuading St. George to go. On May 11, Father Maguire wrote from New York to the Coadjutor Bishop Turgeon regarding the difficult task which lay ahead of him in retrieving Moffatt.

> However repugnant it is to me to intervene in the affairs of our Sisters in Boston—I will take upon me your invitation & the wishes of the Sisters of St. Ursula [he had received a letter from the Mother Superior and Mere de l'Incarnation in Quebec regarding the situation] I will leave this evening for Boston—persuaded that my efforts toward Madame St. George will be useless.—It seems she has decided to stay at her post. She has written to two friends in New York—who have told me in con-

fidence what others do not know who know less of her disposition.—I can not offer any opinion in this regard. Whatever will
be the result of my trip—I pray that God will spare his church
the scandal that a resistance on her part would invariably
cause. . . . The papers report that the menancing of the house in
Roxbury will oblige the religious to flee to Canada—may God
grant this as a manifestation of his will to prepare the good
women for their voyage.[63]

Maguire's letter shows his reluctance to become involved in this unpleasant situation, and he concedes that convincing Moffatt to leave
would be difficult. He and the other Church authorities had indeed
come to a point of desperation, where they themselves welcomed the
menancing and even destruction of her convent as a way of ridding
themselves of this troublesome woman. Notice of Maguire's pending
arrival reached Roxbury the following day, and the superior summoned
Bishop Fenwick to her home.

The *B'p* goes to Brinley Place being sent for by the Superior.
While there the Rev'd Mr. Maguire, Confessor to the Nuns in
Quebec, arrives, on his return from Rome where he has been on
account of the Ecclesiastical affairs of Canada. He had received
on his landing in N. York a letter from the *B'p* of Quebec directing him to repair to Boston in order to conduct the Ursulines still
remaining to Quebec. The *B'p* is exceedingly glad to see him arrived as he hopes it will facilitate the departure of the good Nuns
from this quarter, a thing greatly to be wished in existing circumstances.[64]

With the arrival of Father Maguire, Fenwick became more optimistic
that the departure of Mary Anne Moffatt was imminent, though it
would actually drag out for another ten days.[65]

Shortly before this final parting, both the bishop and the nuns visited
Mount Benedict, though apparently not at the same time. On May 14,
Bishop Fenwick went to Charlestown to survey the ruins in preparation
for erecting a farmhouse where he planned to offer free rent to a custo-
dian who would farm the grounds.[66] On a less practical errand, the three

nuns also visited the ruins to say an emotional farewell to the Mount.[67] During this period, Moffatt also composed letters to her secular friends and supporters to say goodbye. To Mrs. Jonathan Russell, she declined an invitation for herself and the small number of children who would accompany them to Quebec to spend the day in Roxbury, because the trunks were already packed, and she wanted to keep the children's traveling dresses in a "fit state for the journey." At the close of her letter, Moffatt wrote,

> I shall always preserve for you and your family, a most sincere regard, but I do not think I shall be able to correspond with the friends who I now leave behind. My sisters may return to the United States, but I shall not do so. I am returning to a Community in which I was a resident during fourteen years, where I was fondly cherished, and where I shall again be received with open arms; but neither time nor distance, nor novel scenes, will make you, my dear friend lose the place which you occupy in my *affections* and *esteem*. With my kindest regards to your good mother and a kiss to the children, I remain dear Madam, your affectionate friend, The Superior.[68]

Just two days before their departure, the nuns held a moving sale at the home rented from the Dearborns to liquidate all their household furniture.[69] Then the Ursulines prepared to bid adieu to Brinley Place, where the superior had encamped her guards in the great hall during the winter months.

On May 22, 1835, Fenwick recorded that "The *B'p* with Rev'd Mr. Maguire, Rev'd Mr. Wiley & Healy repair to Brinley Place to take their final leave of the Ursulines about to set out for Quebec." The first leg of the journey would take them as far as Dedham, the site where today the Ursulines have a convent and school. From there, the party would continue on to Providence, Rhode Island. Before she stepped into the stagecoach, Moffatt was asked by the bishop to sign an affidavit certifying "that all debts, contracted by me and my Community, both before and since the destruction of theconvent, up to the present day, May 22, 1835, have been discharged, and the Bills receipted."[70] At half past four, the Ursulines left Boston, to Fenwick's great relief.[71] After hearing of the safe arrival of Sisters Mary John and Bernard in Quebec, the day after the last of the Ursulines departed from Boston, Fenwick wrote to Bishop Signay,

> I have the pleasure to announce to your Lordship that Mad. St. George with her remaining religious Sisters left this afternoon in company with Revd Mr. Maguire for Quebec. They are to travel by way of New York, and will, I hope, reach you before too long. I cannot express to your Lordship how grateful I feel for the assistance which you have kindly rendered me in the management of this truly unpleasant business, as well as for your generosity in accommodating our Sisters with an asylum where they can live agreably to their holy rule & enjoy that peace which was not to come here. The Revd Mr Maguire has been particularly useful to me, & although very desirous to proceed after so long an absence from home, yet had the kindness to delay till he could successfully carry the great object which we all had at heart completely into effect. He has my warmest thanks.[72]

The last extant letter in the hand of St. George was written to Bishop Fenwick on the same day from New York. Uncharacteristically, it is in pencil—and written hastily. Dressed in traveling clothes, not in her religious habit, Moffatt wrote to her former friend and colleague this final letter, addressed "Monseigneur":

> We arrived in good season to take the boat in Providence. We were there discovered to be the Ursulines from Boston; by what means, I know not. The children were very particular not to call us by our names, and they have behaved extremely well. We were not sea-sick at all. . . .

After some news about the travel plans and their stay in New York, Moffatt concluded her final correspondence with the bishop:

> Will you be so kind as to write to me at Montreal, as I shall be there some days. It is the only letter I shall request you to write me, and I hope it will be a long one. Please, likewise to enclose

one to the *B'p* of Quebec and the Mere St. Henri, which I may present with my Obedience. This, perhaps, is the last letter I shall ever write you but I shall always be very grateful. Please to tell Mrs. Russell, Fay and our other friends, that we have arrived safely, so far, & to mention what other particulars you please, as it is useless [forgive] to be repeating everything in different letters. All here disapprove of our leaving, and wonder that we should have done so, but I look at it as the will of God.

I remain, Monsieur, your humble, grateful and sincerely attached daughter.

Sr. St. George[73]

Moffatt ended her letter with an apology for the less than proper use of "useless"—the word "forgive" inserted above it in her letter. But "forgive" is no subliminal plea—as her last line still questions the decision of Church authorities to make her leave. There is a certain arrogance here, despite her profession of humility to Fenwick, in Moffatt's statement that only the will of God could have forced her to take this step. Moffatt also wrote to Mrs. Russell from Albany, but that letter does not seem to have survived.[74] The next day, the bishop engaged an Irish carpenter named Patrick McDonough to begin erecting a farmhouse for the caretaker on the grounds of Mount Benedict.[75]

> **Soeur St. Georges (Mary Anne Moffatt)**
> *Entrée: Nov. 20 Oct. 1811 (Vx Récit, p. 406)*
> *Vêture: 25 Janv. 1812*
> *Profession: 20 Janv. 1814*
> *Mission: Mont-Benoit, Boston, 18 mars 1824*
> *Ann. II, p. 26*
> *retour de mission: 5 Juin 1835, p. 170–171*
> *départ définitif: 25 Mai 1836, p. 192*
> *On ne sait ce qu'elle est devenue*

In the archives of the Ursuline Monastery in Quebec is a *fiche*, a small card numbered 175, for Mary Anne Moffatt. In French, it records information about Moffatt's entrance, veiling, profession, and mission to Boston, from *Vx Récit*, the journal reconstructed from the annalist's memory after the original was lost in a fire. *Annals II,* page 26 notes her return on June 5, 1835 and lists her final departure from the monastery on May 25, 1836. The last entry on the card reads *On ne sait ce qu'elle est devenue,* no one knows what became of her.

On June 1, 1835, while the nuns and five students were en route to Quebec City, the civil trials of the convent rioters began in Concord.[76] During this same week, the Catholic Spanish pirates were scheduled for execution, and Fenwick wrote to New York requesting Dr. Varela, who spoke Spanish, to come to Boston to comfort them.[77] By June 5, Moffatt, the other nuns, and the students traveling with them had arrived.[78] The Quebec nuns were thrilled at the return of their beloved confessor Father Maguire after nearly two years, and recorded the momentous return of Sister St. George to her home convent in the annals. The mother superior in Quebec, Louise McLaughlin, who had supported Bishop Fenwick in his bid to expel the Ursulines, was not on hand to greet them, as the annals record she was indisposed. Mother McLaughlin met with Father Maguire and the three nuns privately, in her room. The annals also record that Sister St. George did not seem very much changed, given the ordeal she had been through.[79] But her physical appearance belied the momentous changes that had taken place inside, and her disappointment with the decision of church authorities to recall her to Quebec would result in the loss of her zeal for religious life, though this would take another year to fully surface.

On June 9, 1835 the last of the convent rioters were acquitted in the civil trials, and Bishop Fenwick recorded in his journal,

> Great rejoicing in Charlestown among the blackguards on Saturday in consequence of their acquittal—fifty guns were fired on the occasion! Thus iniquity has prevailed at last! The work on the new Church recommenced.

The same day as the acquittals were announced, the bishop of Ontario, the Reverend Alex McDonnell, wrote to Bishop Fenwick asking, at the request of the British Consul in New York, Mr. Buchanan, that he consider reopening the Ursuline Academy in a proposed City of the Falls in Niagara, Ontario. He included a prospectus for the city, which listed as investors the names of James Buchanan and a James Robinson, perhaps the same Captain Robinson who accompanied his relative Mary Anne Moffatt on her journey from Halifax to Quebec twenty-four years before. It is possible that Moffatt wrote or visited Mr. Buchanan in New York, to solicit his help in opening a convent elsewhere.

What is striking about Bishop McDonnell's views is that they are akin to the loyalist perspective most likely held by Moffatt's father, William Moffatt, on unruly American democracy:

> The destruction of the Ursile [sic] convent & the disgraceful conduct & general hostile feelings of the citizens of Boston & its vicinity against our holy Religion afford a melancholly proof that true liberty or perfect security cannot exist where fierce Democracy is permitted to exhibit its hideous, & savage character beyond the power of the govert of the Country to control it, & the cruel crusade carried on by the fanatics of the Western States of the Union against Catholics is a farther confirmation of the truth of this assertion.[80]

To the British citizen in Ontario, American democracy had manifested a hideous and savage character. There is no record in either Boston or Ontario of Fenwick's answer to the request, and no convent ever opened in the City of the Falls. Two days after McDonnell wrote his letter, the chapter on the Spanish pirates closed with their execution, as Fenwick wrote in his journal:

> June 11th Five of the Spanish Pirates are hanged this day between the hours of 10 & 11. Rev'd Mess'rs Varela & Curtin attend them. . . . The Pirates are interred in the Cath. Burying Ground on Bunker Hill. They died protesting their innocence to the last.

No doubt the bishop meditated often on this perceived inequality of treatment for Catholics punished to the maximum of the law, and the Protestants fully acquitted of their crimes.

During July and August 1835, more reports surfaced that the Protestants were planning violence against Catholic property. The new church on Pond Street was threatened,[81] and a Presbyterian minister named McCalla began a new series of anti-Catholic lectures in Boston.[82] No sooner was the new caretaker's cottage on Mount Benedict complete[83] than rumors of its pending destruction were carried through the town. Moffatt's departure had not had the salutary effect on Protestant-Catholic relations for which Fenwick had hoped. On August 5, 1835 Fenwick wrote,

> Various rumors are circulated this day of the intentions of the lower class of people to celebrate the burning of the U. Convent in Charlestown on the 11th of August that being the anniversary of that horrid transaction. We sincerely hope it is not true, as such a proceeding might lead to very serious consequences on the part of the Catholic population.

Again on the 6th, "Rumour in respect on the celebration of the anniversary still increasing." By the 10th, the rumors intensified and Fenwick wrote, "He understands great preparations are being made which the publick authorities of the City are endeavoring to check." He was relieved to write on the one-year anniversary of the convent burning,

> AUG'T 11TH. The celebration of the anniversary has proved a failure in consequence of the activity of the authorities. The entire day passed without any the least excitement. Thus has the good sense of the community returned at last.

The bishop must have taken some satisfaction that his step of sending the Ursulines back to Quebec had had the desired effect. But his relief was premature. Three days later, Fenwick wryly conceded,

> The B'p learns today that he was shot in effigy by the attemptors at a riot on the day of the anniversary celebration of the burning of the convent. It appears that not being allowed to celebrate it by the authorities of Boston, Roxbury or Charlestown, the outscourings of human Society evinced on that day a determination to do something—they accordingly assembled in a small band on the Chelsea side of the river & there fired at the effigy of the B'p whom they feign not at all to like, for what cause is not

known. However, the *B'p* cares but little for their friendship, so they only confine themselves to sporting with his effigy & will let his person alone.[84]

The warm Charlestown August ended with another dramatic fire, although this time the Catholics were not the primary victims. In his journal for August 25, 1835, Fenwick recorded that much of the city was destroyed by a raging fire:

A most destructive fire broke out about 5 OC'k this day in Charlestown which continued to rage with unabating fury till one or two OC'k this morning & was not brought under till sixty houses including two Hotels & a Bank were utterly consumed. It would seem almost a visitation of God for the horrid outrage committed by the inhabitants of this Town upon the Ursuline Convent on the 11th of last August. It is reported in the Papers that even some lives are lost.

Catholic mythology has continued to link this disaster, along with the suicide of Henry Creesy and the madness of John Runey's daughter, to the actions of the mob on the night of August 11, 1834. The difficult month ended with the Pope "carried in effigy through the Streets of Boston by the Washington Artillary company & finally put up as a Target & fired at."[85]

Whether Mary Anne Moffatt ever heard of these events in far-off Quebec is unknown, and the monastery's annals are silent about St. George until her departure. But Mary Barber, Sister Mary Benedict, whose beauty had so stunned the onlookers at the convent trials, wrote a number of letters to Bishop Fenwick during the nine months before Moffatt's departure. These letters provide a glimpse into the increasing tensions between Mary Anne Moffatt and the Quebec Ursulines. From the letters, it is evident that Barber was not fond of Moffatt. Her tone is critical, even snide. It is difficult to say when Barber lost confidence in the superior, but one of her earliest existing letters, dated August 6, 1835, is very negative. She wrote to Fenwick with a familial closeness that was natural since Fenwick's mother had raised her youngest brother and sister after her parents had assumed separate celibate lives. The letters begin "dear, dear Father," indicating a strong filial relation between Barber and Fenwick—and in the dispute between Moffatt and Fenwick, Barber clearly took Fenwick's side:

> But I feel for *you*—you were cruelly deceived—you were ungratefully treated—you were harassed and tormented by one who should have been a comfort to you; and Religion, in your diocese was on the point of receiving a deadly blow from her who should have been its main support!

Barber's letter also indicates that Moffatt's reception back in Quebec was chilly. Barber, following the request of the Quebec superior, wrote about a problem that had arisen over the compensation of the Roxbury school's dancing instructor, Mrs. Barrymore. Even though Mary Anne Moffatt had signed an affidavit promising all her debts were paid, one was outstanding:

> Our dear Mother wishes me to tell you that the Coadjutor has spoken to St. George about Mrs. Barrymore. She owns she has not paid her, but says she declared that she wished for no payment, unless we were indemnified. In what light can she regard the subscription that was made for us, just before our departure? She says, moreover, that Mrs. Barrymore gave only about sixteen lessons, and that she still had twenty-four to give—But this I know, that more than one note was written to Mrs. Barrymore, expressing regret that payment had to be deferred, and promising that, as soon as money was collected, she should be the *first* whose bill should be discharged—with regard to the number of lessons that had been given, St. George is not to be at all credited. She ought to have paid the poor woman for twenty-five pupils, at least, but the misfortune is, her money has been disposed of in some other way. To be with her, and to witness her conduct, is enough to make one's heart sink. I passed one week pretty much along with her, to assist her to make out her accounts. It was only time lost, but I was most delightfully entertained by the rhetoric and music of her voice. Beyond that, however, she did not dare to proceed.[86]

Mrs. Barrymore had been engaged to give lessons at Brinley Place—and clearly the superior had not anticipated their speedy departure—having contracted the dancing teacher for more lessons. Barber's tone here and her perspective on St. George are reflective of the general view of the Catholic hierarchy—that the nun's behavior had broken all rules and violated her vow of obedience. The situation reached a crisis point when Moffatt was prohibited by Quebec's coadjutor bishop from "approaching the Sacraments" until she had given him a satisfactory "account of her affairs."

In a letter dated September 7, Mary Barber recorded that Sister Bernard remarked with great simplicity, "O Ma Mère, this is a good place—no pride here," making an implicit comparison between Quebec and Charlestown. In the same letter, she wrote of the deteriorating relations between Moffatt and her community:

> There is no alteration in St. George. Her mother has been here, and taken away the two nieces. All three are, I believe, boarding out in Quebec. Mary Anne Fraser, has, if she tells the truth, been travelling ever since she left us on the 13th of May. She passed a week in Newport—that unfortunate place and a good deal of time in New York and Philadelphia.[87]

It is likely that the Mary Anne Fraser referred to in the letter is Moffatt's niece, for whom she bought expensive gifts on the journey north.

In January of 1836, elections for various positions were held in the Quebec monastery. Mary Barber was assigned to work with the *pensionnaires,* the wealthy boarders, and Moffatt with the externs, day pupils, usually charity scholars or poor Irish girls. Formerly in Quebec, Moffatt had been mistress of the *demi-pensionnaires*—wealthy girls attending, but not boarding at the academy. Hers was an important position at the convent that involved meeting with the parents. Perhaps the convent authorities were attempting to teach Moffatt a lesson in humility. Her problems at the convent were reaching a crisis point.

A few days before the assignment to the externs, Mary Barber wrote to Mrs. Russell, who had been a close friend of the superior:

You no doubt, are anxious to know how Madam St. George is. Her health was never so good as at present. She has no employment in the school, and indeed, no particular occupation. Her mother and nieces reside in a house very near us, and come to see her frequently. Many persons in and about Boston imagine that she is still "Superior," but not so; she is like every other private member in the house. A religious Community is, my dear Madam, a republic in miniature: the Superior and officers are elected by votes, and each holds her charge during three years—six at most. Our community in Boston, being small, we could not, without inconvenience, subject ourselves to those changes.[88]

It seems that the humbling of Moffatt was on the minds of various members of the convent.

But Moffatt was not the only source of trouble among the Charlestown personnel, as an apologetic letter from Fenwick to the bishop of Quebec indicates. On February 18, 1836, Fenwick regretted the ingratitude of three of the Charlestown sisters "by the expression of their dissatisfaction at the difference of manners on a national account."[89] In a different letter to Bishop Rosati, Fenwick lamented that the American nuns, Elizabeth Harrison and others, had been unsuccessful in learning French. Their dissatisfaction was becoming such a problem that the Quebec community was considering withdrawing its hospitality.[90]

The greatest problem, however, remained Sister St. George. In early May, 1836, she took the highly unusual step of asking Bishop Signay to approve her departure from the Quebec monastery and a transfer to the Ursuline convent in New Orleans. As the Ursuline convents were autonomous communities, the vows taken for life were taken within specific convents, not to the order generally. Requests for transfers to other houses were practically unknown. Signay, however, granted Moffatt's request to travel on May 9, 1836, saying, in effect, that Moffatt had his permission to go to the monastery of the same order, established at New Orleans. In French, Signay wrote that he had closely considered the motives which argued in favor of the *excorporation*—discharge of this sister from the community.[91]

In recounting this highly unusual decision, the Annals of the Quebec

Ursulines differ in interesting ways from letters in Quebec's and Boston's archdiocesan archives and the *Cahiers des Assemblées du Conseil* of the same date. According to the annals, on May 10, 1836, the bishop of Quebec came to the conference room where he assembled the *Discretoire* (sisters with ten years of profession) who would confer on the matter of St. George. He announced that because of the circumstances of "poor afflicted" St. George, he had given her an obedience to go to New Orleans. When he had asked Moffatt why she wished to leave, she replied that it was too difficult for her to see her dear sisters of Boston, who constantly reminded her of the unhappy fire in her monastery—which there was now no hope of reestablishing. The sight of these sisters, Moffatt reportedly said, would fill her with bitter sorrow for the rest of her life.

The bishop noted he had addressed the obedience to Quebec's mother superior, St. Gabriel, along with a letter demanding that before she received her obedience, St. George would need to give St. Gabriel an open declaration for the principal motivations for her request. All this must be done to St. Gabriel's satisfaction. The community needed assurance that nothing Moffatt would later do would affect the character of the monastery or her own character before God. The Annals express the hope that this step would turn to St. George's advantage for the remaining time Providence destined her to live. According to them, Moffatt's departure took place May 25, 1836. It is added that it was a source of great sorrow to the house that she could not be retained in her mother community, but that all the other sisters of Boston were staying voluntarily, happy to find asylum in Quebec.[92]

In the same way that the annals paint a rosier picture of the reality of the Boston sisters' happiness, so they present a more positive picture of St. George's departure than other documents. In a letter Signay addressed to Mère St. Gabriel, superior of the Ursulines of Quebec, he referred to St. George's repeated solicitations to leave. He asked the mother superior to give permission to St. George, but only after "she has done that which I believe you are going to require of her." His letter indicates that he was not satisfied with his interview with St. George, and asked Mère St. Gabriel to have St. George make a declaration of the principal motives for her request, couched in fraternal terms, not in terms shaded with discontent. That being done, she might have the obedience for New Orleans.

Signay continued,

> When you have received from the religious that declaration—
> and show that she has also satisfied the *discrétoire*, you may give
> her the obedience. The woman will not fail to appreciate the jus-
> tice of my reasons, and will understand that this act of deference
> for the will of her superior will turn to her advantage after her
> departure from the monastery. I ask you to please acknowledge
> on my part, to her mother, that I have received with all the re-
> gards that it merits, the letter that Woman has addressed to me.
> That which I am giving to her daughter, at the present, will serve
> as a response to the contents of that letter.[93]

As the above translation shows, the failure of Moffatt to keep her vow of
obedience was on the minds of the Church hierarchy. Furthermore, the
bishop did not seem pleased that Moffatt's mother had also solicited
him. This letter, "received with all the regards that it merits," appears to
be missing from the archives of the Archdiocese of Quebec.

The official sources differ significantly from a private correspondence sent by Mary Barber to Bishop Fenwick, dated May 19. That letter indicates that Moffatt departed not on May 25, as the annals record,
but a week earlier.

> Last week, I wrote to you by Rev. Mr. Holmes, and mentioned in
> my letter that St. G. was to leave . . . for New Orleans. Last
> evening, at 5 o'clock, she departed; and in order that you may be
> prepared for whatever may happen, I lose no time in conveying
> to you the intelligence. To the very last, she behaved with re-
> markable *sang-froid;* & it appears, her mind is now quite familiar-
> ized to what no one else would be able to think of without
> shuddering. Mary Anne declared she would not accompany her
> aunt. I am glad she has sense enough to take this resolution, for
> otherwise, she would certainly be the victim of her imprudence.
> Strange as it may appear to you, Mrs. Washington used to treat
> her and Josephine about the same—that is, *alone, and in her room;*
> but every where else, like a *princess,* as you well know. In one

sense, I doubt not that she was *greatly indebted* to her, & perhaps, *owed her everything;* but she had much to suffer. Mrs. Washington is, in effect, a second Cleopatra. . . . Our dear Mère St. Henry is much grieved at the departure of St. G. It is deplored by all, but she feels it more than any one. Be so kind as to pray for her, and for St. G. also.[94]

With the departure of Moffatt, the proud "Cleopatra," Barber records what was, to everyone involved, a shocking end. This letter further suggests Mary Anne Fraser may be St. George's niece, the Mary Anne who would not accompany her aunt. The *Supplement to "Six Months in a Convent"* also alludes to Miss Fraser as the superior's "special and mysterious *favorite.*"[95] Ann Janet Kennedy, Reed's friend who left Mount Benedict to enter the convent of the Sisters of Charity, apparently gave Miss Fraser special instruction in music.[96] And in an alleged account by one of the students, Sister Mary Benedict is said to neglect her classes in order to work privately with Miss Fraser.[97] Finally, the superior's list of students refers to a Jane Fraser, not Josephine, so this is perhaps an error on Barber's part. Barber's sarcastic reference to Moffatt as "*Mrs. Washington*" probably comes from the practice of terming the superior "*Mrs. President,*" alluded to in the trial of the convent rioters.

On June 23, 1836, Barber wrote again about the convent's elections.

What a difference between the good Mère St. Henry and St. George! The former is as amiable as happy, as calm, as easy and as *noble,* as before divested of the glittering, but cumbersome trappings of superiority. I could not but admire her when Mrs. Williams called, and the Mère St. Gabriel entered the parlour. "Here, Madam, is the Superior of our community," said the Mère St, Henry, with a tone and manner which did her honor, and which bespoke a dignity of soul, to which neither rhetoric nor painting can render justice. . . .

In addition to constrasting the pride of Moffatt with the superiors of Quebec, Barber adds this additional piece of evidence that Mary Anne Fraser is Moffatt's niece.

I supposed Mr. Kielchen has informed you of the reason why Mr. & Mrs. Williams did not bring on Sarah with Penelope, as they first intended—How deep malice can dive! When they arrived, they were undecided about placing Penelope, but after I had conversed an hour with Mrs. Williams, she was convinced that all M.A. Fraser had said was false. Penelope is now in the convent, and says that nothing would induce her to forego the advantage of remaining here some months or a year. . . . Of poor, unfortunate St. George, we hear nothing. I am sure she will never go to New Orleans, and we are dreading the next intelligence that Providence may send us of her.[98]

As the Russian consul may have told the bishop, Miss Fraser seems to have spread some unpleasant stories, presumably related to the departure of her aunt. As far as convent archives indicate, Providence never sent any additional intelligence of the whereabouts of St. George. No records exist of Moffatt ever soliciting the New Orleans convent to accept her. No record of her arrival or admission to that community has ever surfaced. The uprisings between French and English-speaking Canadians in 1837 appear to have made it impossible to finally track her whereabouts. In 1838, it seems that even Quebec's Bishop Signay sent an inquiry to Bishop Fenwick, asking for news of Moffatt's whereabouts, for in response Fenwick wrote,

Of Mad. St. George I learn nothing, since her departure from Quebec. Various rumors represent her as being in St. Louis, & as having thrown off all restraint—while other accounts have stated that she is dead. I know not which to credit, or whether I ought to credit any.[99]

While a seamstress named Moffatt does appear in the St. Louis directories for this period, the 1840 census that lists her age and the ages of her two children rules her out as the missing mother superior.[100]

One of the most intriguing questions about Moffatt's disappearance remains the motive behind her request to go to New Orleans. If she had intended to leave convent life, why not relinquish her lifetime vow to the cloister, and publicly choose to live life as a lay woman? If she had really intended to go to New Orleans, why didn't she write to arrange it in advance? Perhaps Moffatt needed to assess her future alone, outside the monastery walls where she had spent over twenty-five years. An obedience to another convent would have left her the option to remain in religious life, should she choose to do so. But Moffatt apparently never returned to monastic life. During the summer of 1836, she turned forty-three years old and stepped onto a new path. The historical record is silent about whether that path was scented with rose petals or strewn with thorns.

Bishop Fenwick named Mary Barber superior of the Boston convent, and the community returned to Boston to reopen an academy in September 1838. The last mention of Moffatt in Catholic sources comes in a letter from Mary Barber to the Quebec community, recounting in French the following anecdote:

> I have recently visited with a woman who told me that St. George was in Bordeaux, in France, according to what a gentleman, a Mr. Blain, had told her. "Oh really," I asked, "And how had this gentleman made the Sister's acquaintance?" She replied that the gentleman had known St. George a long time, and said [in English] that *she is associated with his earliest & dearest recollections.* The gentleman had been an intimate friend of St. George's brother, the nobleman Chevalier de St. George. It had been in order to rejoin her brother, that Madame de St. George left for Bordeaux. I felt like telling her, "Madame, you are mistaken. St. George is the name that was given to the Superior when she entered religious life. Therefore she could not be a relative of the Chevalier de St. George." But as the bishop has forbidden us to speak of St. George, I listened in silence and did not enlighten the woman.[101]

IN 1836, Harriet Martineau declared that American women were free to engage in only seven occupations: teaching, needlework, keeping boarders, working in cotton mills, bookbinding, typesetting, and housework.[102] While this statement was an oversimplification, and many women did work in other occupations, there were decidedly few opportunities for educated women in the United States and Canada.[103] When Mary Anne Moffatt left the convent life behind in Quebec, Canada in May 1836, less than two years after her convent had been burned in Charlestown, Massachusetts, she needed to begin her life over again. What would the forty-two-year-old Mary Anne Moffatt do with her life outside the cloister? Of the seven occupations above, her personality and sense of culture would probably rule out most. Her life after the monastery doors closed behind her remains, for now, shrouded in mystery.

# EPILOGUE

AFTER A FEW PIECES of consecrated host were found in the suicide Henry Creesy's breast pocket, the ciborium was located the following day. Near the smoldering ruins, the profaned vessel was found in a thick hedge by a friend of the Catholics. It passed into the hands of the pastor of St. Mary's, Charlestown, and was held safely in that church for a century before it was returned to the Ursulines.[1] In 1938, the parish of St. Mary's church returned the vessel to the Ursuline order as they celebrated the fiftieth anniversary of their arrival in Maine. In her documentation of the exchange, an Ursuline annalist noted "Merici tonight receives this marred ciborium, bruised and corroded as it is, with heartfelt joy that compensates for the want of pomp it once knew."[2] When the pastor of St. Mary's, Father Allchin, wrote to return the vessel to the Ursulines, he said this "is a gift to you. . . . After what the Bostonians did to the Ursulines, this is the least that might be done in reparation."[3] In the 1950s, when the Ursulines reopened an academy in Dedham, Massachusetts, the battered silver ciborium with its history dating to the American Revolution was returned to its rightful home. This antique French ciborium from the chapel at Mount Benedict is the most sacred artifact that remains in the possession of the Ursulines from the destroyed convent.

IN JUNE 1835, Alvah Kelley and Rebecca Reed's brother-in-law, Prescott Pond, filed an appeal in court for compensation for the 144 days they spent in jail awaiting trial in the burning of the Ursuline convent. A Committee of the House reported favorably, as Robert H. Lord notes, "proposing to pay these martyrs five hundred dollars; religious journals applauded; but the majority of the legislators were unwilling to inflict on Massachusetts this supreme ignominy."[4]

\*   \*   \*

R EBECCA REED died February 28, 1838, three years after the
publication of her book, *Six Months in a Convent*. A brief notice
appeared in several local papers:

> In Boston, on Wednesday morning, of consumption, contracted
> while a novice in the Charlestown Nunnery, Miss Rebecca
> Theresa Reed, aged 26. The Sacrament of the Church of which
> she was a member, was administered to her by the worthy Pastor,
> when her last hour was expected, and she then attested to the
> truth of her narrative.

This simple obituary is remarkable for its easy attribution of Reed's
death to the "Nunnery" and its assumption that every reader would understand the allusion to her infamous book.[5]

D URING A VISIT TO QUEBEC during the summer of 1837,
Bishop Fenwick began mulling over the possibility of reestablishing an Ursuline academy in Boston with some members of the original
community. Mary Barber, whom he had chosen as superior the day he
relieved Moffatt of her duties, had begun suffering symptoms of tuberculosis. In a letter written in September 1837, which she claimed was a
confidential last missive from her deathbed, she squarely sized up the
relative strengths and weaknesses of any sister Fenwick might consider
appointing as superior. By the end of her forty-page letter, she had
managed to rule all out but herself as a suitable candidate. Upon the return of the community to Boston in August 1838, Barber was appointed
the new Ursuline superior. Sister Mary Joseph returned as her assistant,
as did choir sisters Mary Ursula, Mary John, and Mary Austin and lay
sisters Mary Claire and Mary Ambrose.

The new school, in its rented quarters, lacked much of the luster of
its former incarnation. Parents feared sending their daughters again, and
the economic downturn of 1837 made it less affordable for many. Barber, who had been critical of Mary Anne Moffatt's style of leadership,
could not keep her staff; the unhappy women of the community

pleaded with the bishop to allow them to join other convents. By October 1841, she was the sole member of the community remaining in Boston. And she who had been critical of Moffatt's insubordination herself became an exasperating problem for the bishop. Defying Fenwick's orders to withdraw to a cloister, and under threat of excommunication, Barber moved in with a brother of the O'Keefe sisters and his wife, a former convent student, and attempted to operate a school. The year before, she had allowed Mr. O'Keefe's illegitimate niece Maria to reside in the convent. This "niece" whom she describes as growing like a "Maypole" is referred to in two of Barber's letters to Fenwick—June 10 and July 5, 1840.[6] Although the age of young Maria is not given, it is intriguing to speculate on the parentage of this mysterious child, and whether or not she was actually born in the convent. That the brother of two of the nuns instructing at the convent married one of the students may itself have raised eyebrows in light of some of the darker accusations directed at the Mount Benedict community.

Toward the end of 1843, Barber, ill and utterly sunk into poverty, wrote to Fenwick that she was prepared to relinquish her role as trustee of Mount Benedict in exchange for his paying off her obligations, which amounted to about a thousand dollars. Elizabeth Harrison (Sister Mary John) had already signed an instrument in Quebec giving Fenwick power of attorney over the property. And the mother of the deceased Sister Mary Frances (Catherine Wiseman) had also signed over her rights to the other trustees. In March 1844, Barber relinquished all claims to Mount Benedict. She returned in 1845 to Quebec, where she died a little more than a year later. With her transaction, the property passed forever out of the hands of the Ursuline community. By the 1870s, the property had been sold, and the proceeds used by the diocese to help pay for Boston's new Cathedral of the Holy Cross.[7] The Ursulines received none of the profits from the sale. Some bricks from the old convent at Mount Benedict were even reused to form the arch in the entranceway to the new cathedral.

B ISHOP BENEDICT FENWICK died at age sixty-four on August 11, 1846, exactly twelve years to the day after the convent burned and nineteen years after the death of Margaret Ryan, Moffatt's beloved friend. During the two days that the bishop's body lay in state in the Cathedral of the Holy Cross, an estimated fifty thousand people paid their respects, and ten thousand reportedly attended his funeral.[8] He is buried on the campus of the College of the Holy Cross, in Worcester, Massachusetts, which he founded in 1843.

THE "MYSTERIOUS LADY," Sister Mary John (Harrison), died in Quebec; Sister Mary Joseph (Ellen O'Keefe) and Sister Mary Ursula (Chase) finished their lives in the convent in Trois Rivières. Sister Mary Claire (DeCosta) and Sister Ambrose (Bennett) went to New Orleans. Sister Ambrose died in the Galveston, Texas, convent founded by the New Orleans sisters. Sister Mary Austin (Frances O'Keefe) joined others from her community in New Orleans and became its superior in 1875, dying in 1887.

*The remains of Mount Benedict in a rare photograph, thought to be commercially produced around 1860.*

IN 1842, the area where the ruins stood was incorporated into the town of Somerville. In 1870, a commentator wrote, "The Convent walls, blackened by the conflagration, are still standing, and the once beautiful grounds are wild and desolate."⁹ In 1874, another writer recorded that the remains of the convent tomb were still visible, and noted that "when we last visited the spot the scene was one of utter loneliness. Year by year the walls have been crumbling away, until the elements are fast completing what the fire spared."¹⁰ During this decade the next bishop of Boston, Archbishop Williams, sold the property for landfill and housing. Today this section of East Somerville is still known to locals as the Nunnery Grounds.

The Ursulines did not return to Boston until 1947, when they opened an academy in the city. In the 1950s, they purchased an estate in Dedham, where today they maintain a convent and a girls' school.


IN NOVEMBER 1851, the Reverend William Croswell, Rebecca Reed's former pastor at Christ Church, was joined by two clergymen on a Saturday excursion to a Boston bookstore. As they were about to part, one of the clerics asked Croswell which way he was walking.

"I must go home and finish my last sermon," replied Croswell. This answer at once arrested the attention of the other clerical brother, who laid his hand familiarly on the Doctor's shoulder, saying, "You do not mean, my brother, your *last* sermon, but your last sermon *this week.*"

To this, Dr. Croswell made no reply. As he walked away, little did his friends think that it would be their last meeting.¹¹

The next day, he performed his Sunday duties in the morning, and met with a group of children from his parish at Boston's Church of the Advent. Though earlier in the day he had pronounced himself in better health than he had been for some time, to the children he seemed unwell, pressing his hand to his head as if in pain. Afterward, some of them recalled seeing tears in his eyes.¹² A few hours later, as he gave the Benediction at the afternoon service, he could not rise from his knees unassisted. He was helped into a coach and rode to his house, where, after a severe turn of vomiting, he died just before six o'clock, the result of an aneurysm at the base of his brain.¹³ He was forty-seven years old.

After four years at Auburn, citing his wife's health as a reason, William Croswell had returned to Boston in 1844 to found the Church of the Advent, and at once became embroiled in a serious and public controversy with the Reverend Manton Eastburn, Episcopal Bishop of the Diocese of Boston. With his choice of Croswell as rector, senior warden and founder Richard Henry Dana, Jr., the judge and author of *Two Years Before the Mast,* signaled "a less Protestant, more Catholic parish in Boston, and indeed, northern New England."[14] Dana, Croswell, and the other founders expressed fervent interest in the Oxford Movement, a movement toward High Church principles within the Church of England which had originated at Oxford University in 1833. The founders avidly consumed Oxford Movement literature and moved to incorporate its principles in the Church of the Advent. This church was unique in the Episcopal Diocese because of its closed system of governance and administration, which allowed church members to insulate their Tractarian liturgical practices. It became the first Episcopal church in the diocese to offer free sittings, relying on the support of voluntary contributions from regular worshipers rather than pew rentals.[15] Less than two years after the church's founding, in 1846, Senior Warden Dana's daughter Charlotte, the church organist, converted to Roman Catholicism, further raising conservative Episcopal eyebrows.[16] In 1847, the church moved to a site on Green Street, the same street on which, coincidentally, the Reverend John Thayer's first Catholic church in Boston had been located during the 1790s.

In a public letter, Bishop Eastburn attacked what he called "idolatrous" practices of the Church of the Advent, including the presence on its "Romish altar" of ornate candlesticks and a cross.[17] Eastburn discouraged other Episcopal priests from preaching at the church, and refused to come himself to perform confirmations. This parochial stress, in combination with his "private family bereavements," affected Croswell's health and worsened the nervous tic that marred his appearance. When Bishop Eastburn came to the Church of the Advent for William Croswell's funeral in November 1851, it was a rare visit indeed. Following the solemnities, William Croswell's body was taken by train to New Haven, for burial in the Croswell family plot.[18]

*       *       *

IN 1854, the last attempt on the part of the Catholics to gain compensation for the destruction of the Ursuline convent failed to pass in the Massachusetts legislature.

BRINLEY PLACE in Roxbury, where Moffatt had tried to reestablish her convent, went on to have an interesting history. It was purchased in 1869 by the Redemptorist Fathers, and in 1876, the cornerstone was laid for a cathedral on the property that abutted the old mansion. Following the dedication by Archbishop Williams, an accidental fire broke out in the Brinley Mansion, burning half of it to the ground. The second floor was later taken off the remaining half, and the Redemptorist Fathers used the surviving structure for a while as a rectory. The remainder of the house stood until 1903, when it was torn down and a new rectory built. Today, this church, called Our Lady of Perpetual Help, is still located in Mission Hill, Roxbury.[19]

IN 1877, a reunion of former pupils was held at the house of one of their number in Boston. In attendance were Miss Russell and Miss Maria Fay, the judge's daughter, who had never married. Others who attended were Lucy Thaxter Titcomb, Louisa Goddard Whitney, and Maria Cotting Holmes.[20]

IN 1870, the following item appeared in the *Suncook Valley Times,* of Pittsfield, New Hampshire:

> Times Change—Fifty years make great changes. Many can remember the difficulty in finding paying employment, and that it was quite common for a young man in search of work, to go on foot, with a bundle of clothing, done up in a bandanna handkerchief, to some of the larger towns in Massachusetts. . . . Several of the Pittsfield boys worked for several seasons at Charlestown, in the numerous brickyards, situated where is now the heart of the city. Perhaps some may remember some young bucks, by the name of Snell, Eaton, Buzzell or Tilton, who were full of pluck

and fun, and often displayed their muscular powers in the popular pastimes of the day, wrestling and fighting. The history of their frolics and adventures would be as interesting as the "Tale of the Arabian Nights." Next to the Battle of Bunker Hill, the most important event at Charlestown, was the burning of the Ursuline Convent. It created excitement. . . . The Pittsfield boys had many a glorious fight with the Irish bruisers, and were implicated in the plot to destroy the Catholic Convent. . . . John R. Buzzell was arrested, and tried as the ring leader, and the man who first fired the building. His trial was a test case. The ablest counsel was employed, and intense interest created; but the abundant testimony of his brother brickmakers, and the united sympathy of the whole Protestant community, favored his acquittal. Recently a history of the convent, published by the leading catholic house in Boston, gives a long and detailed account of the whole transaction. . . . The author states that "Buzzell died in New Hampshire some years afterward, and that he confessed his participation in the events of the Convent burning." Mr. Buzzell is still living. He is at this time a resident of Centre Harbor, and among the most respected men in that town, and was at the last annual election, chosen representative to the legislature. We refer to this matter in justice to Mr. B., as well as to illustrate the inaccuracies of history.[21]

After serving as a representative in the New Hampshire legislature, John R. Buzzell appeared in the records during the late 1880s, extolled in an article in the *Boston Globe*. The *Globe* reporter wrote this account of John R. Buzzell's golden years,

He has spent his declining years in the home of his niece, having laid up what is a competence for his modest wants. Here the children of the neighbors love to congregate, and with his grand-nephews and grand-nieces, gather around the old man's knee while he tells them of the victories of his youth. The older people, too, are not averse to hearing Uncle John's spirited stories, which are told with buoyancy and humor, and with no touch of that garrulousness so common to old age. Of course the story of the burning of the nunnery is the favorite with his hearers, and when, in the long winter evenings, a goodly company of the neighbors have gathered together if conversation lags some one is sure to say, "Now, Uncle John, tell us the story of the Charlestown nunnery." . . . For many years he feared to tell the story before strangers, but now, protected by his venerable white hair, he narrates his part of those exciting scenes with the greatest freedom.[22]

Buzzell ended his *Globe* interview with this reminiscence,

I was down at Charlestown last summer and all over the old nunnery grounds, which are just as the fire left them, except that the old foundations and ruins have settled down and been overgrown in the intervening years. The old brickyards are gone, and handsome buildings occupy their sites, but I can only think of it as it used to be fifty years ago, when every spot and corner was as familiar to me as the faces of my friends. Of those who were with me on that night I can give you but little information. One is still living in this town, and another died here a few years ago. The others have slipped away from me, one at a time, and I have about lost sight of them all.[23]

John R. Buzzell seemed to have outlived all the other persons connected with the burning of the Ursuline convent. He lived to be nearly ninety, dying in Northwood, New Hampshire, in 1894.

THE PORTRAIT OF Mary Edmond St. George by James Bowman seems to have remained in the Quebec monastery as late as 1964, when it too disappeared. In 1973, a curator from the Museum of Quebec interviewed the Ursuline archivist in connection with a book he was compiling on artwork owned by religious communities in the city. The monastery archivist, who is now deceased, told the curator that the portrait of Moffatt was given to the Ursulines in Dedham, Massachusetts, along with Fenwick's in 1964.[24] Records in the annals of the Dedham Ursulines and correspondence between the convents confirm that the Bowman Fenwick was a gift from the Quebec Ursulines, but these contain no reference to the St. George. Lists of artwork owned by the Quebec monastery also show no record of the painting. The lost portrait of St. George only deepens the mystery surrounding her disappearance from the Quebec monastery. The fate of Mary Anne Moffatt remains unknown. The veil of history humbles her in a way the veil of the Ursulines could not.

# APPENDIX:
## PARTIAL LIST OF STUDENTS

Caroline Adams, Sarah Adams, Sarah Arms, Josephine Barber, Sarah Barker, Maria Barnard, Hannah Bartlett, Lucretia Beckford, Ellen Bennett, Rebecca Bennett, Frances Bent, Maria Bent, Susan Bridge, Sophia Brown, Sarah Brownell, Martha Brundell, Mary Bullard, Catherine Callahan, Sarah J. Chase, Sarah Colburn, Mary Ann Coleman, Martha E. Cotting, S. Maria W. Cotting, Charlotte Crehore, Thesta Dana, Julia Danforth, Ann Dean, Sarah Dean, Adelaide Disbrow, Mary Jane Dill, Millicent Dublois, Harriet Edes, Nancy Elwell, Rebecca Elwell, Ann Emmet, Helen Endicott, Penelope English, Eliza D. Fay, Maria D. Fay, Catherine Ferguson, Susan Ferguson, Jane Fraser, Mary Ann Fraser, Lucy Gay, Anna Gibbs, Josephine Gibbs, Ann Gordon, Rachel Graham, Mary Green, Ann Grinnell, Cynthia Hall, Cornelia Hammond, Georgiana Hammond, Martha Harris, Elizabeth Harrison, Mary Hartshorn, Juliet Hutchings, Mathilda Hutchings, Virginia Hutchings, Frances Ireland, Ellen Jackson, Susanna Johnson, Mary Kelly, Mary King, Caroline Little, Mary Jane Mariner, Catalina Mason, Harriet Mason, Elizabeth Maguire, Maria McMurtrie, Emily Mead, Lucy Mears, Garafilia Mohalbi, Susan Moody, Sarah Morfield, Mary A. Morrell, Louisa Murdock, Elizabeth Newton, Julia O'Boit, Mary O'Brien, Frances Ostinelli, Elizabeth Page, Ann Augusta Parkman, Hannah Parkman, Julia Pearce, Mary Peduzzi, Gertrude Pend, Charlotte Penniman, Jane Penniman, Martha Penniman, Frances Percival, Mary Percival, Susan Perrault, Eloise Peters, Harriet Peters, Mary Jane Peterson, Ann Eliza Prentiss, Mary Ann Quin, Ardelle Rhodes, Heloise Rhodes, Julia Robbins, Martha E. Robinson, Geraldine Russell, Ida Russell, Caroline Sanderson, Frances Sargent, Sarah Sawyer, Mary B. Shinkwin, Elizabeth Sisson, Anita Smith, Mary Soule, Ellen Stacy, Harriet Stearns, Emily Stickney, Frances Stoddard, Malvina Storer, Rosalina Storer, Margaret Stuart, Sarah Stuart, Lucy Thaxter,

Mary Thaxter, Hannah Thompson, Margaret Thompson, Sarah Thompson, Sarah Tilden, Catherine Trull, Lydia Turner, Maria Tyler, Abby Utley, Mary Utley, Mary Ann Wales, Catherine Walley, Mary Walley, Miriam Walley, Susan Webster, Ellen Weld, Ann Maria White, Mary Whitmarsh, Margaret Whymbs, Mary Wilcox, Louisa Wilcox, Elizabeth W. Williams, Julia Williams, Melaney Williams, Penelope Williams, Sarah Williams, Sarah S. Williams, Susan Williams, Elizabeth Willis, Elizabeth Woodbury, Sarah Woodbury, Nancy Worthen.[1]

# NOTES

## Prologue

1. "Material About the Ursuline Convent, Mount Benedict, Charlestown, Mass." Translated from *Les Ursulines des Trois Rivieres,* Vol. 2, 1892, 219, 231. Unpublished ms. in Somerville Public Library.

## Chapter One: The Seed Is Planted

1. See S. Willard's *Plans and Sections of the Obelisk on Bunker's Hill with the Details of Experiments Made in Quarrying the Granite* (Boston, 1843), 31. In the collection of the Somerville Public Library.
2. "Statement by the Leader of the Knownothing Mob, Destruction of the Charlestown Convent," *U.S. Catholic Historical Society, Historical Records and Studies,* Vol. 12, 1918, 66–75.
3. *Boston Evening Transcript,* August 15, 1834.
4. Robert C. Winthrop, "Compensation for the Destruction of the Ursuline Convent; a speech delivered in the House of Representatives of Massachusetts, March 12, 1835." In his *Addresses and Speeches of 1852,* Vol. 1 (Boston: Little, Brown, 1852–86), 174–186, 174.
5. Commentators on the convent burning include Isaac Frye, *The Charlestown Convent; Its Destruction by a Mob, on the Night of August 11, 1834* (Boston: Patrick Donohoe, 1870); Ray Allen Billington, *The Protestant Crusade, 1800–1860: A Study of the Origins of American Nativism* (New York: Macmillan, 1938); Robert H. Lord, John E. Sexton, and Edward T. Harrington, *History of the Archdiocese of Boston,* Vols. 1–3 (Boston: Pilot, 1945); Wilfred J. Bisson, *Countdown to Violence; the Charlestown Convent Riot of 1834* (New York: Garland, 1989); Jenny Franchot, *Roads to Rome: The Antebellum Protestant Encounter with Catholicism* (Berkeley: University of California Press, 1994); Daniel A. Cohen, "Miss Reed and the Superiors: The Contradictions of Convent Life in Antebellum America," *Journal of Social History,* Vol. 30, No. 1 (Fall 1996), 149–184; and Jeanne Hamilton, O.S.U., "The Nunnery as Menace: The Burning of the Charlestown Convent, 1834," *U.S. Catholic Historian,* Vol. 14 (Winter 1996), 35–65.
6. Mary Ewens, *The Role of the Nun in Nineteenth Century America* (1971; reprint, New York: Arno Press, 1978), 22.
7. Ewens notes that "one of the most persistent rumors of the time concerned Samuel Adams and his future ordination to the Catholic priesthood" (26) and that George Washington had been presented with a "Masonic apron of satin wrought in silver and gold, which had been hand-made by the Ursuline nuns of Nantes, France" (26). Thomas Jefferson placed both of his daughters in convent schools during his stay in France (27) and promised protection for the Ursulines of New Orleans after the Louisiana Purchase. See also Henry Churchill Semple, S.J., *The Ursulines in New Or-*

*leans and Our Lady of Prompt Succor, A Record of Two Centuries, 1727–1925* (New York: P.J. Kenedy & Sons, 1925), 60–62.

8. Ewens, 43.

9. Annabelle N. Melville, *John Carroll of Baltimore* (New York: Scribner's, 1955), 170, quoted in Ewens, 35.

10. Ewens, 32.

11. Reverend Matthew Russell, "Saintly Influences: Father Thayer and the Ursulines," *Irish Monthly,* Vol. 11 (1883), 625–629, 626.

12. Sister Mary Christina Sullivan, "Some Non-Permanent Foundations of Religious Orders and Congregations of Women in the United States (1793–1850)," *Historical Records and Studies,* Vol. 31, ed. Thomas Meehan (New York: United States Catholic Historical Society, 1940), 13, 19. Quoted in Ewens, 41.

13. Henry Coyle, Theodore Mayhew, and Frank S. Hickey,. *Our Church, Her Children and Institutions,* Vol. 2 (Boston: Angel Guardian Press, 1908), 37.

14. Lord, Sexton, and Harrington, Vol. I, 358.

15. James Fitton, S.J., *Sketches of the Establishment of the Church in New England* (Boston: Patrick Donohoe, 1872), 84.

16. Jeanne Hamilton, O.S.U., "The Nunnery as Menace: The Burning of the Charlestown Convent, 1834," *U.S. Catholic Historian,* Vol. 14 (Winter 1996), 35–65, 35.

17. Hamilton, 35.

18. Rita Bourassa, O.S.U., "The History of the Ursulines." Unpublished material from the Ursuline archives in Dedham, Massachusetts.

19. J. A. Burns, *The Principles, Origins and Establishment of the Catholic School System in the United States* (New York: Benziger Bros., 1912), 280.

20. Coyle et al., Vol. 2, 45.

21. Fitton, 85.

22. Russell, 625. The Maryland convent was the only English-speaking community, which, according to Russell, it is possible Thayer visited.

23. Sr. M. St. Dominic Kelly, O.S.U., *The Sligo Ursulines: The First Fifty Years, 1826–1876,* privately printed, 24. I am indebted to Sister Jeanne Hamilton, O.S.U., for alerting me to this source.

24. Russell, 626.

25. Kelly, 25.

26. Russell, 627.

27. Bourassa, "The Ursulines of Charlestown." Material from the Ursuline archives in Dedham, Massachusetts, 3.

28. *Records of Probate,* Suffolk County, quoted in Lord et al., Vol. I, 680–90. Lord also notes that Thayer had additional property in Ireland to be added to the estate (690).

29. Hamilton, 36.

30. Lord et al., Vol. I, 682.

31. Hamilton, 36.

32. Coyle et al., Vol. 2: "At the death of Father Matignon, Bishop Cheverus became sole trustee, and with characteristic energy purchased a lot land adjoining the Cathedral and erected suitable buildings, and the Ursuline Order was regularly established by the bishop. A school was opened, and became a great success" (45). The figure of one third of the estate is quoted in Hamilton, 36.

33. Sullivan, 45.

34. B. F. DeCosta, "The Story of Mount Benedict," Somerville, Massachusetts, *Citizen Press,* 1893, 2–3.

35. Sullivan, 45.

36. Burns, 281.

37. Superior's Statement in Richard S. Fay, *An Argument before the Committee of the House of*

*Representatives Upon the Petition of Benedict Fenwick and Others* (Boston: J. H. Eastburn, 1835), 34–36, 36.

38. Bishop Fenwick diary, June 21, 1826. Diary of Benedict Fenwick (hereafter FD). In the collection of the archives of the Archdiocese of Boston.

39. Coyle et al.,Vol. 3, 165.

40. Hamilton, 36.

41. Coyle et al.,Vol. 3, say the Very Reverend William Taylor administered the affairs of the diocese for two years before Fenwick's arrival (165).

42. Lord, 726.

43. My translation from the *Annals of the Quebec Ursulines, 1824,* 24–34. Archives of the Quebec Ursulines.

44. "St. George," *The New Catholic Encyclopedia,* Vol. 6, 354.

45. The recounting of this legend is based upon "St. George, Martyr, Protector of the Kingdom of England" in *Butler's Lives of the Saints,* Vol. 2, edited by Herbert Thurston, S.J. and Donald Attwater (Westminster, MD: Christian Classics, 1981), 148–50.

46. See *Supplement to "Six Months in a Convent," Confirming the Narrative of Rebecca Theresa Reed* (Boston: Russell, Odiorne, & Co., 1835), 40.

47. Fenwick's diary of August 14, 1835, states that he was the object of the rioter's animosity. He does not mention Moffatt, who had left for Quebec, specifically. Both their effigies, however, had been displayed and savaged a few months earlier on the Governor's Fast Day (see FD, April 8, 1835).

48. Maria Monk, "A Review of the Whole Subject," in *Awful Disclosures of the Hotel Dieu Nunnery of Montreal* (Salem, NH: Ayer Company; 1836, Arno Press report, 1977), 352. See *Supplement to "Six Months in a Convent,"* 217.

49. Isaac Frye, *The Charlestown Convent; Its Destruction by a Mob, on the Night of August 11, 1834. With a history of the excitement before the burning, and the strange and exaggerated reports relating thereto; the feeling of regret and indignation afterwards; the proceedings of meetings, and expressions of the contemporary press. Also, the Trials of the Rioters, the testimony, and the speeches of counsel. With a review of the incidents, and sketches and record of the principal actors; and a contemporary appendix. Compiled from Authentic sources* (Boston: Patrick Donohoe, 1870). On pager 63, Frye states, "Her worldly name was Grace O'Boyle, her religious one, Sister Bernard." The other names appear on page 81.

50. William Augustine Leahy, "Chapter XIV: The Burning of a Convent" in William Byrne's *History of the Catholic Church in the New England States* (Boston: The Hurd & Evets Co., 1899), 55. Sister St. Henry was actually the niece of the original foundresses, Mary and Catherine Ryan.

51. "Stephen Burroughs, Alleged Counterfeiter and Cattle Rustler Was Also School Teacher and Youth Leader," *Stanstead Journal* (Canada), September 7, 1939, 1.

52. Burroughs was born in 1765, the second son and child to Eden Burroughs, who in 1772 was named pastor of the Hanover, New Hampshire, Protestant Church. Burroughs's mother was the former Abigail Davis of Massachusetts, and the aunt of Stephen's future wife, his cousin Sally. In his *Memoirs of the Notorious Stephen Burroughs,* first published in 1791, Burroughs described his youthful indiscretions with relish and the book went into several editions, including one in 1924 introduced by the American poet Robert Frost. His third child, born in 1794, was named Belinda. Her birth date, May 4, 1794, corresponds roughly to Mary Anne Moffatt's in August 1793. After a picaresque life on the wrong side of the law that included travel to Georgia and Philadelphia, as well as making and just as quickly losing a fortune ($30,000) on land speculation in Louisiana, Burroughs settled in Hanover, New Hampshire, with his growing family. But trouble with his father prompted a move to Stanstead, Lower Canada, in 1799. There he studied medicine, began to counterfeit silver dollars, and applied for a grant of land which he successfully acquired in Shipton County near

Danville around 1804–1805. He continued his counterfeiting business of U.S. bank notes, where, according to the *Stanstead Journal,* his daughter, presumably ten-year-old Belinda, supported herself "in style and elegance by the simple business of signing the bills, in which art she has arrived to great perfection."

About 1808, Burroughs again moved his family to Trois Rivières, where he opened a private school. In 1815, twenty-one-year-old Belinda and her sister Sally, then eighteen, were baptized into the Catholic Church. Belinda, Moffatt's contemporary, never married and became a schoolteacher. She died in Quebec City in 1857, at the age of sixty-three. Sally Burroughs, perhaps the inspiration for the allegations that Moffatt was really Sarah Burroughs, entered the Convent of the Ursulines at Trois Rivières. As Sister St. Claire, she became the institution's archivist, one of the highest officers of the convent before her death at age sixty, also in 1857, the same year as Belinda's death. The fact that Sally became an Ursuline nun gave this rumor about Moffatt's identity much of its staying power.

53. Frye lists Moffatt's birth date as August 27, 1793 (p. 80) but Fenwick's Diary says August 28..

54. Sister Loyola, "Bishop Benedict J. Fenwick and Anti-Catholicism in New England, 1829–1845," *U.S. Catholic Historical Records and Studies,* Vol. 27 (1937), 99–256, 244–45. I am indebted to Sister Jean Hamilton, O.S.U. for alerting me to this reference.

55. The record of the abjuration is in Notre-Dame de Quebec, *Extrait du Registre des baptêmes, mariages, d'abjurations et sépultures de la paroisse de Notre-Dame de Québec,* 1810.

56. In a lawsuit filed by Henry Caldwell against William Moffatt in 1809, Moffatt's last known address is listed as Mr. Dow's boarding house in Quebec City.

57. See J-Edmond Roy, *Histoire de la Seigneurie de Lauzon,* Vol. 2, Levis (1898), xxvi; Vol. 3 (1900), 361 note, and 377 note; and Vol. 5 (1904), 140–142.

58. Lower Canada Land Papers, Canadian National Archives (CNA), 1792. RG 1L 3L, Vol. 10. CS88 Q4 L5 12, # 3243. Microfilm in the collection of the New England Historic Genealogical Society.

59. Alexander Clarence Flick, *Loyalism in New York during the American Revolution. Studies in History, Economics and Public Law,* Vol. 14, No. 1 (1901, reprint, New York: AMS, 1970), 9.

60. Lower Canada Land Papers, CNA, 1792, CS88 Q4 L5 12, # 70293 lists a son, Robert, age nineteen; # 70261 gives Moffatt's residence as White Creek, in the colony of New York, until 1777. In the collection of the New England Historic Genealogical Society. See also Petition of William Moffatt, Lower Canada Land Papers, CNA, 1802. CS88 Q4 L5 12, # 70259.

61. Petition of William Moffatt, Lower Canada Land Papers, CNA, 1802, CS88 Q4 L5 12, # 70262. In the Collection of the New England Historic Genealogical Society.

62. Petition of William Moffatt, Lower Canada Land Papers, CNA 1802. CS88 Q4 L5 12, # 70260–70264. See also the Affidavit of John Savage, Lower Canada Land Papers, CNA CS88 Q4 L5 12, # 70256. In the collection of the New England Historic Genealogical Society.

63. Lower Canada Land Papers, CNA, 1792, CS88 Q4 L5 12, # 70293 and the affidavit of Major Edward Jessup, # 70254. In the collection of the New England Historic Genealogical Society.

64. Petition of William Moffatt, Lower Canada Land Papers, CNA. CS88 Q4 L5 12, # 70253. In the collection of the New England Historic Genealogical Society.

65. Lower Canada Land Papers, CNA, CS88 Q4 L5 12, # 70304. In the collection of the New England Historic Genealogical Society.

66. Lower Canada Land Papers, CNA, CS88 Q4 L5 12, # 224.

67. Fred Q. Bowman, *Landholders of Northeastern New York, 1735–1802* (Baltimore: Genealogical Publishing Co, 1983), 125, 87.

68. See Lower Canada Land Papers, CNA, CS88 Q4 L5 12, 70295–70296.

69. Lower Canada Land Papers, CNA, CS88 Q4 L5 12, 84187–84188, 84190–84193.
70. Papers of M. LeGuay, March 6, 1797, CNA, # 660.
71. Notary Papers of Léon Lalanne, March 25, 1802. Archives Nationales du Quebec (ANQ). Microfilm in the collection of the New England Historic Genealogical Society.
72. Lower Canada Land Papers, CNA, CS88 Q4 L5 12, # 1667, 5189, 70309, 70317, 2131.
73. Lower Canada Land Papers, CNA, CS88 Q4 L5 12, # 70304.
74. The original is probably in the archives of the Ursulines of Quebec, and was published in Sister Loyola, "Bishop Benedict J. Fenwick and Anti-Catholicism in New England," Appendix II, 244.
75. Edmund Burke to the Bishop of Quebec, August 17, 1811. In the collection of the Archdiocese of Quebec, N.E., IV-51.
76. Edmund Burke to the Bishop of Quebec, September 9, 1811. In the collection of the Archdiocese of Quebec, N.E., IV-57.
77. Letter from Major A. S. King to Sir T. Saumarez, February 2, 1814. National Archives in Ottawa, RG 8, Vol. C333, 121–127.
78. Because of constraints placed upon me by the privacy laws in Quebec, the Quebec monastery would not release a transcription of the full record of Moffatt's extraordinary journey. This reconstruction of the trip relies on a summary provided by the monastery, my own partial notes, and the generous assistance of Sister Jeanne Hamilton, O.S.U.
79. My translation from a letter in the Trois Rivières archives, Madame St. Henry to the Superior of Three Rivers, March 16, 1824, III-B-2. 1–8.
80. Reverend William Taylor to Reverend J. O. Plessis, May 17, 1824, E.U.II-46, collection of the Archdiocese of Quebec.
81. Taylor to Plessis, June 19, 1824, and April 15, 1825. Lord Collection in the archives of the Archdiocese of Boston.
82. Taylor to Plessis, June 9, 1824. Lord Collection in archives of the Archdiocese of Boston.
83. Superior's Statement in Richard S. Fay, 34–36.
84. Fay, 36.
85. "A Sacred Bequest." Unpublished material from the Ursuline archives in Dedham, Massachusetts.
86. "A Sacred Bequest."
87. Ibid.
88. Arthur Muir Whitehill, "A Memorial to Bishop Cheverus with a catalog of the books given by him to the Boston Athenaeum." Boston: Boston Athenaeum, 1951, vii. This booklet describes Cheverus's generosity in donating rare books to the library, so giving the ciborium as a gift to the Ursulines would have been in keeping with the bishop's generous nature.
89. Lord et al., Vol. 1, 375. Quoted in Fidelma Conway, CSJ, "'Marine de Brest' Ciborium: An Attempt to Trace its Provenance." Unpublished material in the archives of the Archdiocese of Boston.
90. Lord et al., Vol. 1, 384, quoted in Conway.
91. Lord et al., Vol. 1, 384.
92. Ibid., 375.
93. Ibid., 380.
94. Ibid., 395, 405.
95. Coyle et al., Vol. 2, say of Cheverus, "Before his departure he distributed all he possessed to the clergy, his friends, and the poor, and took with him only a small trunk, which twenty-seven years before he had brought with him" (42).

96. *Trial of John R. Buzzell before the Supreme Court of Massachusetts for Arson and Burglary in the Ursuline Convent at Charlestown* (Boston: Russell, Odiorne and Metcalf, 1834), 12, hereafter *Trial of JRB*.

97. "Material About the Ursuline Convent, Mount Benedict, Charlestown, Mass." Translated from *Les Ursulines des Trois Rivières*, 4. Unpublished manuscript in the Somerville Public Library.

## Chapter Two: Mount Benedict Blooms

1. Rebecca Reed, *Six Months in a Convent*, in Nancy Lusignan Schultz, ed., *Veil of Fear: Nineteenth Century Convent Tales* (West Lafayette, IN: Purdue University Press, 1999), 51.

2. Reverend James Fitton, *Sketches of the Establishment of the Church in New England* (Boston: Patrick Donohoe, 1872), 121.

3. Coyle et al., Vol. 2, 42.

4. J. Fairfax McLaughlin, "Father George Fenwick, S.J.," *U.S. Catholic History Magazine*, Vol. 1 (1887), 396, quoted in Lord et al., Vol. 2, 374.

5. Orestes A. Brownson, "The Right Reverend Benedict Joseph Fenwick, Second Bishop of the Diocese of Boston," *Brownson's Quarterly Review*, Vol. 3 (October 1846), 526, quoted in Lord et al., Vol. 2, 375.

6. Coyle et al., Vol. 2, 45. The figure of 720 is from Burns, 279.

7. Benedict J. Fenwick, "Notes for a History of the Diocese of Boston," 52, handwritten ms., archives of the Archdiocese of Boston, also quoted in Hamilton, 39.

8. Diary of Benedict Fenwick, hereafter FD. In the archives of the Archdiocese of Boston.

9. Lord et al., Vol. 1, 794.

10. Ibid., 810.

11. Ibid., 811.

12. Sr. Mary St. George (Ursuline) to *B'p* England, February 6, 1826 (copy of letter in Charleston Archdiocesan archives, Lord Papers, archives of the Archdiocese of Boston).

13. Sister St. George Superior to Monseignor Panet, Bishop of Quebec, March 22, 1826, E.U., II, 59, archives of the Archdiocese of Quebec.

14. Thérèse Germain, O.S.U., *Autrefois, les Ursulines de Trois-Rivières, une école, un hôpital, un cloître* (Quèbec: Anne Signier, 1997), 212.

15. Germain, 56.

16. Ibid., 220.

17. FD, May 18, 1826.

18. Hamilton, 39.

19. FD, May 19, 1826.

20. FD, June 21, 1826.

21. FD, August 1, 1826.

22. Unattributed description from Fitton, 125.

23. Unattributed description, Fitton, 124–25.

24. *Trial of JRB*, 15.

25. Letter of the Lady Superior to the *Bunker Hill Aurora*, November 5, 1834, reprinted in *The Works of the Right Rev. John England*, Vol. 5 (hereafter, *England*) (Baltimore: John Murphy, 1849), 243.

26. *England*, Vol. 5, 244.

27. FD, April 4, 1827.

28. FD, April 18, 1827.

29. FD, April 18, 1827.

30. FD, March 17, 1827.

31. FD, July 8, 1827.
32. Letter from Sister Mary John to Madame St. Olivier, superior of the Ursulines of Trois Rivières, September 1, 1827. In the collection of the Ursulines of Trois Rivières.
33. FD, July 8, 1827.
34. Sister Mary John to Madame St. Olivier, September 1, 1827.
35. *England,* Vol. 3, 416, 452.
36. Robert Emmett Curran, "'The Finger of God Is Here': The Advent of the Miraculous in the Nineteenth-Century American Catholic Community," *Catholic Historical Review,* Vol. 73, No. 1 (1987), 41–61.
37. Sister Mary John to Madame St. Olivier, September 1, 1827.
38. Sister Mary John to Madame St. Olivier, September 1, 1827.
39. Description of the funeral rites for Margaret Ryan is based upon the "Memoir of Mother Mary Charles," from *England,* Vol. 3, 269.
40. The evidence for this comes from a letter written by Mary Barber (Sister Mary Benedict), then in Quebec, to Benedict Fenwick, in September 1837. The letter is in the archives of the Archdiocese of Boston.
41. Hamilton, 38.
42. Burns, 285.
43. FD, October 1, 1827.
44. FD, January 1, 1828.
45. FD, January 28, 1828.
46. FD, February 8, 1828.
47. FD, February 20, 1828.
48. FD, March 17, 1828.
49. FD, April 14, 1828.
50. FD, May 21, 1828.
51. FD, July 4, 1828.
52. This description of the veiling of Mary Barber is based upon *England,* Vol. 4, 1849, 208–216.
53. Bourassa, "Life Stories."
54. FD, August 15, 1828.
55. FD, August 18, 1828.
56. FD, October 12, 1828.
57. Records of the Ascot Anglican Church, 4400—0589A, "on this seventeenth day of December one thousand eight hundred twenty eight Robert Moffett of Oxford farmer was buried having died the day previously aged sixty-eight years." Since Moffatt's brother Robert was born in 1774, this may have been an uncle born in 1760.
58. FD, November 8, 12, 15, 1828.
59. In a journal entry of July 4, 1828, Bishop Fenwick mentions Miss McLaughlin specifically as a future novice for the Boston convent, saying that "her Relatives would prefer her being in Boston to her being in Quebec."
60. FD, December 20, 1828.
61. FD, January 1, 1829.
62. FD, January 31, 1829.
63. FD, February 8, 1829.
64. FD, February 22, 1829.
65. FD, March, 29, 1829.
66. FD, March 27, 1829.
67. FD, April 6, 1829.
68. FD, April 8, 1829.
69. FD, April 27, 1829.

70. FD, May 27–June 8, 1829.

71. FD, June 11, 16, 17, 1829.

72. FD, June 25, 1829.

73. Fenwick to Panet, February 8, 1830. E.U. II-63, in the archives of the Archdiocese of Quebec.

74. Panet to Fenwick, February 22, 1830. E.U. II-64, in the archives of the Archdiocese of Quebec.

75. Ursuline Community of Mount Benedict to Bishop Panet, March 13, 1830. In the archives of the Archdiocese of Quebec.

76. Fenwick to Bishop Panet, February 20, 1833. E.U. II-65, in the archives of the Archdiocese of Quebec.

77. FD, recap for 1830.

## Chapter Three: Charlestown in Full Flower

1. "Convent at Charlestown," *Christian Register* (Boston), May 8, 1830. See also *Boston Recorder,* May 5, 1830.

2. Catherine Frances Redmond, *The Convent School of French Origin in the United States, 1727 to 1843.* Dissertation, University of Pennsylvania, Philadelphia, 1936.

3. Loosely based upon a description by Sister M. Monica, Ph.D., "Angela Merici and Her Teaching Idea, 1474–1540" (New York: Longmans, Green and Co., 1927), 369.

4. Louisa Whitney, *The Burning of the Convent* (Boston: James R. Osgood & Co., 1877), 38–39.

5. Mother M. Benedict Murphy, RSHM, *Pioneer Roman Catholic Girls' Academies: Their Growth, Character, and Contribution to American Education. A Study of Roman Catholic Education for Girls from Colonial Times to the First Plenary Council of 1852.* Doctoral dissertation at Columbia University, 1958, 149.

6. Whitney, 40–41.

7. Lucy Thaxter, Letter to G.T. Curtis, published in *The Transcript* (Boston), February 4, 1843.

8. For another view of boarding school life, see *Supplement to "Six Months in a Convent,"* 244–249.

9. Loosely based upon a description by Sister M. Monica, Ph.D., 366–67.

10. Burns, 379–80.

11. Thaxter to Curtis, February 4, 1843.

12. Murphy, 129, citing Thomas Woody, *A History of Women's Education in the United States,* 422.

13. Redmond, 30.

14. The Mount Benedict *Prospectus* lists books the students would be using. Mary Barber, in a letter to Bishop Fenwick, dated September 1837, appends a list of books used. She notes the following, for the first class, Senior department: Murray's Grammar, Blake's Chemistry, Blake's Philosophy, Mrs. Lincoln's Botany, Goldsmith's Natural History, Jamieson's Rhetoric, Jamieson's Logic, McIntire on the Globes, and Hume's England. For the second class, Senior Department: Walker's dictionary, Murray's Grammar, Titler's History, Woodbridge/Willards Ancient Geography & Atlas, Jamieson's Rhetoric, McIntire on the Globes. The books used by the first class, Junior department, were Walker's dictionary, Murray's Grammar, Woodbridge/Willards Ancient Geography & Atlas, Titler's History, Goodrich's History of the US. For a discussion of the difficulty of obtaining nonsectarian textbooks, especially for the study of navigation, geography, and natural philosophy, see Francis J. Donahue, "Textbooks for Catholic Schools Prior to 1840," *Catholic School Journal,* Vol. 40, No. 3 (March 1940), 65–68.

15. Redmond, 46. See the Mount Benedict *Prospectus* for fees and book lists.
16. Monica, 384.
17. Based on a description of a Roman Catholic Girls' Academy in Murphy, 183.
18. Redmond, 36.
19. Redmond, 47–48.
20. Monica, 383.
21. Redmond, 47.
22. Redmond, 32.
23. Monica, 366–67.
24. Redmond, 43.
25. Redmond, 44. The description of Maria Cotting's writing lesson is based on Redmond and Monica.
26. Redmond, 44.
27. Murphy, 182, citing Monica, 378–79.
28. Redmond, 44.
29. Redmond, 44, and Monica, 380.
30. Redmond, 45.
31. Redmond, 45, and Monica, 380–81.
32. Sister Mary Christina, S.U.S.C., "Early American Convent Schools," *The Catholic Educational Review,* Vol. 39 (January 1941), 30–35, 33.
33. Redmond, 33.
34. Burns, 279–80.
35. Redmond, 33–34.
36. Redmond, 33, and Monica, 367.
37. Ursuline Constitution, quoted in Redmond, 34–35.
38. Thaxter to Curtis, February 4, 1843.
39. Sister Christina, 33.
40. Quoted in Redmond, 25.
41. Monica, 370.
42. Redmond, 35.
43. Mount Benedict *Prospectus.*
44. "Convent at Charlestown," *Christian Register* (Boston), May 8, 1830.
45. Annales, 1822 à 1894, 103. Archives of the Quebec Ursulines.
46. A.U. Corr de l'abbé L-J. Desjardins à la R.M. St. Henry, Supérieure. Desjardins II. Lettres de 1831 à 1838. Correspondence of Abbe L-J Desjardins to Mother St. Henry, Superior, II, 1831–1838. Quoted in Museum of Quebec exhibition catalogue, *Trésors des Communautés Religieuses de la Ville de Québec,* 1973.
47. Lucretia Beckford's report card from the Ursuline convent, August 7, 1828, in the collection of the Peabody Essex Museum.
48. Thomas Woody, *A History of Women's Education in the United States,* Vol. 1 (1929; reprint, New York: Octagon, 1966), 108.
49. Woody, Vol. 1, 146.
50. Woody, 343.
51. Woody, 364–65.
52. Sister Christina, 30.
53. *Constitution of the Ursuline Order,* quoted in Redmond, 24.
54. Barbara G. Walker, *The Woman's Encyclopedia of Myths and Secrets* (San Francisco: Harper & Row, 1983), 1030.
55. Monica, 411
56. Monica, 410.
57. Harriet Beecher Stowe, *Sunny Memories of Foreign Lands,* Vol. 2 (Boston: Phillips, Sampson, and Co., 1854), 330–31.

58. Scholars propose different dates for the actual foundation, ranging from 1534 to 1537.
59. Walker, 1032.
60. Marie de Saint Jean Martin, O.S.U., *Ursuline Method of Education* (Rahway, NJ: Quinn and Boden, 1946), vi.
61. Redmond, 21.
62. Walker, 1031.
63. Monica, 229–30.
64. Monica, 413.
65. Redmond, 20.
66. Redmond, 21.
67. Monica, 190–191.
68. Monica, 197.
69. Sister Mary Ellen Keenan, "French Teaching Communities and Early Convent Education in the United States, 1727–1850." M.A. thesis, Catholic University of America, 1934, 5.
70. Murphy, 112.
71. Keenan, 2.
72. Monica, 44.
73. Redmond, 20.
74. Constitution of the Ursulines, archives of the Ursulines of New Orleans, quoted in Murphy, 112.
75. Constitution of the Ursulines, quoted in Murphy, 112.
76. Monica, 199.
77. Monica, 237.
78. Ibid., 336.
79. Ibid., 240.
80. Lydia Sterling Flintham, "Leaves from the Annals of the Ursulines," *Catholic World,* Vol. 66, No. 393 (December 1897), 319–39, 320.
81. Monica, 345.
82. Martin, 295.
83. Monica, 351–52.
84. On the question of attribution of the ideas, Redmond further notes: "It is not certain how far Frances [Bermond] herself created this supplement, how far it was handed down from the Provence Sisters or to what extent, if at all, it was blended with the pedagogical maxims of Romillon, under whose direction the Provencal daughters of Angela were teaching. This could be learned only by examining critically the first Rule printed in Provence, and this is no longer in existence" (26). See also Monica, 301.
85. Quoted in Redmond, 26.
86. Quoted in Redmond, 25.
87. Quoted in Murphy, 113.
88. Quoted in Murphy, 113.
89. *Règlements,* Ch. III, Art. 39, quoted in Redmond, 36.
90. Murphy, 183, and Wood, 422–34.
91. Redmond, 30, and Monica, 366.
92. Quoted in Redmond, 25.
93. Quoted in Redmond, 28.
94. Quoted in Redmond, 28.
95. Ewens, 98–99.
96. Murphy, 159, citing Woody, 130.
97. Murphy, 159.
98. Murphy, 159.
99. Ewens, 100.

100. Quoted in Ewens, 100.
101. Ewens, 134.
102. Sister Christina, 31.
103. Sister Christina, 32.
104. Mary Barber to Bishop Benedict Fenwick, September 1837, letter in archives of the Archdiocese of Boston.
105. Murphy, 128
106. Quoted in Redmond, 24.
107. Murphy, 148.
108. "The Ursuline Convent," from *Mrs. Hale's Magazine,* in *An Account of the Conflagration of the Ursuline Convent by a Friend of Religious Toleration* (Boston, 1834), 27–33, 31.
109. Whitney, 3.
110. Lydia Russell to Mary Anne Moffatt, April 1834, in the archives of Catholic University of America.
111. Sister Christina, 32.
112. "Convent of the Visitation," *The American Catholic Historical Researches,* Vol. 9 (Philadelphia: M.I.J. Griffin, 1887–1912), 128.
113. Murphy, 147.
114. Thaxter to Curtis, February 4, 1843.
115. Murphy 133, and Woody, 434–435.
116. Murphy, 133 and Woody, 441.
117. *Report of the Committee Relating to the Destruction of the Ursuline Convent, August 11, 1834* (Boston: J.H. Eastern, 1834), 6.
118. Whitney, 46.
119. Whitney, 53.
120. Redmond, 42.
121. Ibid.
122. Report of the Committee, 6–7.
123. Sister Maria Concepta, C.S.C., *The Making of a Sister-Teacher* (Notre Dame, Indiana: Notre Dame University Press, 1965). The schedule is loosely based on a description of the daily schedule for Bertrand Academy in 1850, p. 97. See also Burns, 379–80.
124. Redmond, 40.
125. Redmond, 41, and Monica, 376.
126. Redmond, 41.
127. Superior to Levi Thaxter, March 7, 1831. In the collection of the Somerville, Massachusetts, Public Library.
128. The whereabouts of this medal today are unknown.
129. Sister Christina, 34.
130. St. George to Three Rivers superior, May 19, 1832, in the archives of the Ursulines of Trois Rivières.
131. Thaxter to Curtis, February 4, 1843.
132. Whitney, 20–22.
133. FD, July 1, 1829.
134. FD, May 1, 1830.
135. Provincial Annals of 1832, archives of Saint Joseph's Provincial House, Emmitsburg, Maryland.
136. Unpublished journal, May 18, 1832, Daughters of Charity archives, Albany, NY.

## Chapter Four: A Deadly Miasma

1. FD, May 11, 1832.
2. Byrne, 53. In 1836, *The Jesuit's* name was changed to *The Pilot.*

3. Unpublished journal, May 18, 1832, Daughters of Charity archives, Albany, NY.
4. FD, June 4, 1833.
5. *Bunker Hill Aurora,* November 30, 1833.
6. James Gillespie Blaine II, *The Birth of a Neighborhood: Nineteenth-Century Charlestown, Massachusetts,* Vol. I. Dissertation, University of Michigan, 1978, 6.
7. Blaine, 7.
8. Ibid., 8.
9. Ibid., 9.
10. James Frothingham Hunnewell, *A Century of Town Life: A History of Charlestown, Mass-achusetts, 1775–1887* (Boston, 1888), 14–15. Quoted in Blaine, 9.
11. Blaine, 10.
12. Figures taken from the United States Decennial Census for the year 1830, quoted in Blaine, 13.
13. Blaine, 14.
14. *Bunker Hill Aurora,* March 8, 1828, quoted in Blaine, 15.
15. Blaine, 17.
16. Blaine, 17–18.
17. Rice, quoted in Blaine, 19.
18. Quoted in Blaine, 19.
19. Blaine, 22–23. Blaine points out that the Baptists, the Universalists, and, most impor-tantly, the Unitarians burst the social and theological ties of unity (23). He adds that the nineteenth century witnessed the ranking of certain sects along a social contin-uum, so that a person's religious affilation told much about his social position.
20. *Charlestown Directory of 1831,* quoted in Blaine, 19–20.
21. Blaine, 24.
22. Blaine, 26.
23. Wilfred Bisson, *Some Conditions for Collective Violence.* Dissertation, Michigan State University, 1974, 45.
24. Blaine, 33.
25. Blaine, 56.
26. Blaine, 84. These were Francis Hay, Abijiah Monroe, Samuel Poor, and Stephen Wiley.
27. *Bunker Hill Aurora,* November 16, 1833. Quoted in Blaine, 77.
28. Bisson, 73.
29. Bisson discusses the strike on pages 67–68.
30. "Convent at Charlestown," *Boston Recorder,* May 5, 1830, 1.
31. Ibid.
32. FD, January 9, 1831.
33. FD, February 27, 1831.
34. FD, March 6, 1831.
35. FD, March 27, 1831.
36. FD, June 21, 1831
37. FD, October 9, 1831.
38. Sister Mary Magdalene died of tuberculosis on November 17, 1831, and was buried in the tomb at Mount Benedict. Hers was the sixth corpse laid to rest in the mausoleum.
39. FD, August 23, 1831. See also the entry for August 29, 1831.
40. FD, November 13, 1831.
41. *United States Catholic Intelligencer,* May 25, 1832.
42. Undated letter fragment in the collection of the archives of Catholic University of America.
43. Undated letter fragment in the collection of the archives of Catholic University of America.
44. Letter from "An Episcopalian" described as "an aged and respectable lady whose two

daughters were four years in the Ursuline convent," originally published in the *New York Evening Star* and reprinted in *England,* Vol. 5, 278.

45. *England,* Vol. 5, 278.
46. Mary Anne Ursula Moffatt, *An Answer to "Six Months in a Convent"* (Boston, 1835), 2.
47. FD, January 19, 1832.
48. A letter of Rev. Byrne, March 31, 1835 to the editor of the *Boston Courier* identifies the friend as Mrs. Graham. Reprinted in *England,* Vol. 5, 283. See also *Supplement to "Six Months in a Convent,"* 154–155.
49. Dr. Felix Varela's Remarks, *NY Catholic Diary and Register,* in *England,* Vol. 5, 299.
50. Reed, *Six Months in a Convent,* 36.
51. Reed, 30.
52. Reed, 26. On January 2, 1835, Fay wrote to the *Boston Courier,* "I will take the liberty to refer you to a certain Miss Rebecca Theresa Read, alias Rebecca Mary Agnes Theresa Read (as Goldsmith says, I love to give the whole name), a Catholic Protestant as she termed herself in court the other day, who has been about Boston and the vicinity for the last two and a half years, announcing herself as "the humble instrument in the hands of Providence, to destroy the institution at Mount Benedict." Reprinted in *England,* Vol. 5, 268.
53. *Christian Watchman,* April 2, 1827.
54. *Christian Watchman,* August 6, 1827.
55. Mary Kent Davey Babcock, "William Croswell and Christ Church: Hymns from the Cloisters of the Old North Church . . . —a Lady discovers Old North's Rector Poet." Unpublished ms. in the archives of the Episcopal Diocese of Boston, 15.
56. Babcock, 12.
57. William Foster Otis, *In Memoriam Gulielmi Crucifontis* (Boston, 1857), in the collection of the Boston Athenaeum.
58. Mary Kent Davey Babcock, "History of Christ Church: Rectors and Ministers." Unpublished ms. in the archives of the Episcopal Diocese of Massachusetts, 60.
59. Edited with George Washington Doane, later Bishop of New Jersey, and father of William Croswell's namesake. From Mary Kent Davey Babcock, "William Croswell and Christ Church," 3.
60. Babcock, "History of Christ Church," 60.
61. Babcock, "History of Christ Church," 60.
62. Ibid., 60.
63. Ibid., 61.
64. Ibid.
65. Ibid., 61–62.
66. Ibid., 64.
67. Ibid., 66.
68. Ibid., 67.
69. Ibid.
70. Ibid.
71. Babcock, "Hymns from the Cloisters of the Old North Church," 14.
72. Thomas Hall, *Hall's Index to Proprietor's Records of Christ Church, 1724–1875.* Research notes of the parish historian, n.p. Material in the Episcopal archives of Boston.
73. Thomas Hall, research notes, n.p.
74. Letter to Harry Croswell, April 10, 1839, quoted in Babcock, "History of Christ Church," 67.
75. Letter to Proprietors in early May 1840, quoted in Babcock, "History of Christ Church," 8.
76. Letter to Proprietors, addressed to Dr. Bacon, May 14, 1840. quoted in Babcock, "History of Christ Church," 69.

77. Babcock, "History of Christ Church," 69. Amanda Tarbell was the daughter of Silas P. Tarbell.

78. Babcock, "History of Christ Church," 70–71.

79. Babcock, "History of Christ Church," 71.

80. Published in the *Witness and Advocate,* Boston, November 14, 1851. Clipping in Otis, *In Memoriam*.

81. Betty Hughes Morris, *A History of the Church of the Advent* (Boston: Episcopal Diocese, 1995), 16–17. One of these bereavements was probably the unexpected death of Amanda Tarbell's sister, Mary, less than a week before her marriage to William Croswell.

82. Babcock, 29.

83. Reed, 37.

84. Reed, 37.

85. Ibid., 4.

86. Ibid., 5.

87. Ibid., 14.

88. Ibid., 40.

89. *England,* Vol. 5, 292.

90. "The Ursuline Community," in *The New-England Magazine,* Vol. 8 (January–June 1835), 392–99, 397.

91. Reed, 40–41.

92. "Abstract of the Superintendent's Annual Report, 1829, Fifteenth Year of Christ Church Sunday School, presented at the Adjourned Annual Meeting, May 22, 1829," 15–16. Material in the archives of the Episcopal Diocese of Boston.

93. Reed, 14.

94. The diary of Harry Croswell is in the collection of the Sterling Memorial Library at Yale University.

95. The sales figures are from *England,* Vol. 5, 278, and Billington, 90, 108.

96. *England,* Vol. 5, 359.

97. *England,* Vol. 5, 293.

98. *England,* Vol. 5, 375.

99. Reprinted in *England,* Vol. 5, 278–79.

100. "The Ursuline Community," in *The New-England Magazine,* Vol. 8 (1835), 397–99.

101. *Report of the Committee,* 6.

102. Reed, 127–28.

103. *Report,* 6.

104. *Report,* 6.

105. *Report,* 7.

106. *Report,* 7.

107. *Report,* 8.

108. *England,* Vol. 5, 288–289. For a more sympathetic view of Reed, see Cohen, "Miss Reed and the Superiors."

109. FD, March 8, 1830. The building was covered for $500 and the insurance company had it rebuilt.

110. "A Death in Boston: Cholera and Graveyards as Contributory Factors in the Burning of the Ursuline Convent," in *Lifting the Veil: Remembering the Burning of the Ursuline Convent.* Exhibition catalog edited by Nancy Natale and Nancy Lusignan Schultz, Ph.D., Somerville Museum, Somerville, Massachusetts, 1997, 27.

111. Daly, 27.

112. Selectmen of Charlestown (Mass. St. A. Acts 1832, ch. 150), Lord Papers, Archives of the Archdiocese of Boston.

113. FD, March 15, 1832.

114. FD, May 7, 1832.
115. FD, May 19, 1832.
116. FD, May 19, 1832.
117. FD, May 20–21, 1832.
118. See FD, May 25–26, 1832.
119. FD, June 17 and 23, 1832.
120. FD, April 24, 1833.
121. Daly, 27.
122. Daly, 27.
123. Ibid., 26.
124. Ibid.
125. Ibid.
126. Lawrence M. Tierney, Jr. M.D., *Pocket Guide to the Essentials of Diagnosis and Treatment* (Stamford, CT: Appleton & Lange, 1997), 237.
127. *United States Catholic Intelligencer,* June 22, 1832.
128. Daly, 26.
129. *U.S. Catholic Intelligencer,* June 22, 1832.
130. Daly, 26.
131. Daly, 26.
132. Quoted in Daly, 27.
133. Daly, 26.
134. *U.S. Catholic Intelligencer,* June 22, 1832.
135. *U.S. Catholic Intelligencer,* June 22, 1832
136. Daly, 26–27.
137. *U.S. Catholic Intelligencer,* June 22, 1832.
138. Tierney, 237.
139. FD, August 15, 1832.
140. FD, September 26, 1832.
141. Daly, 27.
142. FD, March 5–6, 1832.
143. FD, August 30, 1832.
144. FD, November 12, 1832.
145. FD, April 25, 1833.
146. FD, November 21, 1832.
147. FD, November 29, 1832.
148. FD, December 10, 1832.
149. FD, December 30, 1832.
150. FD, September 19, 1833.
151. FD, May 22, 1833.
152. FD, June 10, 1833.
153. FD, March 17, 1833.
154. FD, July 1, 1833

## Chapter Five: The Vine Uprooted

1. Fenwick's journals describe the lots as being "in a good location, at the corner of two streets, & having at the same time an Alley way in the rear, for a new Catholic Church. The price is one Doll'r pr. foot—and the size of each lot 20 feet by 85. FD, January 4, 1834.
2. FD, April 3–4, 1834.
3. FD, April 12, 1834.
4. FD, April 30, 1834.

5. FD, May 31, 1834.
6. FD, July 12, 1834.
7. FD, May 8, 1834
8. FD, May 9, 1834.
9. FD, July 8–9, 1834.
10. "Leader of the Knownothing Mob," 68.
11. "Leader of the Knownothing Mob," 69.
12. From *Boston Daily Atlas,* reprinted in *England,* Vol. 5, 250.
13. "Leader of the Knownothing Mob," 69.
14. *England,* Vol. 5, 250.
15. *Trial of JRB,* 28.
16. Ibid.
17. *England,* Vol. 5, 250.
18. Letter of the Lady Superior to the *Bunker Hill Aurora,* November 5, 1834, reprinted in *England,* Vol. 5, 243.
19. Ibid.
20. FD, July 28, 1834.
21. FD, July 28, 1834.
22. FD, July 29, 1834.
23. FD, July 30, 1834.
24. FD, July 30, 1834.
25. FD, July 31, 1834.
26. FD, August 3, 1834.
27. Anna Loring (Mrs. Charles Greely Loring) to Mary Pierce of Litchfield, CT, August 12, 1834 in the collection of the Somerville Public Library.
28. *Trial of JRB,* 36.
29. *Report,* 9.
30. *England,* Vol. 5, 243.
31. Argument of James T. Austin before the Supreme Court of Massachusetts (Boston: Ford & Damrell, 1834), 15–16.
32. FD, August 9, 1834.
33. *Trial of John R. Buzzell, the Leader of the Convent Rioters for Arson and Burglary* (Boston: Lemuel Gulliver, 1834) (hereafter, *Leader of the Convent Rioters*), 18–19.
34. Fitch Cutter quoted in Frye, 86.
35. FD, August 9, 1834.
36. *England,* Vol. 5, 244.
37. *England,* Vol. 5, 244.
38. Ibid.
39. FD, August 10, 1834.
40. The cap and a documentation of its history is in the collection of the Ursulines in Dedham, Massachusetts.
41. "Dr. Beecher's Sermon at Park Street Church, August 11 [*sic*], 1834," *Christian Watchman,* Boston, August 15, 1834. From the Robert H. Lord papers, archives of the Archdiocese of Boston.
42. *Christian Watchman,* August 15, 1834.
43. Anna Loring (Mrs. Charles Greely Loring) to Mary Pierce of Litchfield, CT, August 12, 1834, in the collection of the Somerville Public Library.
44. *Christian Watchman,* August 15, 1834.
45. Ibid.
46. *Christian Examiner,* September 1834, 131–136, 133.
47. *Report,* 9.
48. *England,* Vol. 5, 243.

49. *England,* Vol. 5, 243.
50. *Report,* 9.
51. Thaxter to Curtis, February 4, 1843.
52. *Supplement to "Six Months in a Convent,"* 128.
53. Whitney, 84–85.
54. Austin, 26.
55. Austin, 37.
56. "Leader of the Knownothing Mob," 71.
57. *England,* Vol. 5, 270.
58. *Trial of JRB,* 63.
59. "Leader of the Knownothing Mob," 66–67.
60. Whitney, 103.
61. *Leader of the Convent Rioters,* 31.
62. *England,* Vol. 5, 249.
63. FD, August 11, 1834.
64. FD, August 11, 1834.
65. Whitney, 112.
66. *Report,* 10.
67. *England,* Vol. 5, 247.
68. "Leader of the Knownothing Mob," 71.
69. *Trial of JRB,* 61.
70. *England,* Vol. 5, 243.
71. "Leader of the Knownothing Mob," 72.
72. Thaxter to Curtis, February 4, 1843.
73. The incident is discussed in Bisson, 101–107.
74. The Boston *Atlas* of July 12, 1834 published a satiric *Proclamation of Andrew I,* reprinted in Bisson, 137–138.
75. Austin, 24.
76. FD, August 11, 1834.
77. Whitney, 106–107.
78. Whitney, 130.
79. Moffatt to Austin, November 30, 1834, in the collection of the archives of Catholic University of America.
80. Whitney, 149.
81. Austin, 7–8.
82. *Report,* 11.
83. "Leader of the Knownothing Mob," 72.
84. *Trial of JRB,* 11.
85. *Leader of the Convent Rioters,* 19–20.
86. Whitney, 142.
87. *Leader of the Convent Rioters,* 9.
88. John C. Tenney in "Somerville in 1842: Interesting Interviews with Old Residents— Describing the City As It Was a Half Century Ago," *Somerville Journal,* June 4, 1892.
89. "Leader of the Knownothing Mob," 72–73.
90. "Leader of the Knownothing Mob," 73.
91. Austin, 39.
92. "Leader of the Knownothing Mob," 72.
93. Whitney, 180–182.
94. Anna Loring to Miss Pierce, August 12, 1834.
95. "Destruction of the Charlestown Convent," *U.S. Catholic Historical Society Historical Records and Studies,* Vol. 13 (1919), 106–19, 111.
96. *Report,* 1.

97. Proclamation of Governor John Davis, of Massachusetts, August 15, 1834 (Massachusetts State Archives, Commissions, Proclamations, etc 1833–38) Copy. 1b. 118–19, Lord Papers, archives of the Archdiocese of Boston.
98. "Destruction of the Charlestown Convent," 113–116.
99. FD, August 12, 1834.
100. *Truth Teller* (NY), March 28, 1835, Lord Papers, archives of the Archdiocese of Boston.
101. *Daily Evening Transcript* (Boston), August 15, 1834.
102. *Report,* 3.
103. *Report,* 4.
104. *Supplement to "Six Months in a Convent,"* 30, 63–64.
105. Theodore Russell to Hon. Charles Russell, Esq., August 31, 1834, from the Charles Russell collection in the Massachusetts Historical Society.
106. FD, October 26, 1834.
107. FD, October 27, 1834.

## Chapter Six: The Lost Garden

1. Reprinted in *England,* Vol. 5, 260.
2. "Leader of the Knownothing Mob," 73.
3. *Report,* 4.
4. *Report,* 14.
5. *Report,* 13.
6. *Christian Examiner,* September 1834.
7. Theodore Hammet, "Two Mobs of Jacksonian Boston: Ideology and Interest," *Journal of American History,* Vol. 62 (March 1976), 845–68.
8. *Report,* 13.
9. *Christian Examiner,* September, 1834.
10. FD, September 3, 6, 1834.
11. Indictments returned by the Grand Jury against John R. Buzzell et al. September 1834, Middlesex Superior Court Archives. Lord Papers, archives of the Archdiocese of Boston.
12. "Leader of the Knownothing Mob," 73.
13. Commodore J.D. Elliott to Bp. Fenwick, October 22, 1834. Letters in the archives of the Archdiocese of Boston.
14. Bp. Fenwick to Rev. George Fenwick, Novermber 8, 1834. Lord Papers, archives of the Archdiocese of Boston.
15. Fenwick to Signay, November 18, 1834, E.V. II-67, archives of the Archdiocese of Quebec.
16. FD, October 23, 1834.
17. Moffatt to Austin, November 15, 1834, letter in the collection of Catholic University of America.
18. Fenwick to Signay, November 18, 1834.
19. Bp. Fenwick to Rev. George Fenwick, November 6, 1834, Lord Papers, archives of the Archdiocese of Boston.
20. FD, November 19, 1834.
21. Mary Anne Moffatt to Attorney General J.T. Austin, September 12, 1834, in the collection of Catholic University of America.
22. Moffatt to Austin, undated letter in the collection of Catholic University of America.
23. It is likely these were brought by James Logan.
24. Moffatt to Austin, November 15, 1834, letter in the collection of Catholic University of America.

25. The evidence for the gift giving comes from a letter from Mary Barber to Bishop Fenwick, August 6, 1835, archives of the Archdiocese of Boston.
26. Moffatt to Austin, December 17, 1834, archives of Catholic University of America.
27. List of Articles belonging to Mrs. Russell, undated, in the archives of Catholic University of America.
28. The Superior's List, reprinted in *An Account of the Conflagration of the Ursuline Convent by a Friend of Religious Toleration* (Boston, 1834), 10–11.
29. *England,* Vol. 5, 242.
30. *Truth Teller* (New York), March 28, 1835, Lord Papers, archives of the Archdiocese of Boston.
31. Thaxter to Curtis, February 4, 1843.
32. FD, November 28, 1834.
33. The eclipse of the sun is noted in FD, November 30, 1834. The execution of the Spanish pirate is noted in FD, December 2, 1834.
34. *England,* Vol. 5, 261.
35. "Leader of the Knownothing Mob," 73–74.
36. *England,* Vol. 5, 244.
37. *Leader of the Convent Rioters,* 4.
38. *Boston Atlas,* December 3, 1834.
39. FD, December 2, 1834.
40. *Trial of JRB,* 9.
41. *Trial of JRB,* 11.
42. *England,* Vol. 5, 346.
43. *England,* 246.
44. *Trial of JRB,* 13.
45. *England,* Vol. 5, 246.
46. *Leader of the Convent Rioters,* 30.
47. *Leader of the Convent Rioters,* 7–8.
48. *England,* Vol. 5, 246.
49. *England,* Vol. 5, 247.
50. FD, December 5, 1834.
51. *England,* Vol. 5, 247.
52. *Trial of JRB,* 18.
53. Ibid.
54. *Leader of the Convent Rioters,* 9.
55. *Trial of JRB,* 25.
56. *England,* Vol. 5, 249.
57. *England,* Vol. 5, 249.
58. *Leader of the Convert Rioters,* 10.
59. Ibid., 11.
60. Ibid., 14.
61. *England,* Vol. 5, 247.
62. Ibid., 252.
63. Ibid.
64. Ibid., 253.
65. *Trial of JRB,* 47.
66. *Trial of JRB,* 48. This charge is repeated in *Supplement to "Six Months in a Convent,"* 88 and 129.
67. *England,* Vol. 5, 262.
68. *Trial of JRB,* 54.
69. Ibid., 55.

70. Ibid.
71. *Supplement to "Six Months in a Convent,"* 141.
72. *Trial of JRB,* 73.
73. *Leader of the Convent Rioters,* 24.
74. Ibid., 28.
75. Austin, 3.
76. Ibid., 9.
77. Ibid., 16.
78. *Leader of the Convent Rioters,* 33–35.
79. "Leader of the Knownothing Mob," 74.
80. *England,* Vol. 5, 257.
81. "Leader of the Knownothing Mob," 74.
82. Ibid.
83. Ibid.
84. *England,* Vol. 5, 259.
85. Ibid., 255.
86. Ibid., 262.
87. Ibid., 269.
88. Ibid., 270.
89. Sr. Mary St. George to Dr. Hooker, February 25, 1834 (Mass. State Archives, Pardons, 1835, M. Marcy), Lord Papers, archives of the Archdiocese of Boston.
90. Sr. Mary St. George to Gov. Davis, Feb. 26, 1835 (Mass. State Archives, Pardons, 1835, M. Marcy), Lord Papers, archives of the Archdiocese of Boston.
91. *England,* Vol. 5, 271.
92. Ibid., 301.
93. Isaac Frye, *The Charlestown Convent* (Boston: Patrick Donohoe, 1870), 76.
94. Frye, 80.

## Chapter Seven: The Ashes Scatter

1. Fenwick to Signay, August 27, 1834. E.U., II–66, archives of the Archdiocese of Quebec.
2. The birth dates for Mary and Catherine are from a genealogical chart in "Saintly Influences: Father Thayer and the Ursulines," Russell, 627. Margaret Ryan's birth date is not listed on the chart. The Index for South Boston Cemetery is in the archives of the Archdiocese of Boston.
3. The next visit to Mount Benedict recorded by Fenwick was December 5, 1834. He and a man named Mr. Dyer had gone to the graveyard on Bunker Hill to lay out a lot where a small house might be built for a caretaker to protect the Catholic cemetery. He records nothing in his diary entry of December 5 about the bodies in the Mount Benedict mausoleum.
4. FD, October 11, 1834.
5. FD, October 13, 1834.
6. Bishop Fenwick's obedience for Sister Mary Ursula, Sister Mary Joseph, and Sister Mary Austin, February 27, 1835. E.U., II–69, archives of the Archdiocese of Quebec.
7. Francis Drake, *The Town of Roxbury: Its Memorable Persons and Places.* Published by the author (1878), 327. By 1878, when Drake's book was published, the house was already in severe disrepair and almost unrecognizable.
8. Drake, 333.
9. Emily Pierpont Lesdernier, quoted in Drake, 327–328.
10. FD, October 16, 1834.
11. FD, November 21, 1834.
12. FD, October 23, 1834.

13. Moffatt to Austin, December 17, 1834. Archives of Catholic University of America.
14. "The Roxbury Committee of Vigilance, 1834–1835," *Proceedings of the Massachusetts Historical Society,* Vol. 53 (June 1920), 325–331, 326.
15. "Roxbury Committee of Vigilance," 327.
16. FD, December 21, 1834.
17. FD, December 22, 1834.
18. "Roxbury Committee of Vigilance," 332.
19. "Roxbury Committee of Vigilance," 329.
20. Ibid.
21. FD, December 25, 1834.
22. Bishop Fenwick to George Fenwick, December 29, 1834 (Lord Papers). Archives of the Archdiocese of Boston.
23. *England,* Vol. 5, 264.
24. FD, January 8, 1835.
25. FD, January 11, 1835.
26. "The Ursuline Community," in *The New-England Magazine,* Vol. 8 (January–June 1835), 392–99, 396.
27. FD, January 20, 1835.
28. FD, January 21, 1835.
29. *England,* Vol. 5, 300.
30. Fenwick to Signay, January 28, 1835. E.U., II-68, archives of the Archdiocese of Quebec.
31. Fenwick to Signay, January 28, 1835.
32. This figure is from the *Annals of the Ursulines of Quebec,* Vol. 2, May 10, 1835, 165–166. Archives of the Quebec Ursulines.
33. FD, March 1, 1835.
34. FD, March 16, 1835.
35. *Supplement to "Six Months in a Convent,"* 144.
36. FD, March 17, 1835.
37. FD, March 13, 1835.
38. Fenwick to Signay, March 19, 1835. E.V., II-70, archives of the Archdiocese of Quebec.
39. FD, March 20, 1835.
40. St. George to Signay, March 21, 1835. E.V., II-71, archives of the Archdiocese of Quebec.
41. St. George to James T. Austin, March 21, 1835, in the collection of Catholic University of America.
42. FD, March 26, 1835.
43. My translation of Signay to Fenwick, Quebec, March 28, 1835 (Lord Papers), archives of the Archdiocese of Boston.
44. My translation of Signay to St. George, March 28, 1835 (Lord Papers), archives of the Archdiocese of Boston.
45. FD, April 3–7, 1835.
46. FD, April 7, 1835.
47. "The Ursuline Community," in *The New-England Magazine,* 397.
48. *England,* Vol. 5, 297.
49. Ibid., 289.
50. Ibid., 296.
51. FD, April 8, 1835.
52. FD, April 9, 1835.
53. FD, April 13, 1835.
54. FD, April 14, 1835.

55. FD, April 15, 1835.
56. St. George to J.T. Austin, April 15, 1835, archives of Catholic University of America.
57. FD, April 20, 1835.
58. FD, April 28, 1835.
59. Fenwick to Signay, May 3, 1835. E.U., II-72, in the archives of the Archdiocese of Quebec.
60. FD, May 6, 1835.
61. Annals of the Ursulines of Quebec, Vol. 2, 165–66.
62. The Annals of May 10, 1835 state, "En conséquence, Sr. Grandeur, sachant que le digne Père Maguire devait alors être à New York, lui à écrit de bonheur bien passer par Boston pour rameuter ici les trois dernières Ursulines" (Vol. 2, 165–66).
63. My translation of Father Maguire to Bishop Turgeon, May 11, 1835, ICR, I–149, in the archives of the Archdiocese of Quebec.
64. FD, May 12, 1835.
65. FD, May 13, 1835.
66. FD, May 14, 1835.
67. Mary Barber alludes to the visit in a letter to Fenwick, August 6, 1835, archives of the Archdiocese of Boston.
68. Moffatt to Mrs. Jonathan Russell, May 17, 1835, archives of Catholic University of America.
69. FD, May 20, 1835.
70. Document in the archives of the Archdiocese of Boston.
71. FD, May 22, 1835.
72. Fenwick to Signay, May 23, 1835. E.U., II-73, archives of the Archdiocese of Quebec.
73. Moffatt to Fenwick, dated [incorrectly] March 1835, archives of the archdiocese of Boston.
74. Mrs. Russell to Superior, June 11, 1835, archives of Catholic University of America.
75. FD, May 26, 1835.
76. FD, June 1, 1835.
77. FD, June 3, 1835.
78. England, Vol. 5, 301.
79. Annals, 171–72. Archives of the Quebec Ursulines.
80. McDonnell to Fenwick, June 5, 1835, archives of the Archdiocese of Boston.
81. FD, July 4, 1835.
82. FD, July 29, 1835.
83. FD, August 1, 4, 1835.
84. FD, August 14, 1835.
85. FD, September 10, 1835.
86. Mary Barber to Fenwick, August 6, 1835, archives of the Archdiocese of Boston.
87. Barber to Fenwick, September 7, 1835, archives of the Archdiocese of Boston.
88. Barber to Mrs. Jonathan Russell (Lydia), January 22, 1836, archives of Catholic University of America.
89. Fenwick to Bishop of Quebec, February 18, 1836. E.U., II-76, archives of Archdiocese of Quebec.
90. See Fenwick to Bp. Rosati, May 5, 1836, Lord Papers, archives of the Archdiocese of Boston.
91. Obedience for St. George, issued by Bp. Signay, May 9, 1836, archives of the Archdiocese of Quebec.
92. My translation from Annals of the Ursulines of Quebec, archives of the Quebec Ursulines, 191–192.
93. My translation, Signay to Mother Saint Gabriel. À Reverende Mère Saint Gabriel, from Signay, May 9, 1836, in Letter Register No. 17, June 5–December 10, 1836, No. 301.

94. Barber to Fenwick, May 19, 1836, archives of the Archdiocese of Boston.
95. *Supplement to "Six Months in a Convent,"* 189.
96. Ibid., 192.
97. Ibid., 245–246.
98. Barber to Fenwick, July 17, 1836, archives of the Archdiocese of Boston.
99. Fenwick to Signay, March 9, 1838. E.U., II-77, archives of the Archdiocese of Quebec.
100. St. Louis Census records for 1840.
101. Mary Barber to Madame la Superieure des Ursulines de Quebec, October 30, 1838, in the archives of the Ursulines of Quebec.
102. Martineau, *Society in America,* Vol. 2, 257. Quoted in Woody, Vol. 2, 8.
103. Woody, Vol. 2, 8.

## Epilogue

1. A letter to the Ursulines in Lewiston, Maine, dated March 14, 1938, from Frederic J. Allchin, Pastor of St. Mary's in Charlestown, Massachusetts, gives the history of the ciborium in the twentieth century. From this letter we learn that Sister M. Gonzaga of the Ursuline Convent in Lewiston wrote to ask for the return of the ciborium. It had been in use by the Sisters of St. Mary's and they agreed to give it to the Ursulines as a gift in 1938. In the collection of the Ursulines of Dedham, Massachusetts.
2. Bourassa, "The Ursulines of Charlestown."
3. Father Frederic J. Allchin to Sister M. Gonzaga, March 14, 1938.
4. Lord et al., Vol. 2, 230. Report of the Special Committee on the Petition of Alvah Kelley and Prescott P. Pond, March 1, 1836 (Massachusetts State Archives, House Documents, 1836, 4, 112), Lord Papers, archives of the Archdiocese of Boston.
5. *Boston Daily Advertiser,* March 1, 1838. See also *Salem Gazette,* March 6, 1838.
6. These letters are in the archives of the Archdiocese of Boston. It is tempting to speculate that Maria was the mysterious "Louisa from New Orleans" entrusted to Louisa Whitney's care on the night of the convent burning. See Whitney, 125–34.
7. Hamilton, 60.
8. Lord et al., Vol. 2, 383.
9. Frye, 82.
10. Samuel Adams Drake, *Historic Fields and Mansions of Middlesex* (Boston: James R. Osgood & Co, 1874), 94.
11. William Foster Otis, *In Memoriam Gulielmi Crucifontis.* From the archives of The Church of the Advent, collection in the Boston Athenaeum, n.p.
12. Otis, *In Memoriam,* n.p.
13. Otis, *In Memoriam,* n.p.
14. Morris, 8.
15. Collection Records, The Parish of Advent Church, Boston, Historical Note, 49.
16. Morris, 16.
17. Croswell's letter book in the archives of the Church of the Advent, Boston Athenaeum.
18. Coyle et al., Vol. 3, 179, notes that G. H. Doane, son of Bishop Doane, Croswell's best friend, became a Roman Catholic priest.
19. For the above information, I wish to acknowledge the kind assistance of Father Joseph Adamek of the Mission Hill Church.
20. B. F. DeCosta, *The Story of Mount Benedict* (Somerville, Massachusetts: Citizen Press, 1893), 6.
21. *Suncook Valley Times* (Pittsfield, New Hampshire), June 9, 1870. Thanks to Larry Berkson for alerting me to this reference.
22. "Leader of the Knownothing Mob," 67–68.

23. Ibid., 74–75.
24. *Trésors des Communautés Religieuses,* 99.

## Appendix: Partial List of Students

1. From Monroe, "Destruction of the Convent at Charlestown, Massachusetts, 1834," 649.

# ACKNOWLEDGMENTS

I BEGAN WORK on the convent burning in 1991, and the early research was my sabbatical project from Salem State College in the spring of 1992. In almost a decade, many people have offered generous assistance. The staffs of the American Antiquarian Society, the Boston Public Library, the Massachusetts Historical Society, and the Essex Institute were very helpful in the beginning phases of this project. Early on, John Mahoney, Christopher Wilson, Judith Wilt, and Father James Woods of Boston College provided important support, as did the late Richard Marius. Dorothy Z. Baker, Jane Eberwein, John Hampsey, Robert Johnson-Lally, Patricia Johnston, David Klooster, and Dane Morrison helped with letters of recommendation as I applied for various grants. Thanks to the Somerville Arts Council, the Massachusetts Foundation for the Humanities, and the Bay State Historical League for grant support. At the Somerville Public Library, I wish to thank Barbara Bannick, Ron Castile, Paul DeAngelis, John Murphy, Dora St. Martin, and especially Josie Wrangham. Thanks to Evelyn and Tom Battinelli and the Somerville Museum for hosting the exhibition *Lifting the Veil*.

Various archivists in the United States and Canada have offered invaluable assistance: Steven Nonack at the Boston Athenaeum; Nora Murphy at the Episcopal Archives in Boston; Timothy Meagher at Catholic University of America; Sister Marjorie Fallon of the Archdiocese of Hartford; Sister Wheeler at the Daughters of Charity in Albany, New York; Bonnie Weatherly at the Daughters of Charity in Emmetsburg, Maryland; Sister Joan Marie Aycock and Dr. Charles Nolan in the Archdiocese of New Orleans; Todd Welch at the Oregon Historical Society; Peter Murphy and Karen White in the archdiocese of Halifax; Antonio Lechasseur at the Canadian National Archives in Ottawa; and Larry Berkson of Pittsfield, New Hampshire. Thanks to the staff of the St. Louis Public Library, the St. Louis Historical Society, the Oregon Historical Society, as well as the McLoughlin House. At the College of the Holy Cross, Jim Mahoney and the interlibrary loan staff were a tremendous help. Thanks to Robert Vose for his kind assistance with researching the Bowman paintings and to Georgia Barnhill at the American Antiquarian Society. I would like to especially acknowledge the expertise of Michael Leclerc at the New England Historic Genealogical Society.

At the Boston Archdiocesan archives, the assistance of archivist Robert Johnson-Lally, Phyllis Dannehy, and Mary Lou Jacobs was invaluable. A special thank you to Sister Jeanne Hamilton OSU, for her marvelous scholarship and for helping with an important breakthrough. At the Ursuline Convent in Dedham, Massachusetts, I would also like to thank Sister Mary Gilbert and Sister Angela Krippendorf. Sister Rita Bourassa, an accomplished historian herself, did a great deal of sleuthing and gave expert commentary on portions of the manuscript. At the Ursuline monastery in Quebec, I wish to acknowledge the kind assistance of Sister Marie Marchand and Madame Christine Turgeon. At the Musée du Quebec, Dr. Mario Beland and M. Claude Thibault and at the archdiocesan archives in Quebec, Abbé Armand Gagné provided valuable materials. At the Commission d'Accès in Quebec, I wish to thank Laurent Bilodeau for his interest in my case. Thanks to Katherine LeGrand and Brian Young of the History Department at McGill University. At Trois Rivières, thanks to Sister Germaine Blais. And to Sylvie Tremblay, genealogist extraordinaire—warm appreciation for her commentary, for sharing her wealth of knowledge about Canadian archives, and for her phenomenal detective ability!

For all the support rendered by colleagues at Salem State College, I wish to thank Jon Aske, Bill Coyle, Joyce Cryan, Lucinda Damon-Bach, Mary Devine, Rod Kessler, Claire Keyes, Eileen and Ed Margerum, Patricia Markunas, Patricia Parker, Donnalee Rubin, John Steele, the late Joseph Flibbert, as well as research assistants Jasper Swiniuch and Kim Underhill. I want especially to acknowledge Dean Marion Kilson, who has encouraged this project since its inception. Vice President Albert Hamilton has provided invaluable support and advice. Thanks to President Nancy Harrington, Dean Anita Shea, and English Department Chairperson Patricia Buchanan, and to Martha Jane Moreland, Eleanor Reynolds, and Dean Laverna Saunders of the library. For expert advice on various chapters, I wish to thank colleagues and friends Liz Blood,

Avi Chomsky, Elizabeth Kenney, Ellen Rintell, Peter Walker—and especially Frank Devlin, who generously read and commented extensively on the manuscript.

Nancy Natale was instrumental in getting this project launched with our work together on the *Lifting the Veil* exhibition and catalog. Her artistic vision helped me see the story more clearly. Nancy Allen, of Allen and Chin, designed my book proposal and did fabulous work on the exhibition catalog for *Lifting the Veil*. Lisa Adams of the Garamond Agency is an expert and knowledgeable literary agent, whose advice and friendship I value. At The Free Press, I wish to thank the editorial director, Elizabeth Maguire, and my editor, Chad Conway.

Thanks to Sharon Baert and Nancy Walker Lusignan for sharing their special gifts, and to Tasia Bolotina and Louise Mann. My parents Carolyn and Henry Lusignan faithfully help out as needed and are always enthusiastic readers of my books.

My husband, Jackson Schultz, has supported this project in every possible way—often setting aside his own work to help. I will be forever grateful to him. For sharing their lives with this book, and for enriching mine beyond measure, it is lovingly dedicated to him and to our boys.

# ILLUSTRATION CREDITS

26    *Map of the frontier of Lower Canada, 1815,* courtesy of the collection of the Canadian Public Archives, Ottawa.

35    *The Mount Benedict ciborium* courtesy of the Ursuline Sisters of Dedham, Massachusetts. Photograph by Kay Canavino.

40    *Portrait of Bishop Benedict Fenwick, circa 1831,* courtesy of the collection of the Ursuline Sisters of Dedham, Massachusetts. Photograph by Kay Canavino.

49    *The superior's signature* from a letter courtesy of the collection of the Somerville, Massachusetts Public Library.

75    *Penmanship sample of Maria Cotting* from James Phinney Monroe, "The Destruction of the Convent at Charlestown, Massachusetts, 1834," *New-England Magazine,* February 1901, 643.

99    *Lucretia Beckford's report card* courtesy of the collection of the Peabody Essex Museum, Salem, Massachusetts.

103    *Sister Ann Alexis* photo courtesy of the archives of the Archdiocese of Boston.

116    *Lyman Beecher* photo courtesy of the American Antiquarian Society.

117    *"Dr. Brimstone"* by David Claypoole Johnston from Johnston's *Scraps,* 1835, courtesy of the American Antiquarian Society.

150    *Rossiter's dog* from *The Trial of John R. Buzzell, the Leader of the Convent Rioters for Arson and Burglary, Committed on the Night of the 11th of August, 1834. By the Destruction of the Convent on Mount Benedict, in Charlestown, Massachusetts,* by Lemuel Gulliver, Boston, 1834.

153    *Buzzell flogging the Irishman* from *The Trial of John R. Buzzell, the Leader of the Convent Rioters for Arson and Burglary, Committed on the Night of the 11th of August, 1834. By the Destruction of the Convent on Mount Benedict, in Charlestown, Massachusetts,* by Lemuel Gulliver, Boston, 1834.

164     *Linen baby cap embroidered by Mary Anne Moffatt* courtesy of the collection of the Ursuline Sisters of Dedham, Massachusetts.

185     *The destruction of the Ursuline convent by fire* from *The Trial of John R. Buzzell, the Leader of the Convent Rioters for Arson and Burglary, Committed on the Night of the 11th of August, 1834. By the Destruction of the Convent on Mount Benedict, in Charlestown, Massachusetts,* by Lemuel Gulliver, Boston, 1834.

200     *Mount Benedict Ursuline Community House* from the Mount Benedict Prospectus.

207     *The superior unveiled in court* from *The Trial of John R. Buzzell, the Leader of the Convent Rioters for Arson and Burglary, Committed on the Night of the 11th of August 1834. By the Destruction of the Convent on Mount Benedict, in Charlestown, Massachusetts,* by Lemuel Gulliver, Boston, 1834.

217     *Rebecca Reed* from *The Trial of John R. Buzzell, the Leader of the Convent Rioters for Arson and Burglary, Committed on the Night of the 11th August, 1834. By the Destruction of the Convent on Mount Benedict, in Charlestown, Massachusetts,* by Lemuel Gulliver, Boston, 1834.

233     *Brinley Place* from *The Town of Roxbury: Its Memorable Persons and Places* (1878) by Francis Drake.

272     *The convent ruins* photograph from the collection of William Saunders, courtesy of the Cambridge Historical Commission.

# INDEX